WORKING PAPERS
CHAPTERS 1-6
to accompany

ACCOUNTING PRINCIPLES

6th Edition

JERRY J. WEYGANDT Ph.D., C.P.A.
Arthur Andersen Alumni Professor of Accounting
University of Wisconsin - Madison
Madison, Wisconsin

DONALD E. KIESO Ph.D., C.P.A.
KPMG Peat Marwick Emeritus Professor of Accountancy
Northern Illinois University
DeKalb, Illinois

PAUL D. KIMMEL Ph.D., C.P.A.
Associate Professor of Accounting
University of Wisconsin - Milwaukee
Milwaukee, Wisconsin

Prepared By

DICK D. WASSON M.B.A., C.P.A.
Southwestern College
San Diego State University
University of Phoenix

JOHN WILEY & SONS, INC.
New York • Chichester • Weinheim • Brisbane • Singapore • Toronto

COVER PHOTO © James Bareham/Stone.

To order books or for customer service call 1-800-CALL-WILEY (225-5945).

ISBN 0-471-39632-X

Printed in the United States of America

10 9 8 7 6 5 4 3 2 1

Printed and bound by Courier Kendallville, Inc.

NOTE TO THE STUDENT

These working papers contain solution forms for all Brief Exercises, Exercises, and Problems in Weygandt, et al., *Accounting Principles*, 6th edition, Chapters 1 – 6. The working papers also contain solution forms for each Financial Reporting Problem, Comparative Analysis Problem, Interpreting Financial Statements, Exploring the Web, Group Decision Case, Communication Activity, and Ethics Case. There are no working paper solution forms for any of the Self-Study Questions or chapter Questions at the end of each chapter.

In general, the working papers follow the organization of the textbook. To maximize the use of space, however, forms for the Exercises occasionally appear out of order.

Name

Section

Date

Name

Section

Date

Name Exercises 1-1 to 1-3

Section

Date

#1

#2

#3

Name Exercise 1-4

Section

Date Roberta Mendez & Co.

(a)

(b)

(c)

Name Exercise 1-5

Section

Date

Roberta Mendez & Co.

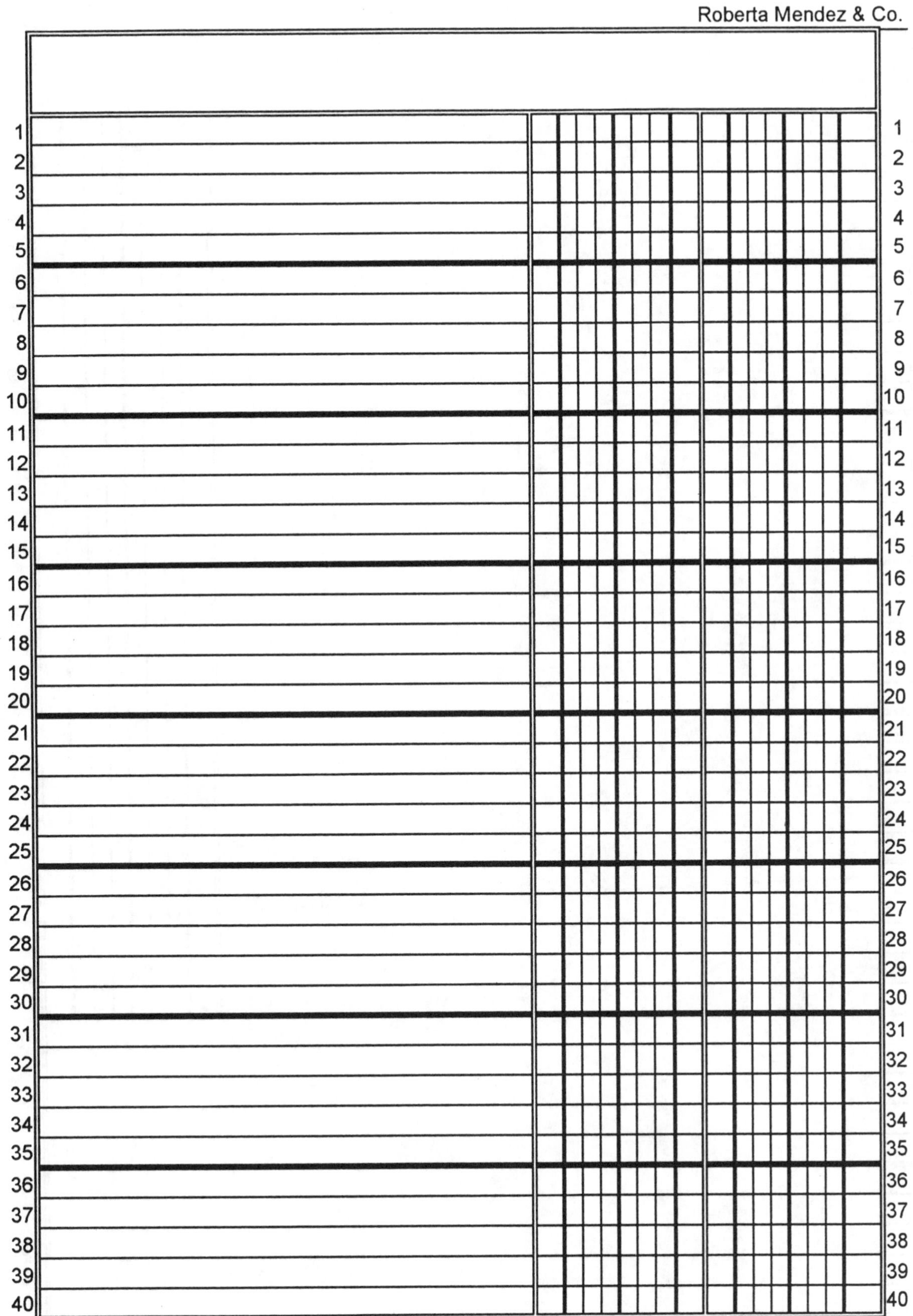

Name Exercise 1-6

Section

Date Padre Company

(a)

(b)

(c)

Name

Section

Date

Exercise 1-7

Neve Campbell & Maxim Enterprises

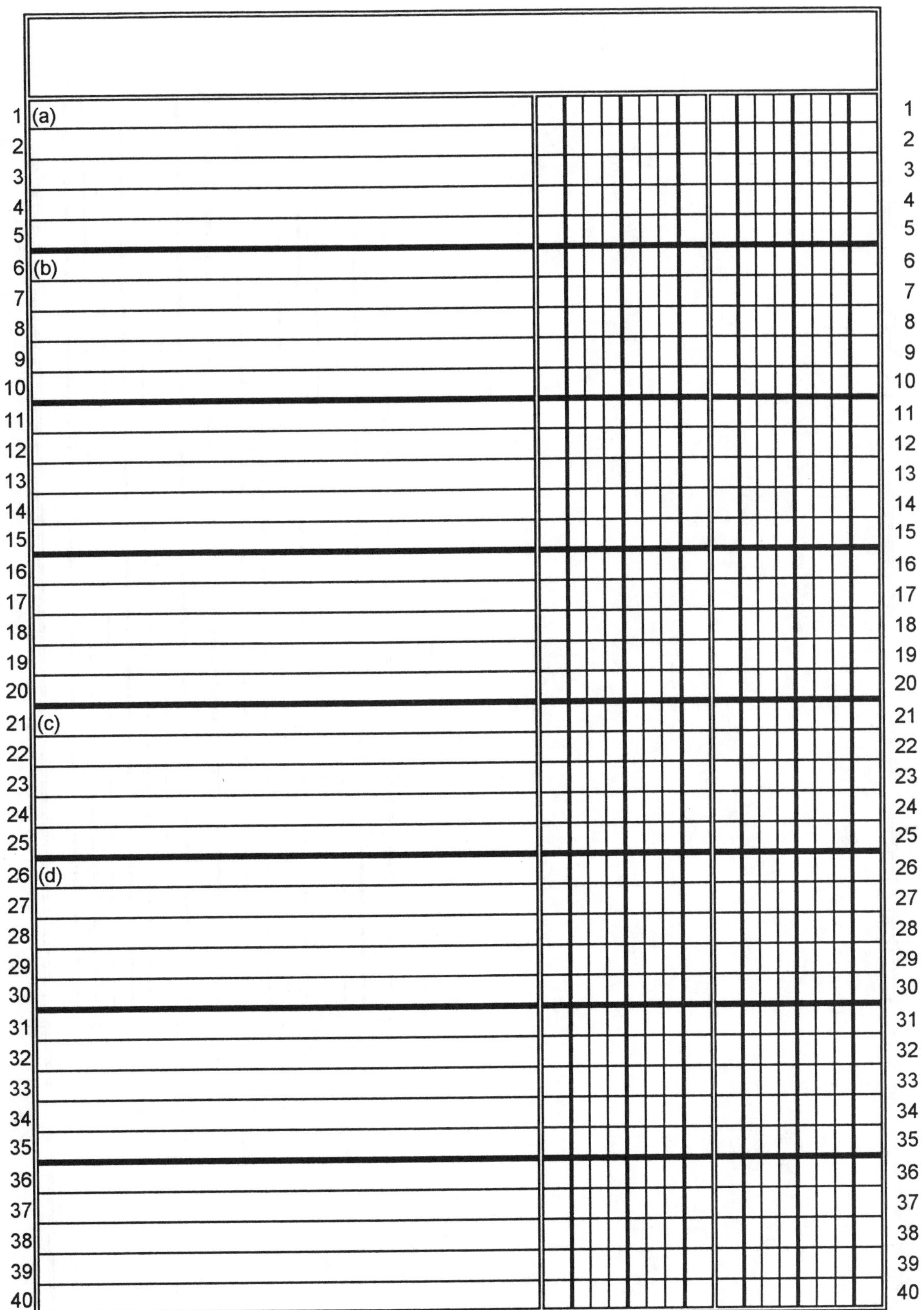

(a)

(b)

(c)

(d)

Name

Section

Date

Exercise 1-8

Stanley Tucci Co.

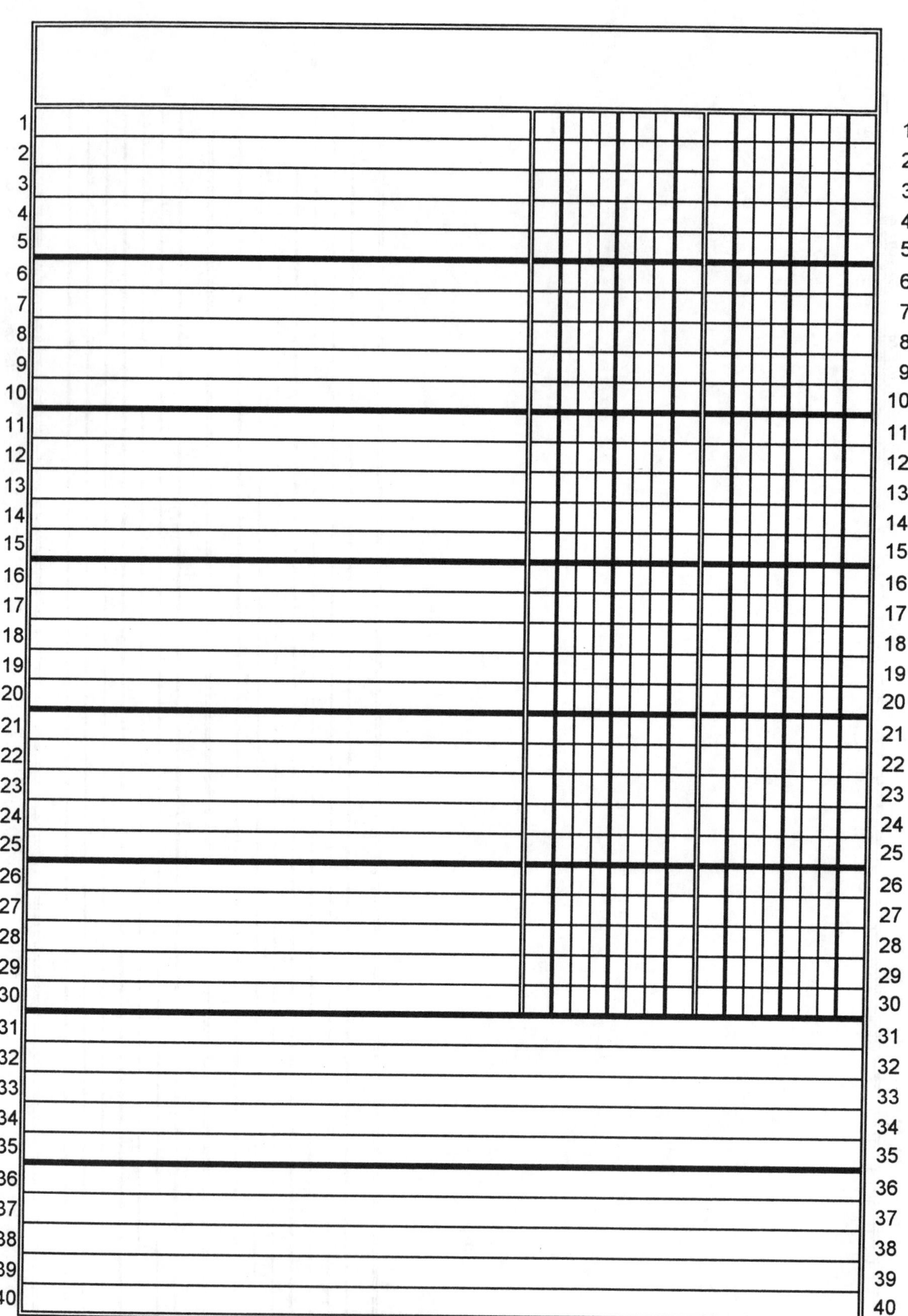

Name

Section

Date

#9

#10

Name
Section
Date

Exercises 1-11 to 1-12

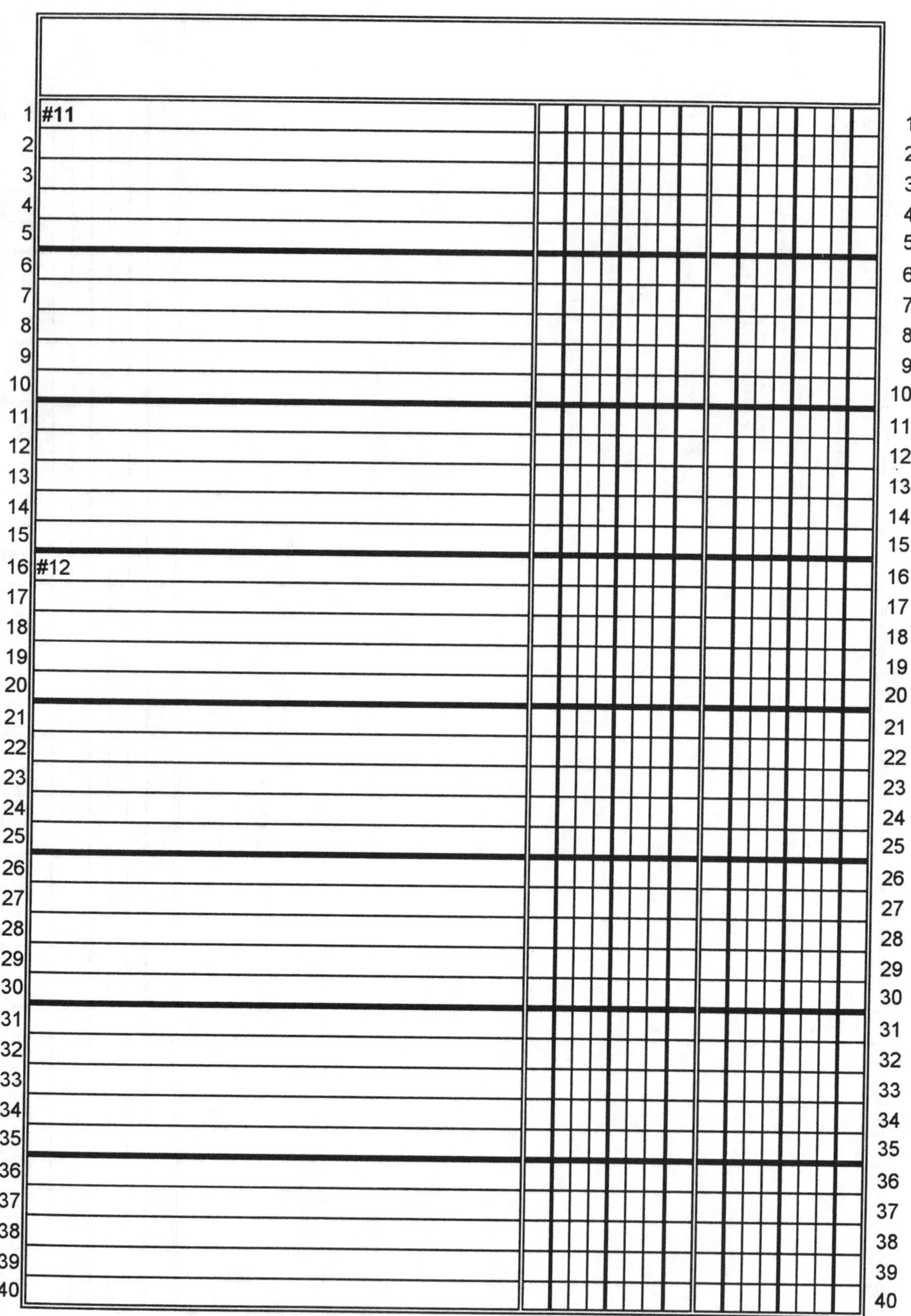

Name

Section

Date

(a)

AFFLECK'S REPAIR SHOP

	Assets				= Liabilities	+ Owner's Equity
Transactions	Cash	+ Accounts Receivable	+ Supplies	+ Equipment	= Accounts Payables	+ U. Kumar, Capital
1.						
2.						
3.						
4.						
5.						
6.						
7.						
8.						
9.						
10.						
11.						

Name

Section

Date

Problem 1-1A Concluded

Affleck's Repair Shop

(b)

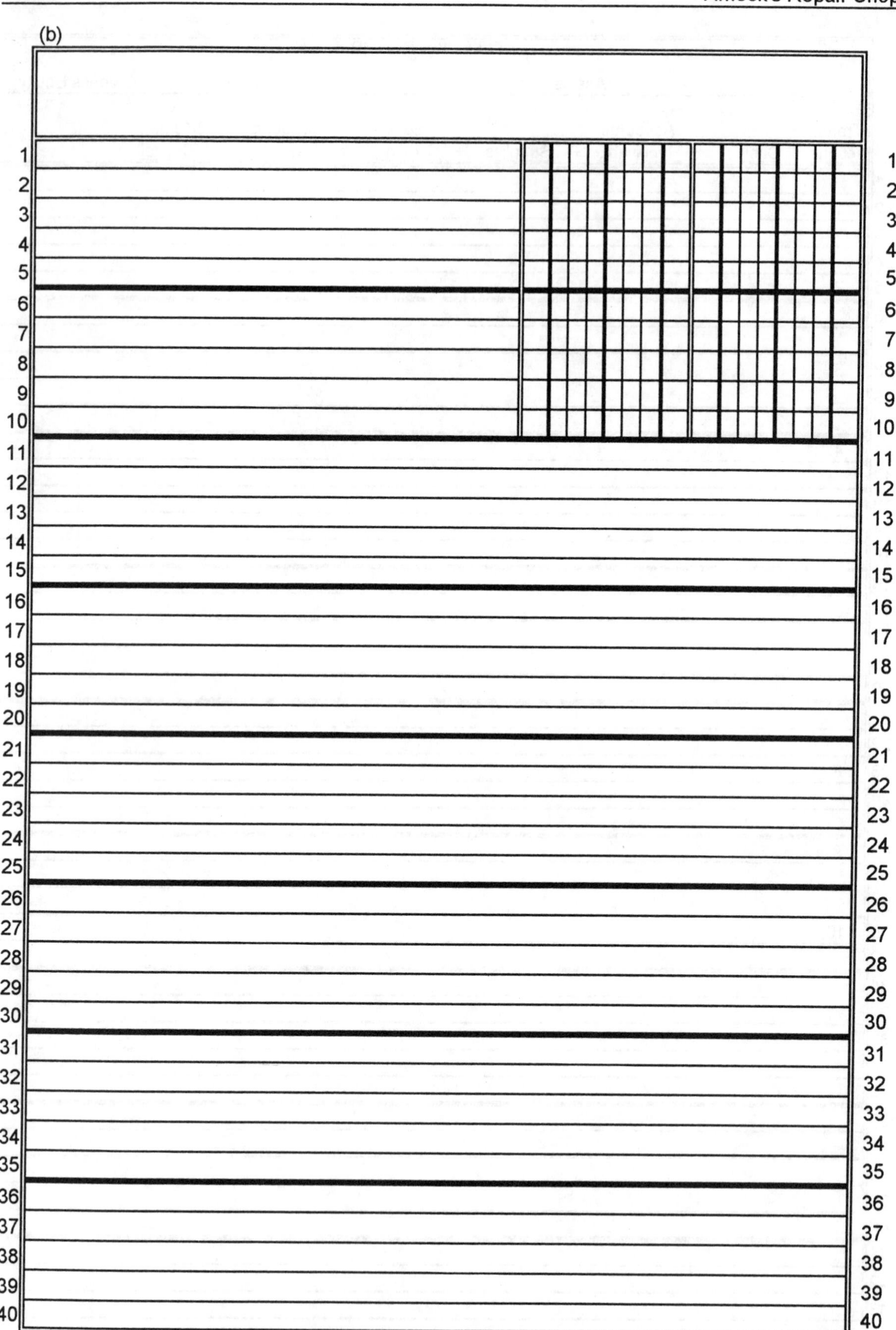

Name
Section
Date

Problem 1-2A

Judi Dench, Veterinarian

(a)

JUDI DENCH, VETERINARIAN

Trans-action	Assets							=	Liabilities			+	Owner's Equity
	Cash	+	Accounts Receivable	+	Supplies	+	Office Equipment	=	Notes Payable	+	Accounts Payable	+	Judi Dench, Capital
Bal.	$ 9,000	+	$ 1,700	+	$ 600	+	$6,000.00	=		+	$3,600.00	+	$ 13,700.00
1.													
2.													
3.													
4.													
5.													
6.													
7.													
8.													

(b)

JUDI DENCH, VETERINARIAN Income Statement For the Month Ended September 30, 2002		
Revenues		
Expenses		
Net Income (Loss)		

JUDI DENCH, VETERINARIAN Owner's Equity Statement For the Month Ended September 30, 2002		

Name Problem 1-2A Concluded

Section

Date Judi Dench, Veterinarian

(b) (Continued)

JUDI DENCH, VETERINARIAN Balance Sheet September 30, 2002		
Assets		
Liabilities and Owner's Equity		

Name | Problem 1-3A
Section
Date | Skyline Flying School

(a)

SKYLINE FLYING SCHOOL
Income Statement
For the Month Ended May 31, 2002

Revenues

Expenses

Net Income (Loss)

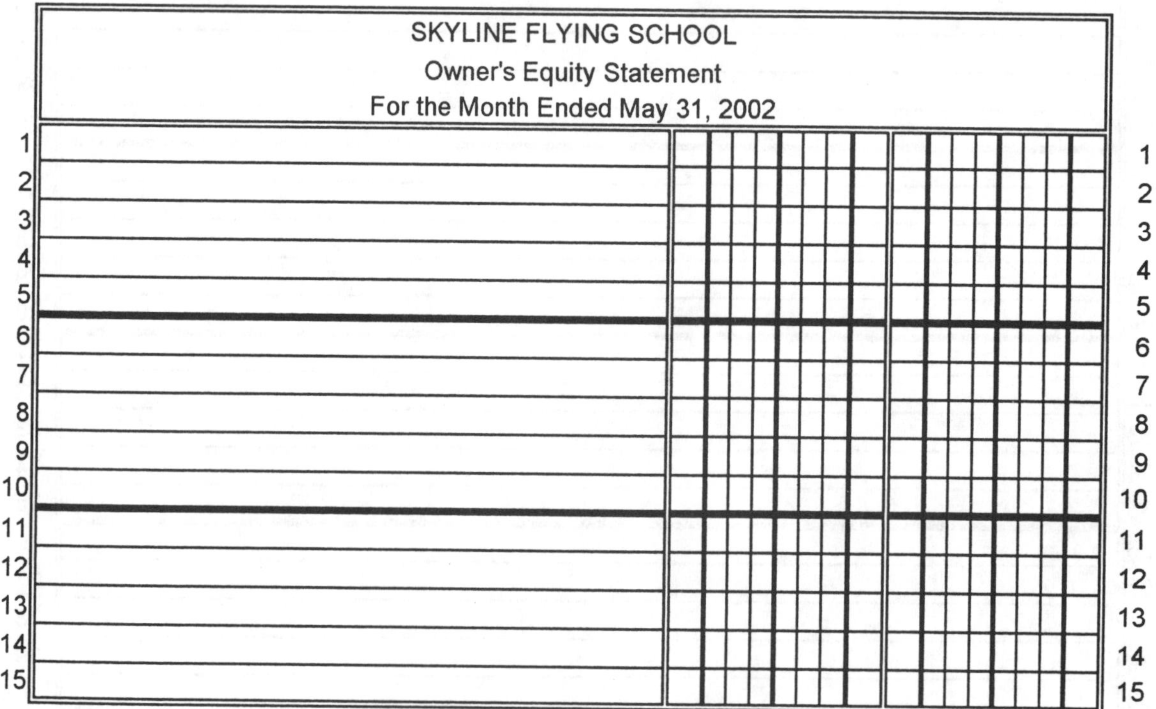

SKYLINE FLYING SCHOOL
Owner's Equity Statement
For the Month Ended May 31, 2002

(a) (Continued)

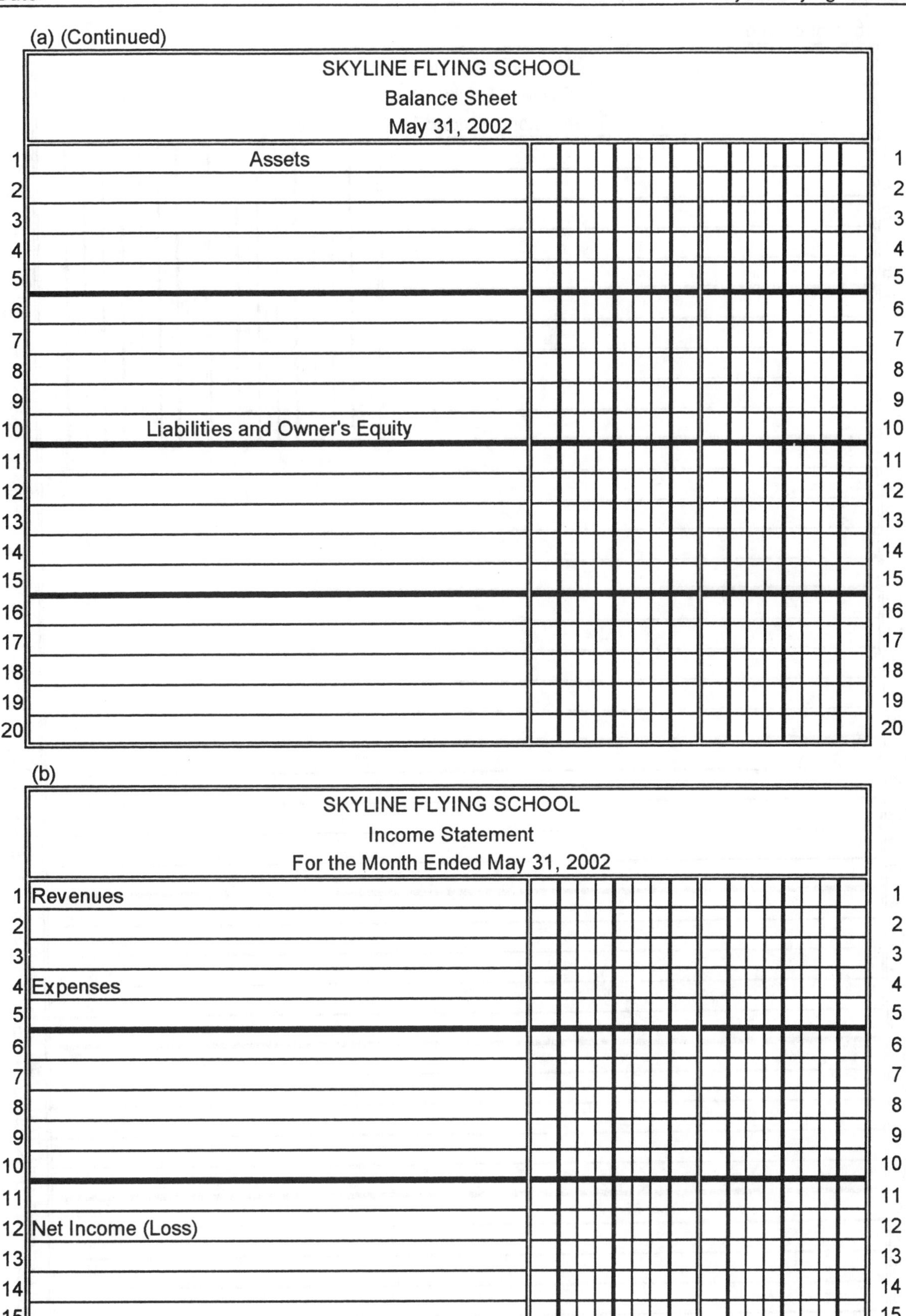

SKYLINE FLYING SCHOOL
Balance Sheet
May 31, 2002

Assets

Liabilities and Owner's Equity

(b)

SKYLINE FLYING SCHOOL
Income Statement
For the Month Ended May 31, 2002

Revenues

Expenses

Net Income (Loss)

Name

Section

Date

Problem 1-3A Concluded

Skyline Flying School

(b) Concluded

SKYLINE FLYING SCHOOL

Owner's Equity Statement

For the Month Ended May 31, 2002

Name
Section
Date

Problem 1-4A

Salem Deliveries

(a)

SALEM DELIVERIES

Date	Assets				=	Liabilities		+	Owner's Equity	
Date	Cash	+ Accounts Receivable	+ Supplies	+ Delivery Van	=	Notes Payable	+ Accounts Payable	+	R. Salem, Capital	Explanation
May 1										
2										
3										
5										
9										
12										
15										
17										
20										
23										
26										
29										
30										

(b)

SALEM DELIVERIES
Income Statement
For the Month Ended June 30, 2002

Revenues		
Expenses		
Net income		

SALEM DELIVERIES
Balance Sheet
June 30, 2002

Assets		
Liabilities and Owner's Equity		

Name | Problem 1-5A
Section
Date | Zarle Company and Others

(a)

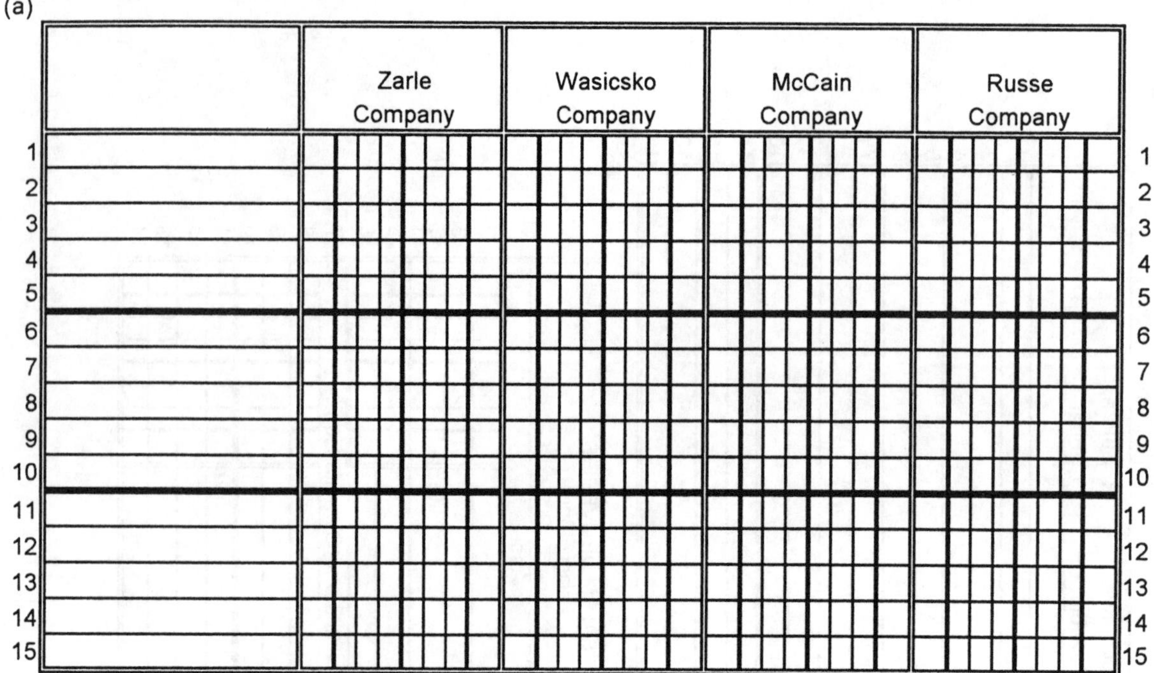

	Zarle Company	Wasicsko Company	McCain Company	Russe Company

(b) and (c)

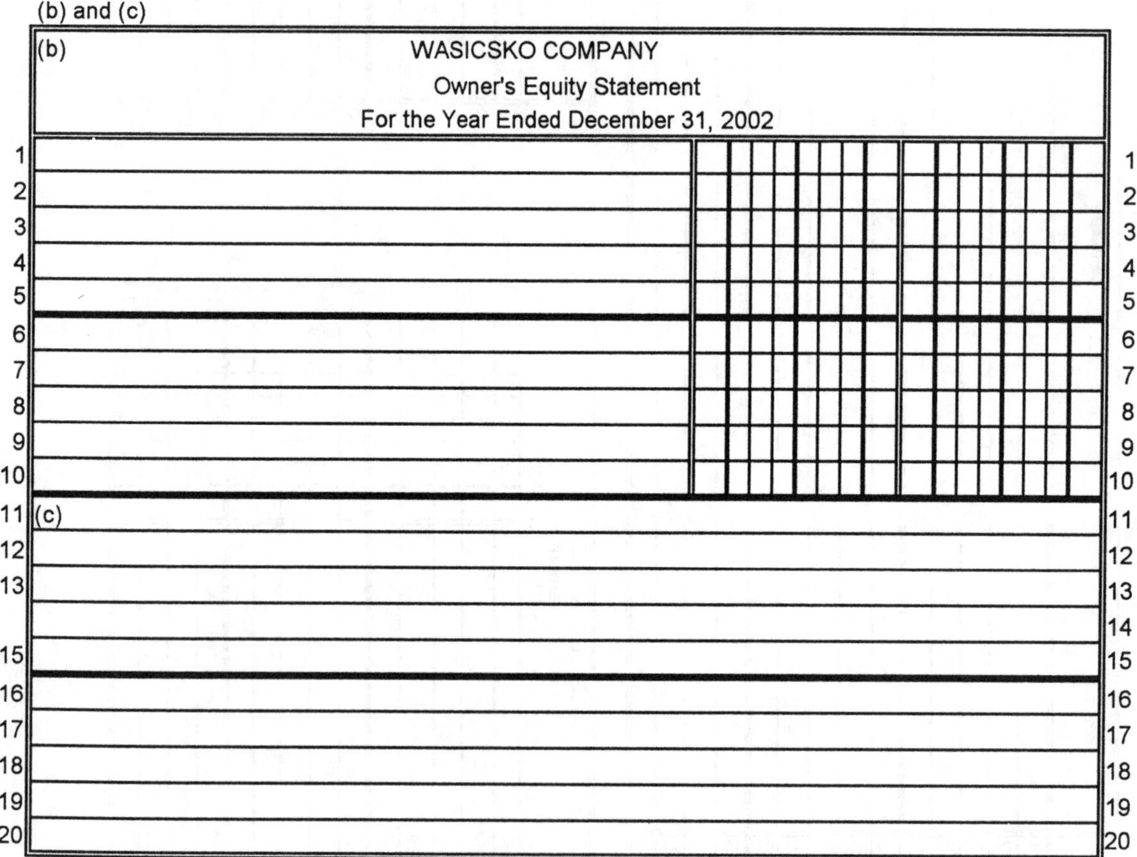

(b)

WASICSKO COMPANY

Owner's Equity Statement

For the Year Ended December 31, 2002

(c)

Name Problem 1-1B

Section

Date Matrix Travel Agency

(a)

	MATRIX TRAVEL AGENCY										
	Assets						=	Liabilities	+	Owner's Equity
Trans-actions	Cash	+	Accounts Receivable	+	Supplies	+	Office Equip-ment	=	Accounts Payables	+	Dolly Parton Capital
1.											
2.											
3.											
4.											
5.											
6.											
7.											
8.											
9.											
10.											

Name Problem 1-1B Concluded

Section

Date Matrix Travel Agency

(b)

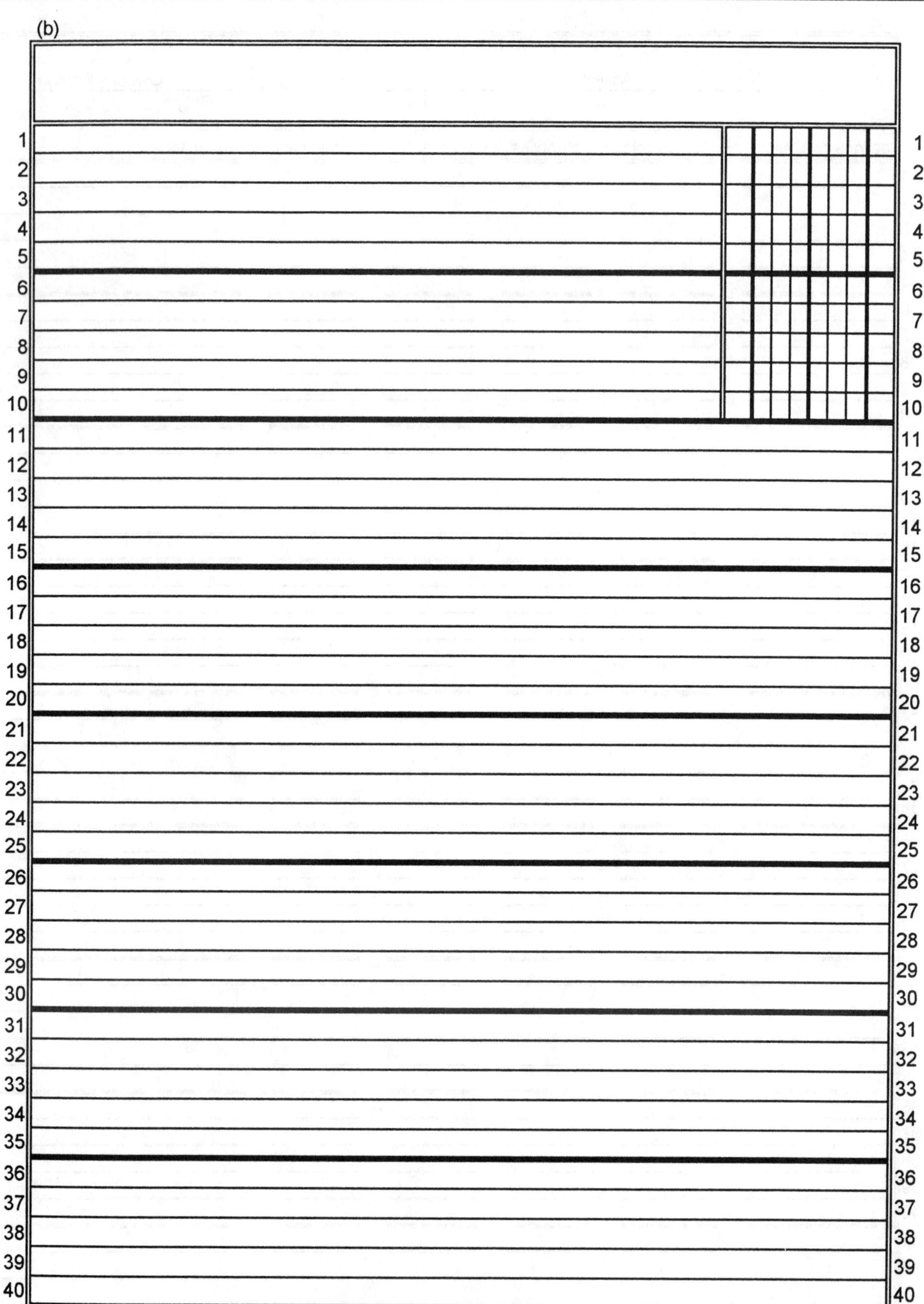

Name

Section

Date

Problem 1-2B

Michelle Pfeiffer, Attorney at Law

(a)

MICHELLE PFEIFFER, ATTORNEY AT LAW

	Assets							=	Liabilities			+	Owner's Equity
Trans-action	Cash	+	Accounts Receivable	+	Supplies	+	Office Equipment	=	Notes Payable	+	Accounts Payable	+	Michelle Pfeiffer, Capital
Bal.	$ 4,000	+	$ 1,500		$ 500		$ 5,000	=		+	$ 4,200	+	$ 6,800
1.													
2.													
3.													
4.													
5.													
6.													
7.													
8.													

(b)

MICHELLE PFEIFFER, ATTORNEY AT LAW
Income Statement
For the Month Ended August 31, 2002

Revenues		
Expenses		
Net Income (Loss)		

MICHELLE PFEIFFER, ATTORNEY AT LAW
Owner's Equity Statement
For the Month Ended August 31, 2002

(b) (Continued)

MICHELLE PFEIFFER, ATTORNEY AT LAW
Balance Sheet
August 31, 2002

Assets

Liabilities and Owner's Equity

Name Problem 1-3B

Section

Date Divine Cosmetics Co.

(a)

DIVINE COSMETICS CO.
Income Statement
For the Month Ended June 30, 2002

Revenues

Expenses

Net Income (Loss)

DIVINE COSMETICS CO.
Owner's Equity Statement
For the Month Ended June 30, 2002

Name | Problem 1-3B Continued

Section

Date | Divine Cosmetics Co.

(a) Continued

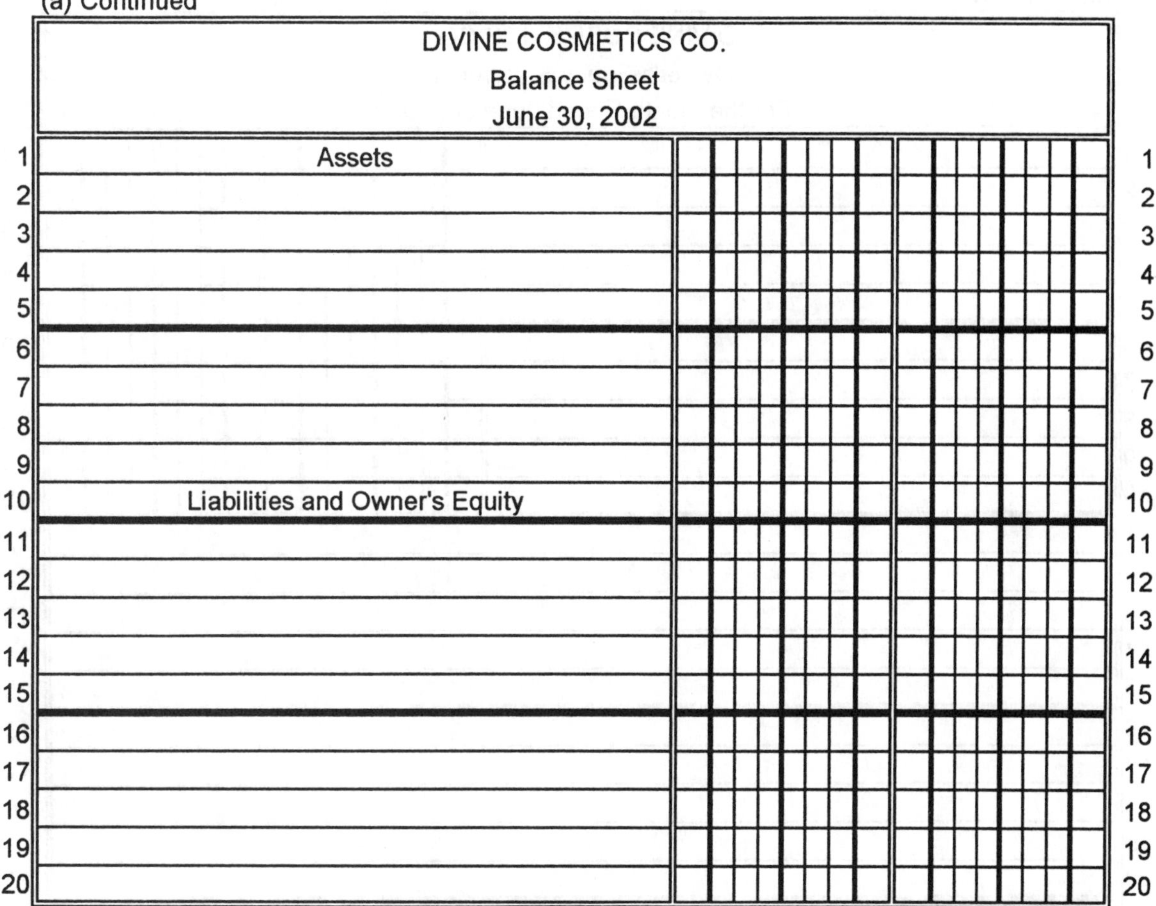

(b)

DIVINE COSMETICS CO.

Income Statement

For the Month Ended June 30, 2002

Revenues

Expenses

Net Income (Loss)

Name

Section

Date

Problem 1-3B Concluded

Divine Cosmetics Co.

(b) Concluded

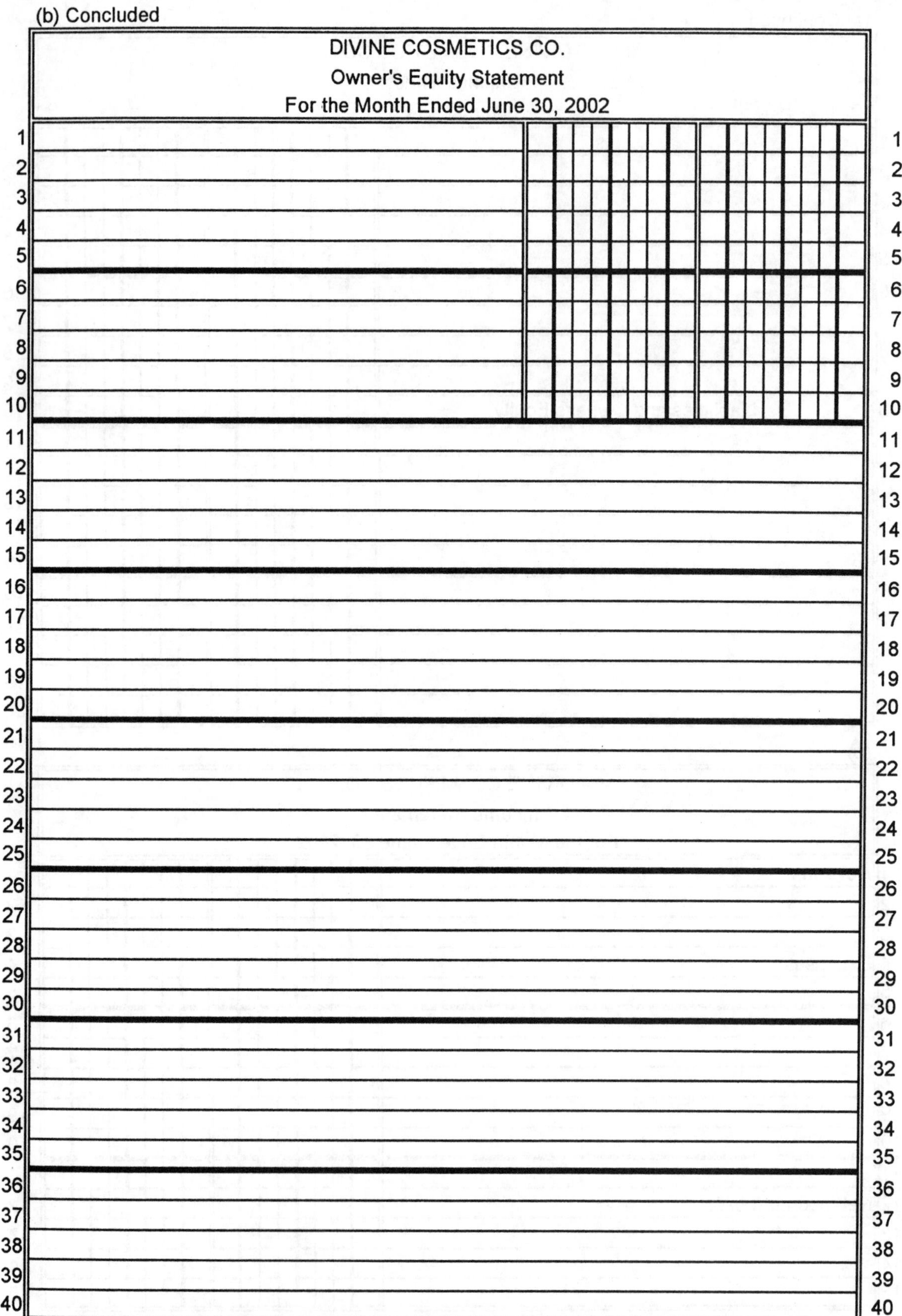

Name

Section

Date

Problem 1-4B

Spengel Consulting

(a)

SPENGEL CONSULTING

Date		Assets				=	Liabilities		+	Owner's Equity	
	Cash	+ Accounts Receivable	+ Supplies	+ Office Equipment		=	Notes Payable	+ Accounts Payable	+	J. Spengel, Capital	Explanation
May 1											
2											
3											
5											
9											
12											
15											
17											
20											
23											
26											
29											
30											

(b)

SPENGEL CONSULTING
Income Statement
For the Month Ended May 31, 2002

Revenues	
Expenses	
Net income	

SPENGEL CONSULTING
Balance Sheet
May 31, 2002

Assets	
Liabilities and Owner's Equity	

Name — Problem 1-5B

Section

Date — Yanni Company and Others

(a)

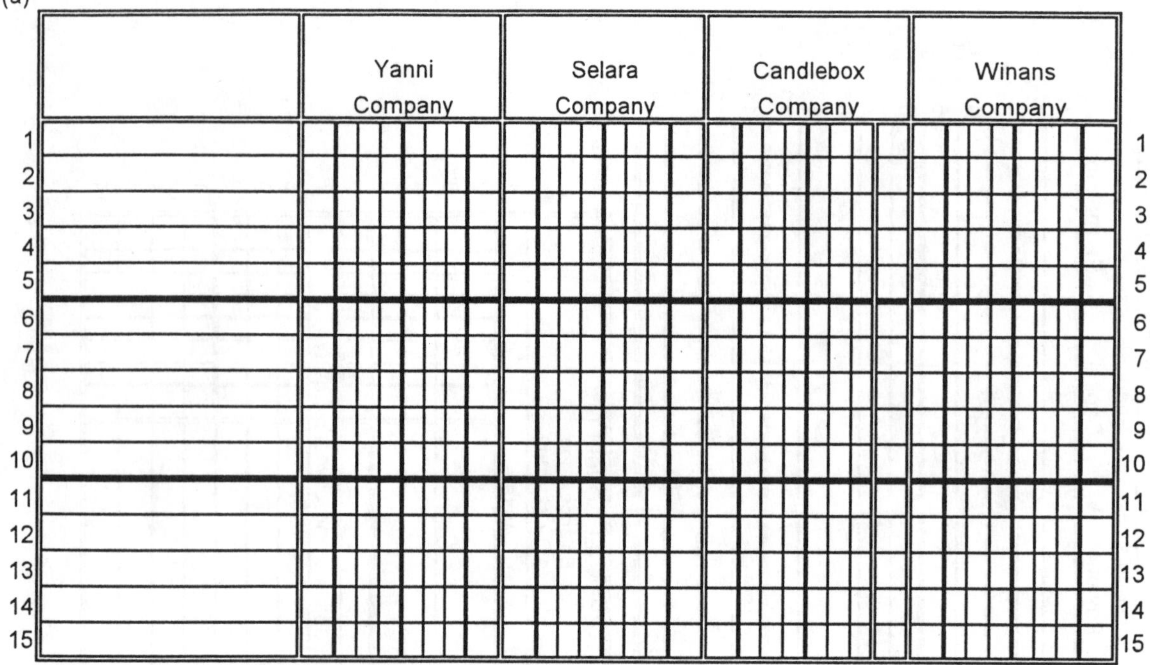

(b) and (c)

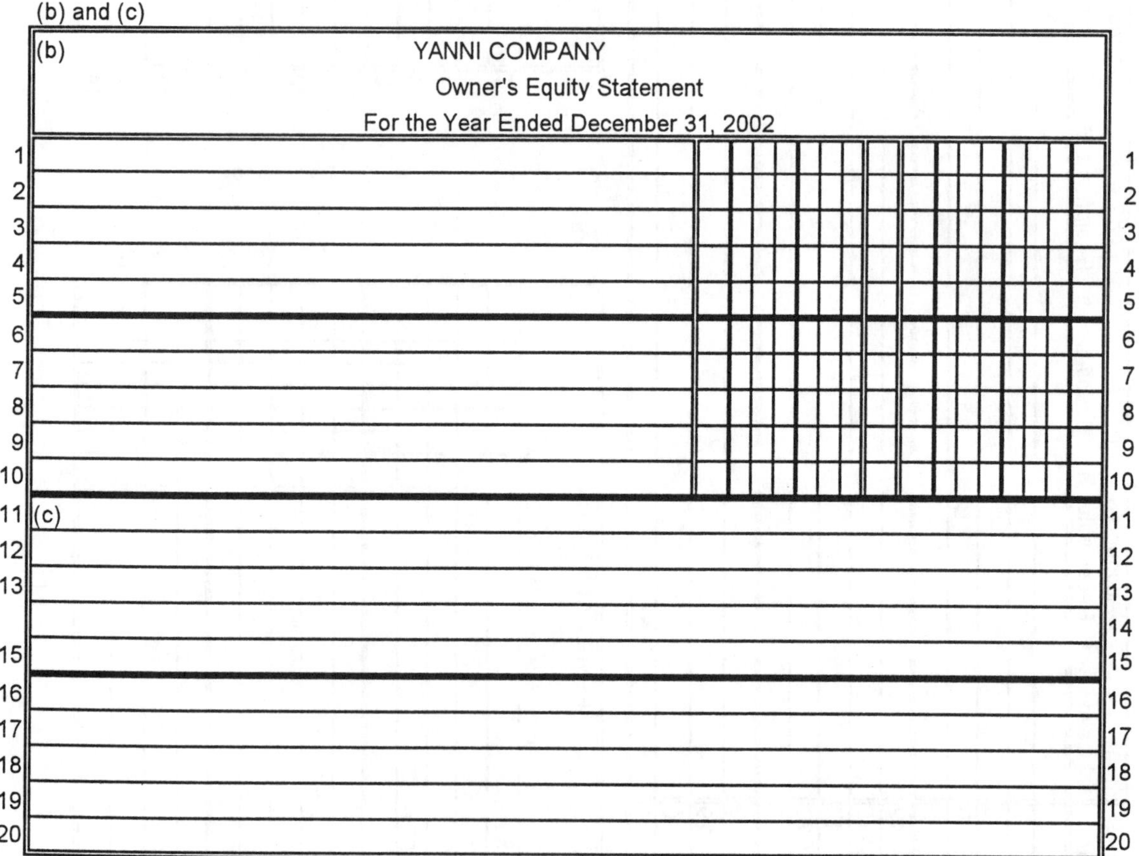

Name

Section

Date

Lands' End

(a)

(b)

(c)

(d) Net sales - 1998 (in thousands)

1999 (in thousands)

2000 (in thousands)

(e)

Name

Section

Date

Chapter 1 Comparative Analysis Problem

Lands' End vs Abercrombie & Fitch

(a) (in thousands)	Lands' End	Abercrombie & Fitch
1. Total assets		
2. Accounts receivable (net)		
3. Net sales		
4. Net income		
(b)		

Name

Section

Date

Nestle

(a)

(b)

(c)

Name

Section

Date

Accounting Career Information

(a)

(b)

(c)

(d)

(d) Continued

(e)

Name

Section

Date

Chapter 1 Group Decision Case

Chip-Shot Driving Range

(a)

(b)

CHIP-SHOT DRIVING RANGE
Balance Sheet
March 31, 2002

Assets

Liabilities and Owner's Equity

Name

Section

Date

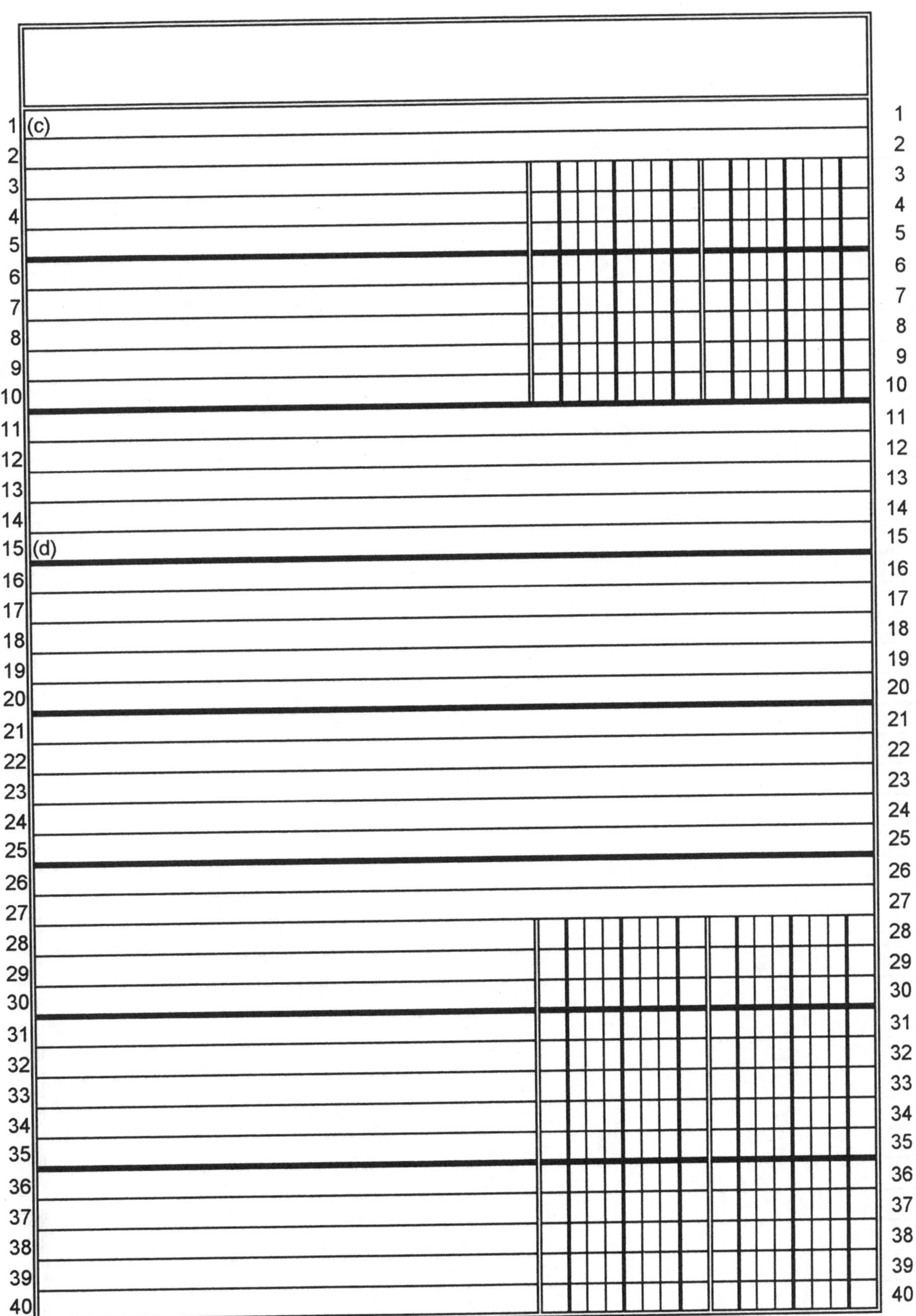

Name

Section

Date

Chapter 1 Communication Activity

New York Company

Name

Section

Date

NEW YORK COMPANY
Balance Sheet
December 31, 2002

Assets		
Liabilities and Owner's Equity		

Name

Section

Date

Chapter 1 Ethics Case

Warren Filler, Job Interviewee

(a)

(b)

(c)

Name

Section

Date

Name

Section

Date

Name

Section

Date

General Journal

Date	Account Titles and Explanations	Ref.	Debit	Credit

Date	Explanation	Ref.	Debit	Credit

Date	Explanation	Ref.	Debit	Credit

Date	Explanation	Ref.	Debit	Credit

Name

Section

Date

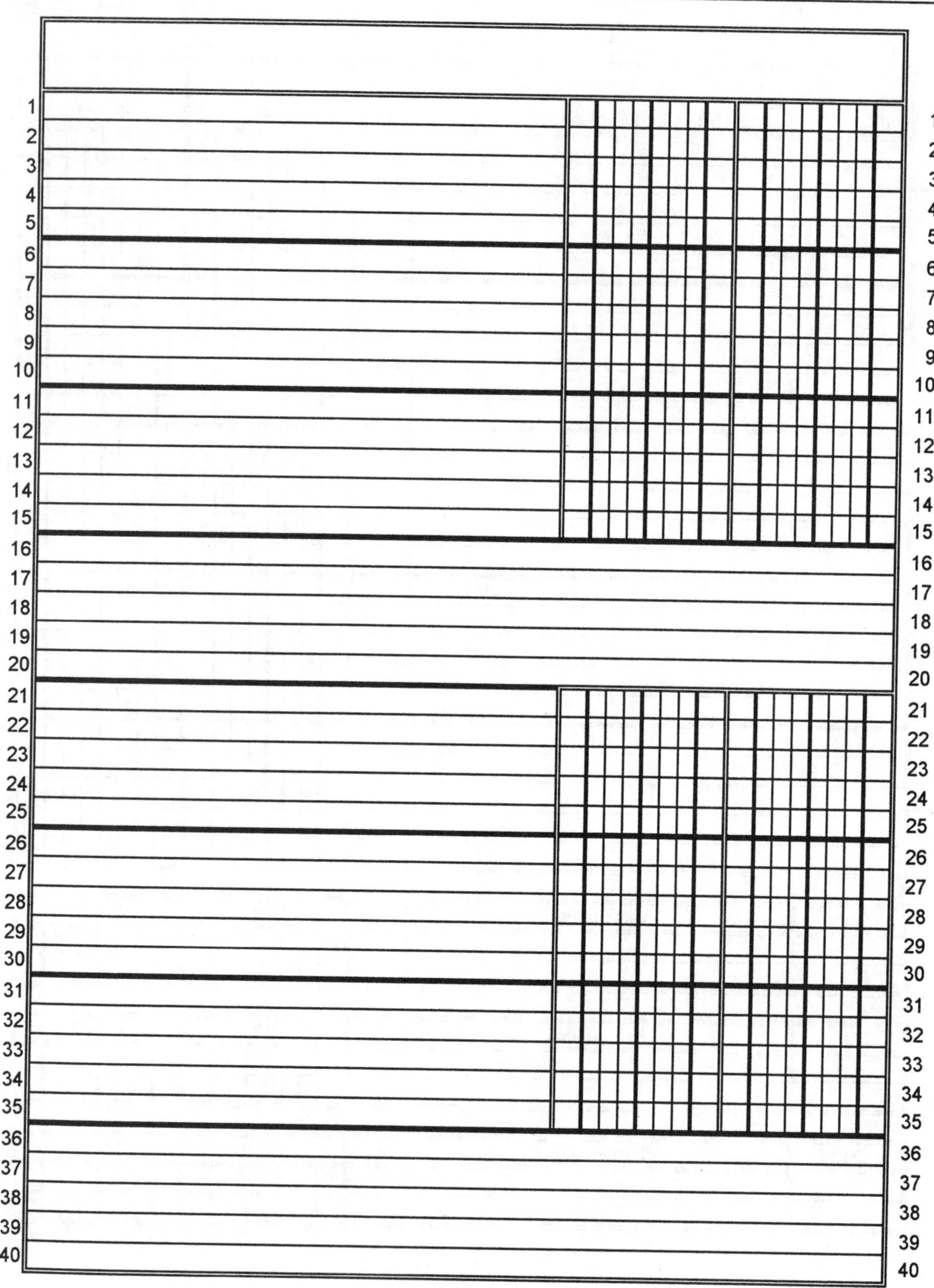

Name

Section

Date

Exercise 2-1

A. Mane, Interior Decorator

Transaction Date	Account Debited (a) Basic Type	Account Debited (b) Specific Account	Account Debited (c) Effect	Account Debited (d) Normal Balance	Account Credited (a) Basic Type	Account Credited (b) Specific Account	Account Credited (c) Effect	Account Credited (d) Normal Balance
Jan.								
2	Asset	Cash	Increase	Debit	Owner's	A. Mane,	Increase	Credit
d					Equity	Capital		
3								
9								
11								
16								
20								
23								
28								

Name

Section

Date

Exercise 2-2

A. Mane, Interior Decorator

Date	Account Titles and Explanation	Ref.	Debit	Credit

Name

Section

Date

#3

#4

Date	Account Titles and Explanation	Ref.	Debit	Credit

Name
Section
Date

Exercise 2-5

J.L. Kang, Invesment Broker

(a)

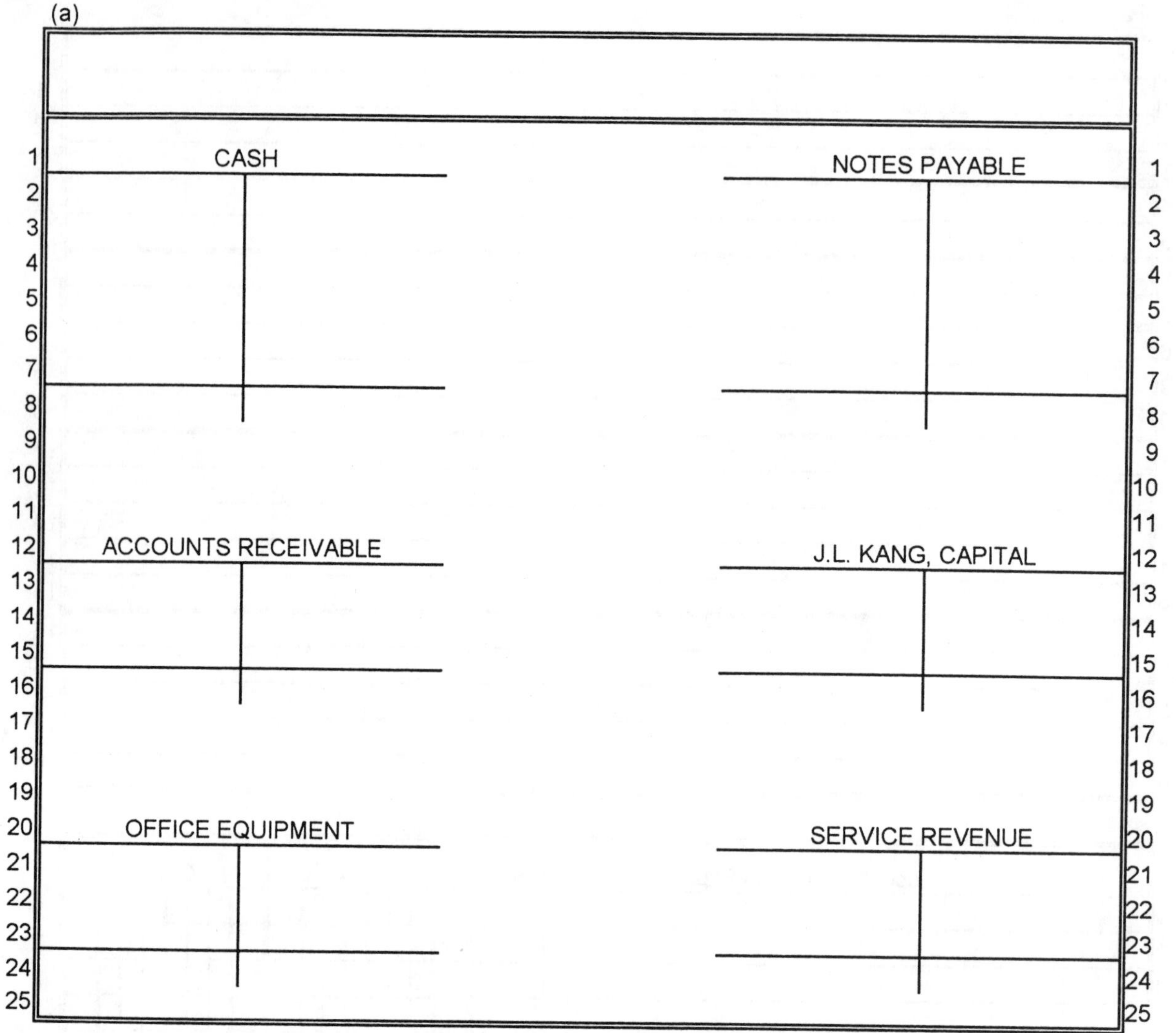

(b)

J. L. KANG, INVESTMENT BROKER
Trial Balance
August 31, 2002

	Debit	Credit

Name

Section

Date

Exercise 2-6

Kim Landscaping Company

(a)

General Journal

Date	Account Titles and Explanation	Ref.	Debit	Credit

(b)

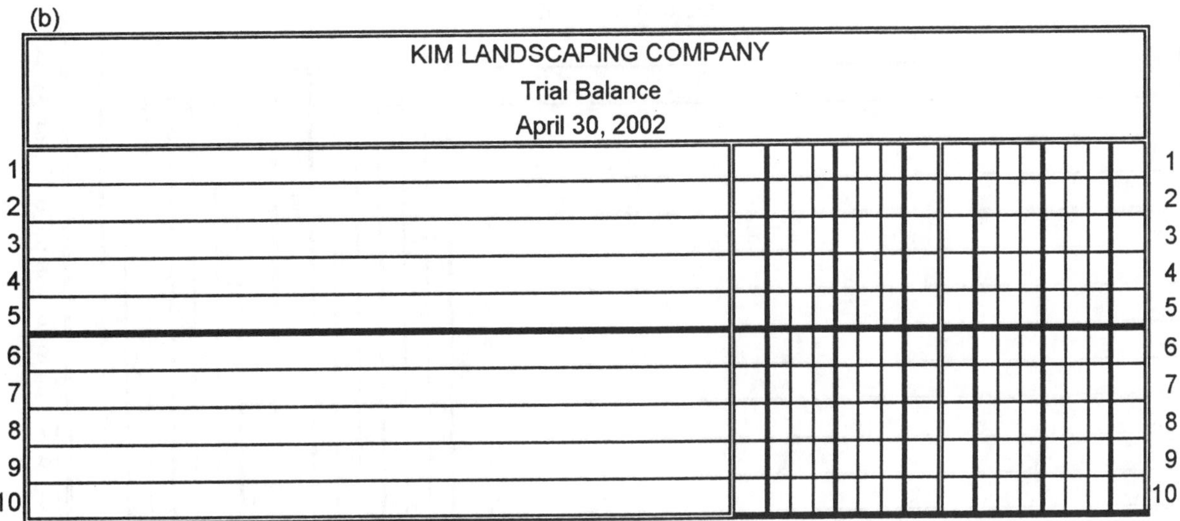

KIM LANDSCAPING COMPANY

Trial Balance

April 30, 2002

Name

Section

Date

Exercise 2-7

Holly Co.

(a)

General Journal

Date	Account Titles and Explanation	Ref.	Debit	Credit

(b)

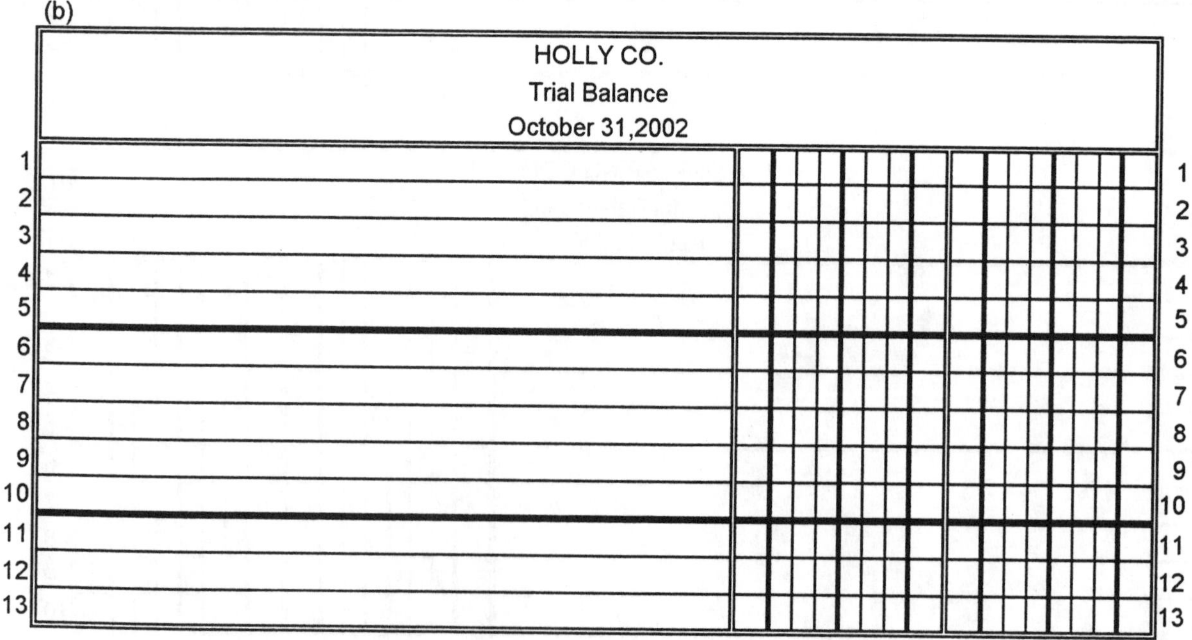

HOLLY CO.

Trial Balance

October 31,2002

Name

Section

Date

Exercise 2-8

Craig Stevenson Company

(a)

General Journal J1

Date	Account Titles and Explanation	Ref.	Debit	Credit

(b)

Cash No. 101

Date	Explanation	Ref.	Debit	Credit	Balance

Equipment No. 157

Date	Explanation	Ref.	Debit	Credit	Balance

Accounts Payable No. 201

Date	Explanation	Ref.	Debit	Credit	Balance

Craig Stevenson, Capital No. 301

Date	Explanation	Ref.	Debit	Credit	Balance

Craig Stevenson, Drawing No. 306

Date	Explanation	Ref.	Debit	Credit	Balance

Name

Section

Date

Exercises 2-9 to 2-10

Tardy Delivery Service

9

Error	(a) In Balance?	(b) Difference	(c) Large Column
1. Credit posting of $400 to Accounts Receivable was omitted	No	$400	Debit

10

TARDY DELIVERY SERVICE

Trial Balance

July 31, 2002

	Debit	Credit

Problem 2-1A

Frontier Park

…eral Journal J1

…tion	Ref.	Debit	Credit	
				1
				2
				3
				4
				5
				6
				7
				8
				9
				10
				11
				12
				13
				14
				15
				16
				17
				18
				19
				20
				21
				22
				23
				24
				25
				26
				27
				28
				29
				30
				31
				32
				33
				34
				35
				36
				37
				38
				39
				40

Name | Problem 2-2A
Section
Date | Iva Holz, CPA

(a)

General Journal

J1

Date	Account Titles and Explanation	Ref.	Debit	Credit

(b)

Cash — No. 101

Date	Explanation	Ref.	Debit	Credit	Balance

Accounts Receivable — No. 112

Date	Explanation	Ref.	Debit	Credit	Balance

Supplies — No. 126

Date	Explanation	Ref.	Debit	Credit	Balance

Accounts Payable — No. 201

Date	Explanation	Ref.	Debit	Credit	Balance

Unearned Revenue — No. 205

Date	Explanation	Ref.	Debit	Credit	Balance

Iva Holz, Capital — No. 301

Date	Explanation	Ref.	Debit	Credit	Balance

(b) (Cont)

Service Revenue No. 400

Date	Explanation	Ref.	Debit	Credit	Balance

Salaries Expense No. 726

Date	Explanation	Ref.	Debit	Credit	Balance

Rent Expense No. 729

Date	Explanation	Ref.	Debit	Credit	Balance

IVA HOLZ, CPA
Trial Balance
April 30, 2002

	Debit	Credit
Cash		
Accounts Receivable		
Supplies		
Accounts Payable		
Unearned Revenue		
Iva Holz, Capital		
Service Revenue		
Salaries Expense		
Rent Expense		

Name	Problem 2-3A
Section	
Date	Byte Repair Service

(a)

(b) and (d)

Cash

Accounts Receivable

Parts Inventory

Prepaid Rent

Shop Equipment

Accounts Payable

Leo Mataruka, Capital

Leo Mataruka, Drawing

Repairs Service Revenue

Advertising Expense

Miscellaneous Expense

Repair Parts Expense

Rent Expense

Wage Expense

Name | Problem 2-3A Continued

Section

Date | Byte Repair Service

(c) General Journal J1

Date	Account Titles and Explanation	Ref.	Debit	Credit

(e)

BYTE REPAIR SERVICE
Trial Balance
January 31, 2002

	Debit	Credit
Cash		
Accounts Receivable		
Parts Inventory		
Prepaid Rent		
Office Equipment		
Accounts Payable		
Leo Mataruka, Capital		
Leo Mataruka, Drawings		
Repair Service Revenue		
Advertising Expense		
Miscellaneous Expense		
Repair Parts Expense		
Rent Expense		
Wage Expense		

(f)

(g)

Name | Problem 2-4A

Section

Date | Santos Company

SANTOS COMPANY
Trial Balance
May 31, 2002

	Debit	Credit

Name

Section

Date

Problem 2-5A

Lake Theater

(a) and ©

Cash — No. 101

Date	Explanation	Ref.	Debit	Credit	Balance

Accounts Receivable — No. 112

Date	Explanation	Ref.	Debit	Credit	Balance

Prepaid Rentals — No. 136

Date	Explanation	Ref.	Debit	Credit	Balance

Land — No. 140

Date	Explanation	Ref.	Debit	Credit	Balance

Buildings — No. 145

Date	Explanation	Ref.	Debit	Credit	Balance

Equipment — No. 157

Date	Explanation	Ref.	Debit	Credit	Balance

Accounts Payable — No. 201

Date	Explanation	Ref.	Debit	Credit	Balance

(a) and (c) (Continued)

Mortgage Payable No. 275

Date	Explanation	Ref.	Debit	Credit	Balance

Avtar Sandhu, Capital No. 301

Date	Explanation	Ref.	Debit	Credit	Balance

Admission Revenue No. 405

Date	Explanation	Ref.	Debit	Credit	Balance

Concession Revenue No. 406

Date	Explanation	Ref.	Debit	Credit	Balance

Advertising Expense No. 610

Date	Explanation	Ref.	Debit	Credit	Balance

Film Rental Expense No. 632

Date	Explanation	Ref.	Debit	Credit	Balance

Salaries Expense No. 726

Date	Explanation	Ref.	Debit	Credit	Balance

Name Problem 2-5A Continued

Section

Date Theater

(b) General Journal J1

Date	Account Titles and Explanation	Ref.	Debit	Credit

(b) (Concluded)

General Journal

J1

Date	Account Titles and Explanation	Ref.	Debit	Credit

(d)

LAKE THEATER
Trial Balance
April 30, 2002

	Debit	Credit
Cash		
Accounts Receivable		
Prepaid Rentals		
Land		
Buildings		
Equipment		
Accounts Payable		
Mortgage Payable		
Avtar Sandhu, Capital		
Admission Revenue		
Concession Revenue		
Advertising Expense		
Film Rental Expense		
Salaries Expense		

Name | Problem 2-1B

Section

Date | Surepar Minature Golf and Driving Range

General Journal | J1

Date	Account Titles and Explanation	Ref.	Debit	Credit

Name Problem 2-2B

Section

Date Patricia Perez, Architect

(a) General Journal J1

	Date	Account Titles and Explanation	Ref.	Debit	Credit	
1						1
2						2
3						3
4						4
5						5
6						6
7						7
8						8
9						9
10						10
11						11
12						12
13						13
14						14
15						15
16						16
17						17
18						18
19						19
20						20
21						21
22						22
23						23
24						24
25						25
26						26
27						27
28						28
29						29
30						30
31						31
32						32
33						33
34						34
35						35
36						36
37						37
38						38
39						39
40						40

Name Problem 2-2B

Section

Date Patricia Perez, Architect

(b)

Cash No. 101

Date	Explanation	Ref.	Debit	Credit	Balance

Accounts Receivable No. 112

Date	Explanation	Ref.	Debit	Credit	Balance

Supplies No. 126

Date	Explanation	Ref.	Debit	Credit	Balance

Accounts Payable No. 201

Date	Explanation	Ref.	Debit	Credit	Balance

Unearned Revenue No. 205

Date	Explanation	Ref.	Debit	Credit	Balance

Patricia Perez, Capital No. 301

Date	Explanation	Ref.	Debit	Credit	Balance

(b) (Cont)

Service Revenue No. 400

Date	Explanation	Ref.	Debit	Credit	Balance

Salaries Expense No. 726

Date	Explanation	Ref.	Debit	Credit	Balance

Rent Expense No. 729

Date	Explanation	Ref.	Debit	Credit	Balance

PATRICIA PEREZ, ARCHITECT
Trial Balance
April 30, 2002

		Debit	Credit	
1	Cash			1
2	Accounts Receivable			2
3	Supplies			3
4	Accounts Payable			4
5	Unearned Revenue			5
6	Patricia Perez, Capital			6
7	Service Revenue			7
8	Salaries Expense			8
9	Rent Expense			9
10				10
11				11

Name — Problem 2-3B

Section

Date — Bablad Brokerage Services

(a) General Journal J1

Date	Account Titles and Explanation	Ref.	Debit	Credit

Name

Section

Date

Babl ad Brokerage Services

(b)

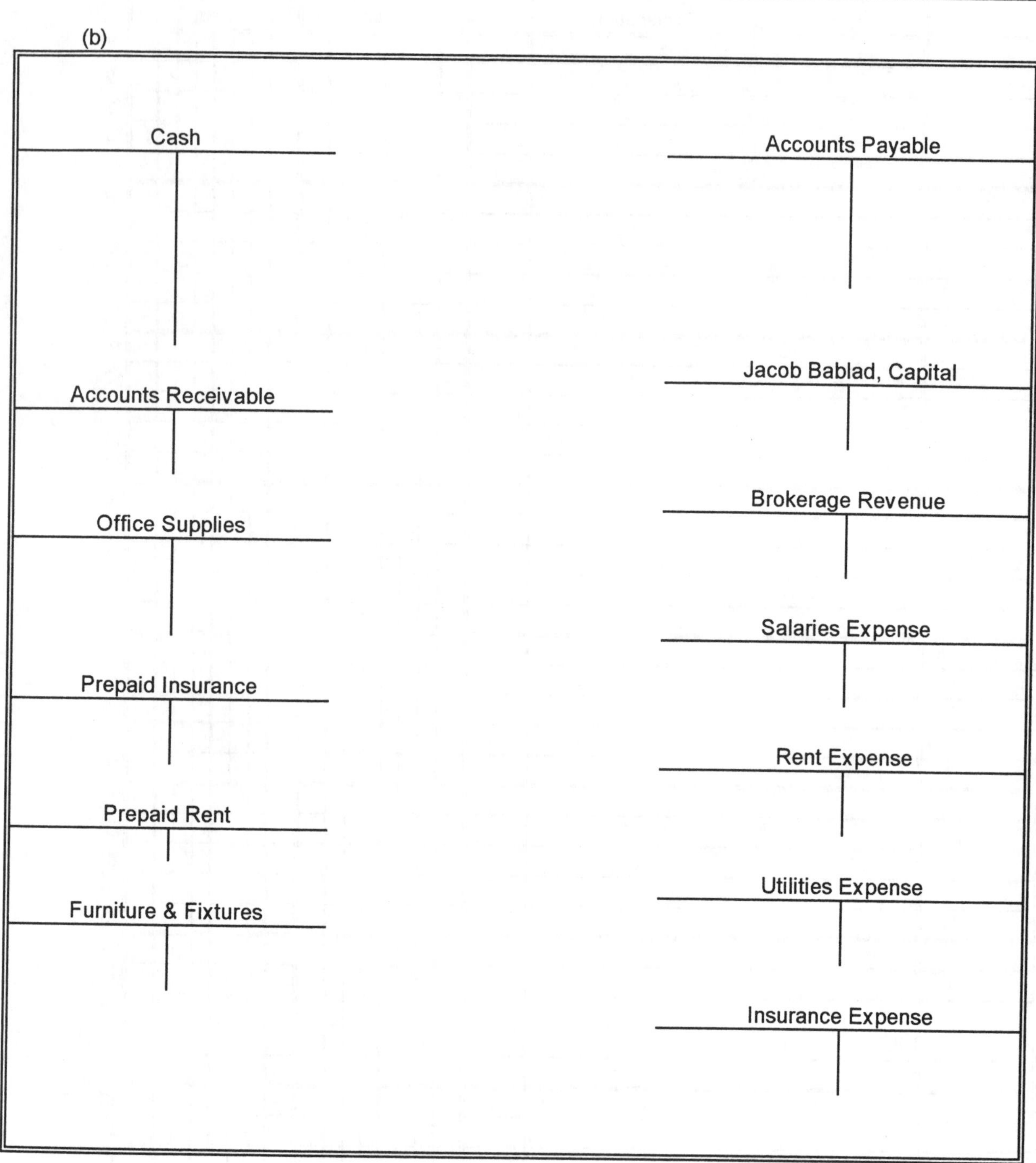

Name

Section

Date

(c)

BABLAD BROKERAGE SERVICES

Trial Balance

May 31, 2002

	Debit	Credit
Cash		
Accounts Receivable		
Office Supplies		
Prepaid Insurance		
Prepaid Rent		
Furniture and Equipment		
Accounts Payable		
Jacob Bablad; Capital		
Brokerage Revenue		
Salaries Expense		
Rent Expense		
Utility Expense		
Insurance Expense		

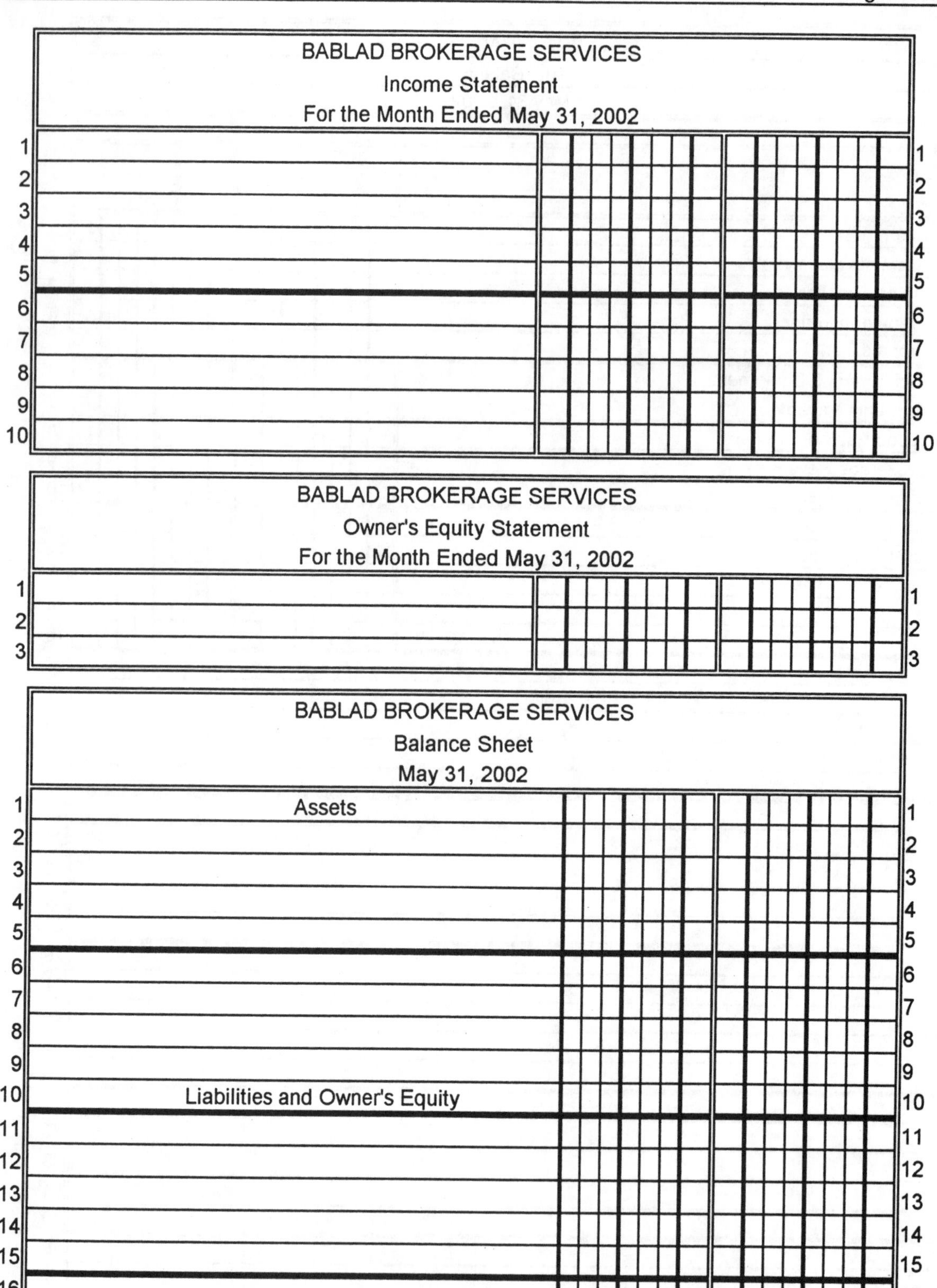

BABLAD BROKERAGE SERVICES
Income Statement
For the Month Ended May 31, 2002

BABLAD BROKERAGE SERVICES
Owner's Equity Statement
For the Month Ended May 31, 2002

BABLAD BROKERAGE SERVICES
Balance Sheet
May 31, 2002

Assets

Liabilities and Owner's Equity

Name

Section

Date

Problem 2-4B

Thom Wargo Co.

THOM WARGO CO.

Trial Balance

June 30, 2002

	Debit	Credit

Journal Entry Aids:

Name

Section

Date

Problem 2-5B

Sabo Theater

(a) and (c

Cash — No. 101

Date	Explanation	Ref.	Debit	Credit	Balance

Accounts Receivable — No. 112

Date	Explanation	Ref.	Debit	Credit	Balance

Land — No. 140

Date	Explanation	Ref.	Debit	Credit	Balance

Buildings — No. 145

Date	Explanation	Ref.	Debit	Credit	Balance

Equipment — No. 157

Date	Explanation	Ref.	Debit	Credit	Balance

Accounts Payable — No. 201

Date	Explanation	Ref.	Debit	Credit	Balance

Name
Section
Date

Problem 2-5B Continued

Sabo Theater

(a) and (c) (Continued)

A. Sabo, Capital — No. 301

Date	Explanation	Ref.	Debit	Credit	Balance

Admission Revenue — No. 405

Date	Explanation	Ref.	Debit	Credit	Balance

Concession Revenue — No. 406

Date	Explanation	Ref.	Debit	Credit	Balance

Advertising Expense — No. 610

Date	Explanation	Ref.	Debit	Credit	Balance

Film Rental Expense — No. 632

Date	Explanation	Ref.	Debit	Credit	Balance

Salaries Expense — No. 726

Date	Explanation	Ref.	Debit	Credit	Balance

Name
Section
Date

Problem 2-5B Continued

Sabo Theater

(b)

General Journal

J1

Date	Account Titles and Explanation	Ref.	Debit	Credit

Name | Problem 2-5B Concluded

Section

Date | Sabo Theater

(b) (Continued) General Journal J1

	Date	Account Titles and Explanation	Ref.	Debit	Credit	
1						1
2						2
3						3
4						4
5						5
6						6
7						7
8						8
9						9
10						10
11						11
12						12
13						13
14						14

(d)

SABO THEATER
Trial Balance
March 31, 2002

		Debit	Credit	
1	Cash			1
2	Accounts Receivable			2
3	Land			3
4	Buildings			4
5	Equipment			5
6	Accounts Payable			6
7	A. Sabo, Capital			7
8	Admission Revenue			8
9	Concession Revenue			9
10	Advertising Expense			10
11	Film Rental Expense			11
12	Salaries Expense			12
13				13
14				14
15				15
16				16
17				17

Name

Section

Date

Chapter 2 Financial Reporting Problem

Lands' End

(a)

Account	Side of Account for		Normal Balance
	Increase	Decrease	
Accounts Payable			
Accounts Receivable			
Property, Plant, and Equipment			
Income Taxes Payable			
Interest Expense			
Inventory			

(b) and (c)

	Accounts	Effect
(b) When		
Acccounts Receivable is decreased		
Accounts Payable is decreased		
Inventories are increased		
(c) When		
Interest Expense is increased		
OR		
Property, Plant and Equipment is increased		
OR		

(a) Lands' End

1.

2.

3.

4.

Abercrombie & Fitch

1.

2.

3.

4.

(b)

Section

Date

(a)

(b)

(c)

(d)

Name

Section

Date

Company Information

Name
Section
Date

Chapter 2 Group Decision Case

Lucy Lars Riding Academy

(a) General Journal

	Date	Account Titles and Explanation	Ref.	Debit	Credit	
1						1
2						2
3						3
4						4
5						5
6						6
7						7
8						8
9						9
10						10
11						11
12						12
13						13
14						14
15						15
16						16
17						17
18						18
19						19
20						20
21						21
22						22
23						23
24						24
25						25
26						26
27						27
28						28
29						29
30						30
31						31
32						32
33						33
34						34
35						35
36						36
37						37
38						38
39						39
40						40

(b)

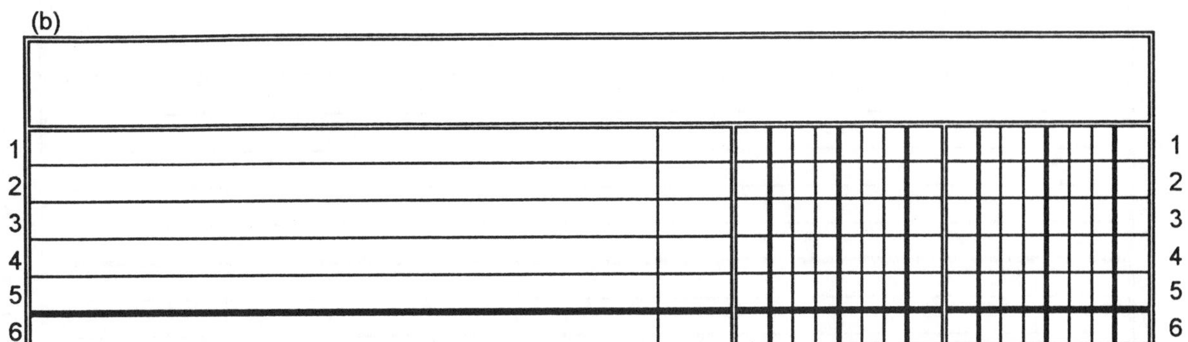

(c) and (d)

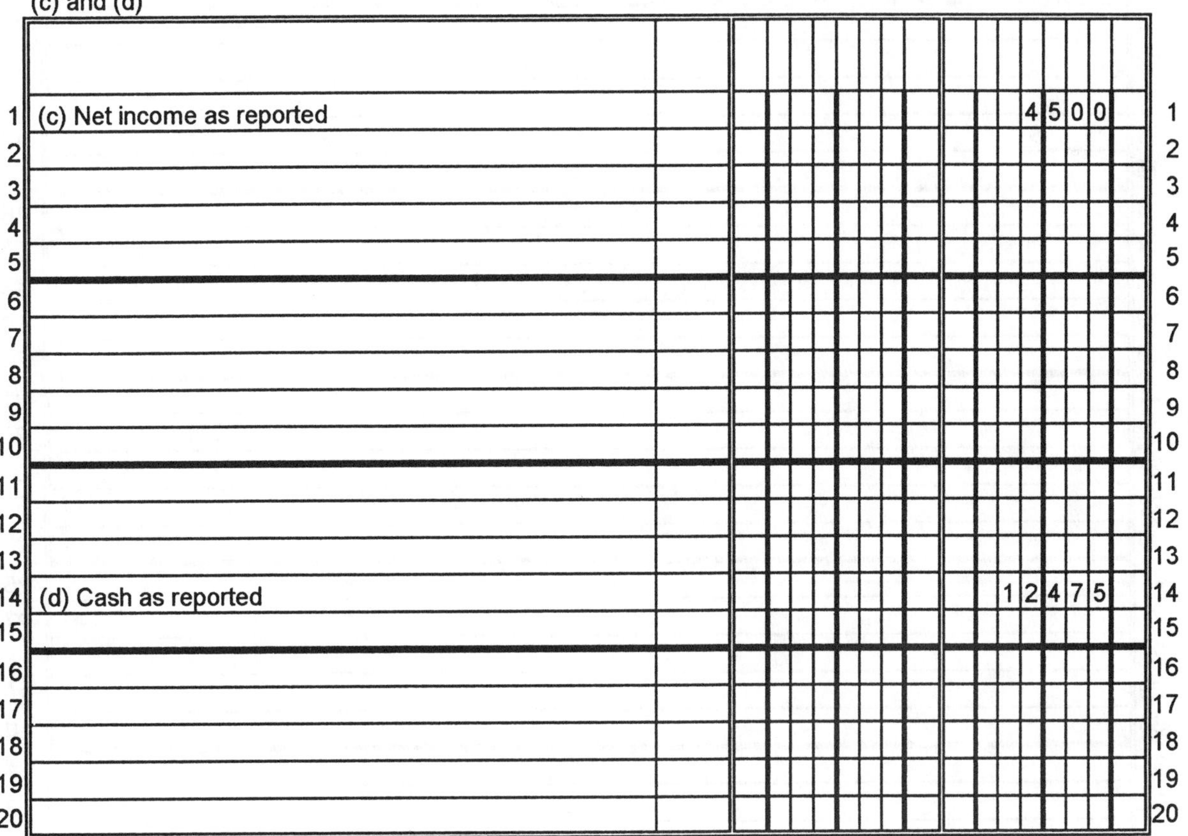

(c) Net income as reported		4500
(d) Cash as reported		12475

Name

Section

Date

Merlynn's Maid Company

Name | Chapter 2 Ethics Case

Section

Date | Hokey Company

(a)

(b)

(c)

Name

Section

Date

Name

Section

Date

Name

Section

Date

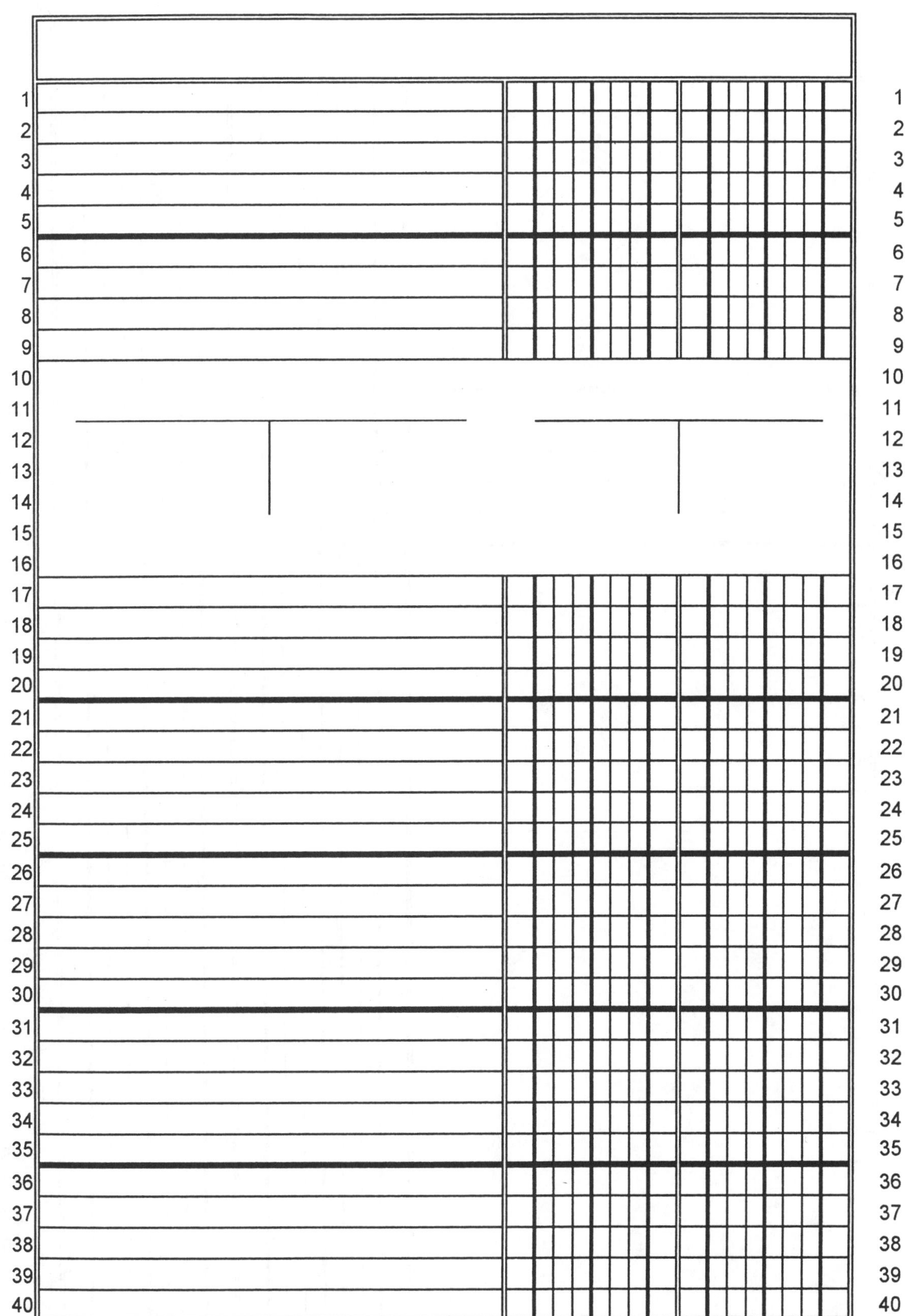

Name

Section

Date

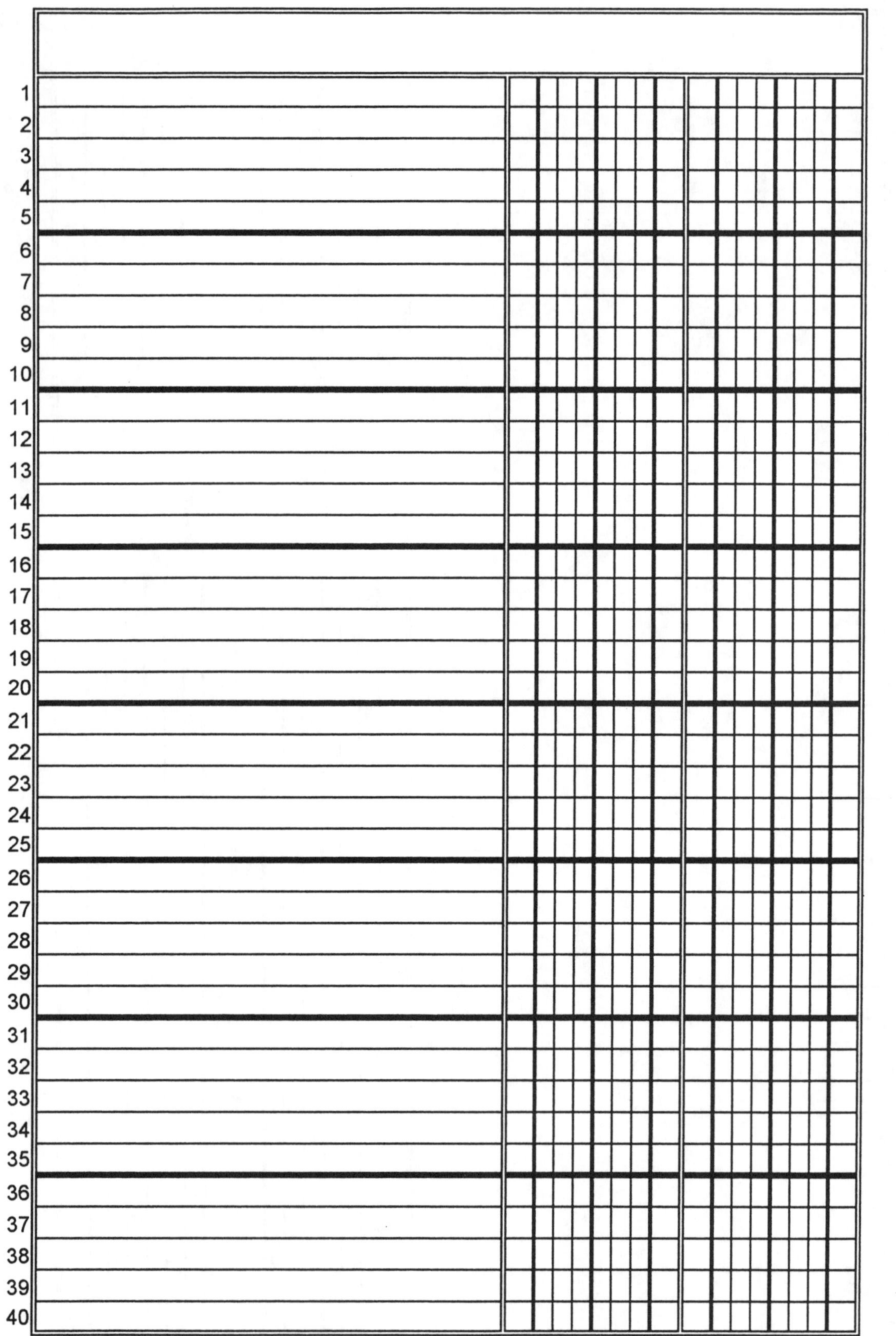

Name Exercise 3-1

Section

Date Cash vs Accrual

Name

Section

Date

Exercises 3-2 to 3-3

#2

Adj.	(a) Type of Adjustment	(b) Accounts before Adjustment

#3

General Journal

Date	Acccounts and Explanations	Ref.	Debit	Credit

Name

Section

Date

General Journal

Date	Account Titles and Explanations	Debit	Credit
#4			
#5			

Name

Section

Date

Exercises 3-6 to 3-7

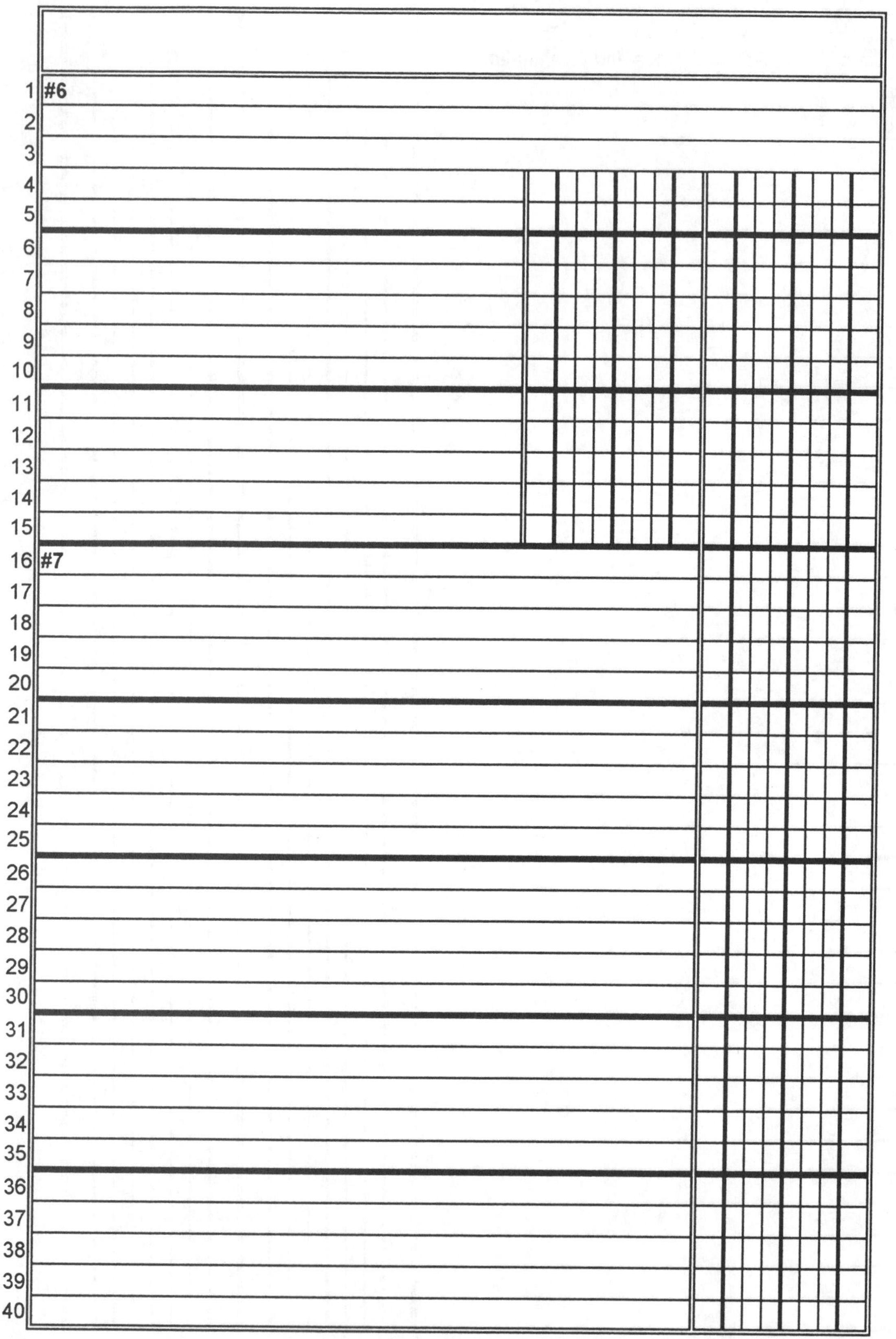

Name Exercises 3-8 to 3-9

Section

Date

General Journal

Date	Account Titles and Explanations	Debit	Credit
#8			
#9			

Name

Section

Date

Exercise 3-10

Tang Company

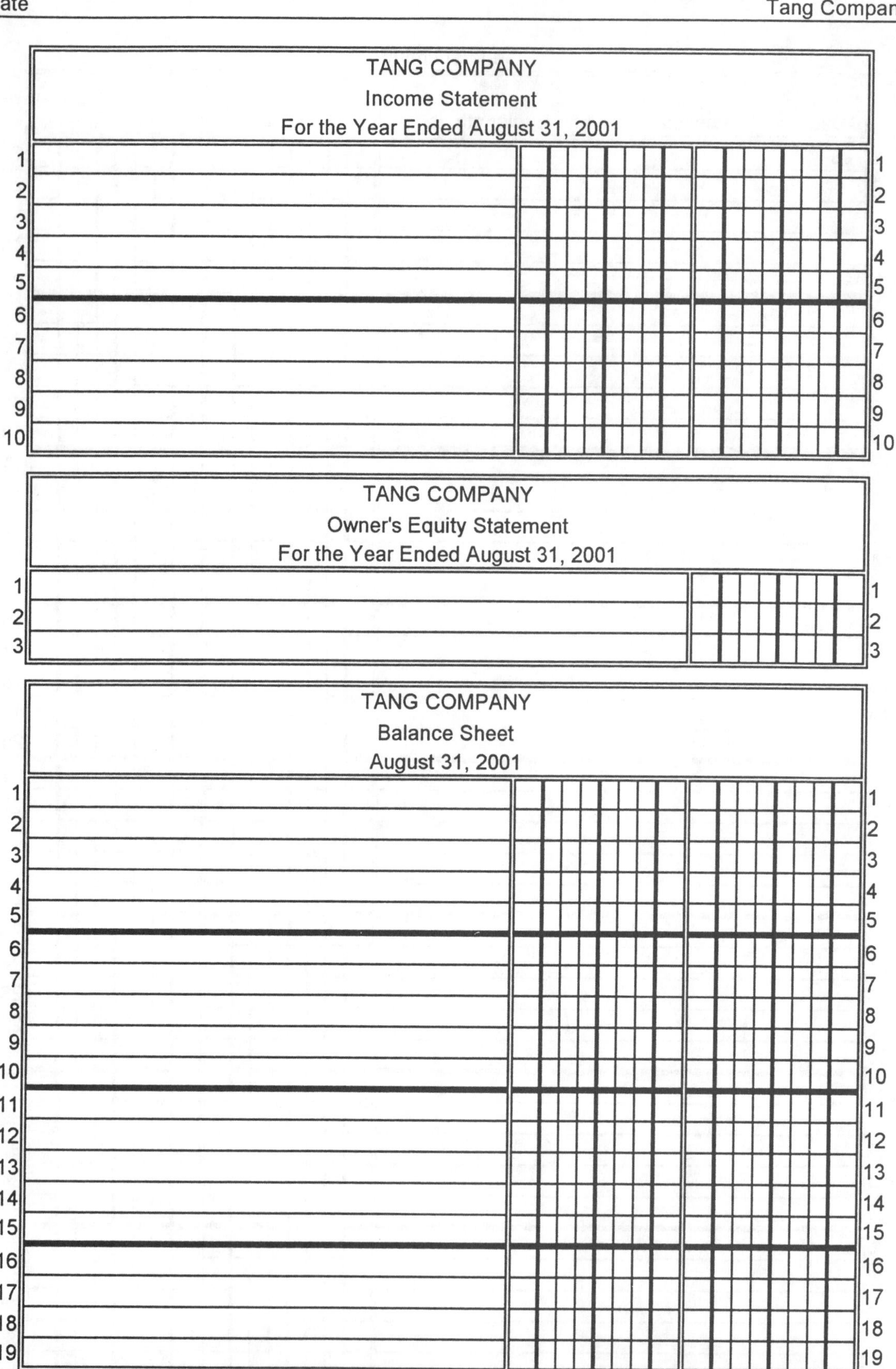

TANG COMPANY
Income Statement
For the Year Ended August 31, 2001

TANG COMPANY
Owner's Equity Statement
For the Year Ended August 31, 2001

TANG COMPANY
Balance Sheet
August 31, 2001

Name

Section

Date

Exercise 3-11

Breakers Billiards Club

General Journal

Date	Account Titles and Explanations	Debit	Credit

Name

Section

Date

Exercise 3-12

Devereaux Company

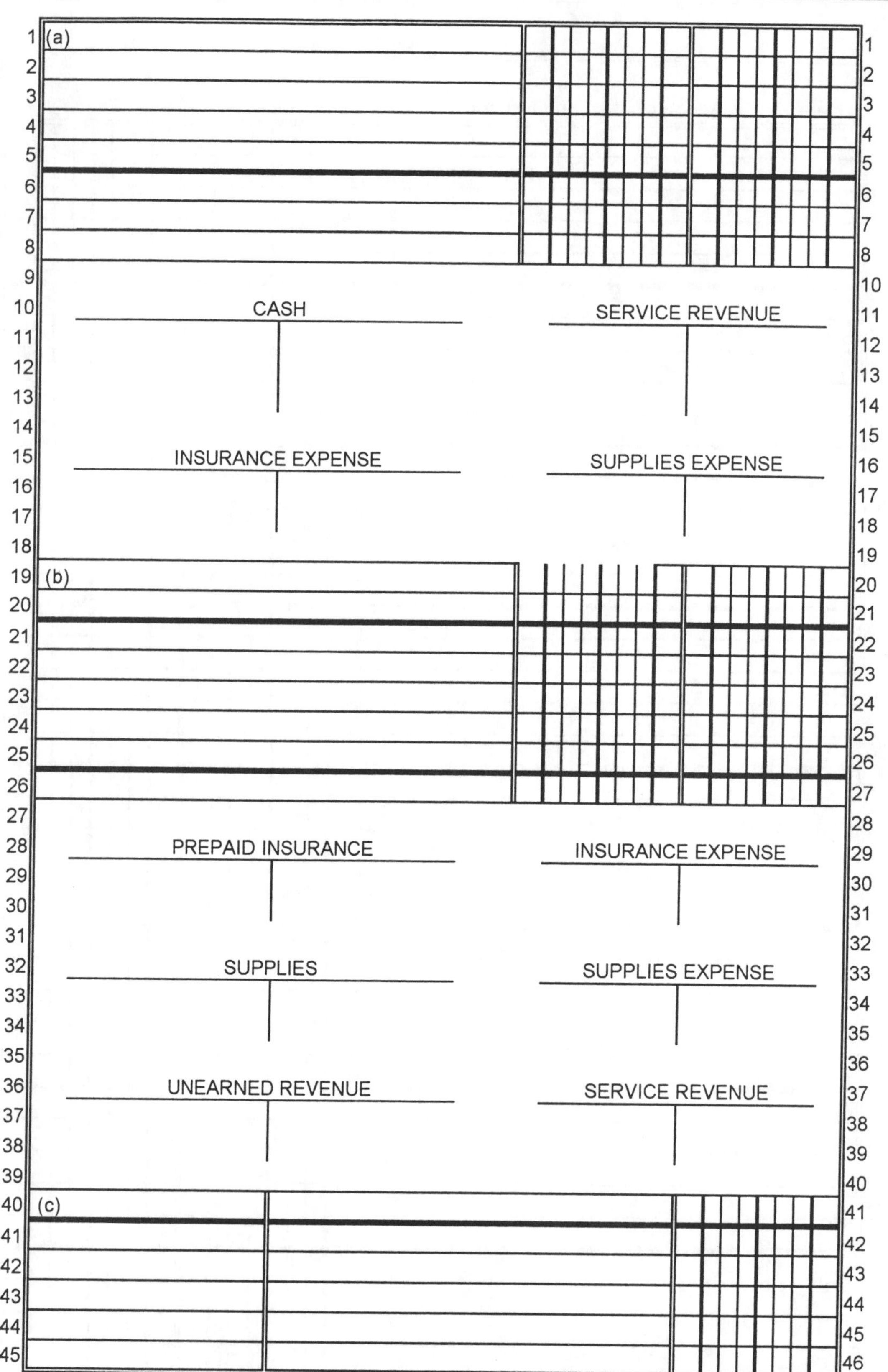

Name | Problem 3-1A

Section

Date | Solo Company

(a) General Journal J3

Date	Account Titles and Explanations	Ref.	Debit	Credit

Name
Section
Date

Problem 3-1A Continued

Solo Company

(b)

Cash — No. 100

Date	Explanation	Ref.	Debit	Credit	Balance

Accounts Receivable — No. 110

Date	Explanation	Ref.	Debit	Credit	Balance

Prepaid Insurance — No. 120

Date	Explanation	Ref.	Debit	Credit	Balance

Supplies — No. 130

Date	Explanation	Ref.	Debit	Credit	Balance

Office Equipment — No. 135

Date	Explanation	Ref.	Debit	Credit	Balance

Accumulated Depreciation - Office Equipment — No. 136

Date	Explanation	Ref.	Debit	Credit	Balance

Accounts Payable — No. 200

Date	Explanation	Ref.	Debit	Credit	Balance

Name

Section

Date

Problem 3-1A Continued

Solo Company

(b) (Continued)

Utilities Payable — No. 210

Date	Explanation	Ref.	Debit	Credit	Balance

Salaries Payable — No. 220

Date	Explanation	Ref.	Debit	Credit	Balance

Unearned Service Revenue — No. 230

Date	Explanation	Ref.	Debit	Credit	Balance

H. Solo, Capital — No. 300

Date	Explanation	Ref.	Debit	Credit	Balance

Service Revenue — No. 400

Date	Explanation	Ref.	Debit	Credit	Balance

Salaries Expense — No. 510

Date	Explanation	Ref.	Debit	Credit	Balance

Rent Expense — No. 520

Date	Explanation	Ref.	Debit	Credit	Balance

Name

Section

Date

Problem 3-1A Continued

Solo Company

(b) (Continued)

Depreciation Expense — No. 530

Date	Explanation	Ref.	Debit	Credit	Balance

Insurance Expense — No. 540

Date	Explanation	Ref.	Debit	Credit	Balance

Utilities Expense — No. 550

Date	Explanation	Ref.	Debit	Credit	Balance

Supplies Expense — No. 560

Date	Explanation	Ref.	Debit	Credit	Balance

Name

Section

Date

(c)

SOLO COMPANY

Adjusted Trial Balance

June 30, 2002

	Debit	Credit

Name

Section

Date

Problem 3-2A

Muddy River Resort

(a)

General Journal

J1

Date	Account Titles and Explanations	Ref.	Debit	Credit

Cash

No. 101

Date	Explanation	Ref.	Debit	Credit	Balance

Accounts Receivable

No. 112

Date	Explanation	Ref.	Debit	Credit	Balance

(b)

Supplies No. 126

Date	Explanation	Ref.	Debit	Credit	Balance

Prepaid Insurance No. 130

Date	Explanation	Ref.	Debit	Credit	Balance

Land No. 140

Date	Explanation	Ref.	Debit	Credit	Balance

Cottages No. 143

Date	Explanation	Ref.	Debit	Credit	Balance

Accumulated Depreciation-Cottages No. 144

Date	Explanation	Ref.	Debit	Credit	Balance

Furniture No. 149

Date	Explanation	Ref.	Debit	Credit	Balance

Accumulated Depreciation-Furniture No. 150

Date	Explanation	Ref.	Debit	Credit	Balance

Name
Section
Date

Problem 3-2A Continued

Muddy River Resort

(b) (Continued)

Accounts Payable — No. 201

Date	Explanation	Ref.	Debit	Credit	Balance

Unearned Rent — No. 208

Date	Explanation	Ref.	Debit	Credit	Balance

Salaries Payable — No. 212

Date	Explanation	Ref.	Debit	Credit	Balance

Interest Payable — No. 230

Date	Explanation	Ref.	Debit	Credit	Balance

Mortgage Payable — No. 275

Date	Explanation	Ref.	Debit	Credit	Balance

P. Javorek, Capital — No. 301

Date	Explanation	Ref.	Debit	Credit	Balance

P. Javorek, Drawing — No. 302

Date	Explanation	Ref.	Debit	Credit	Balance

Name

Section

Date

Problem 3-2A Continued

Muddy River Resort

(b) (Continued)

Rent Revenue No. 429

Date	Explanation	Ref.	Debit	Credit	Balance

Depreciation Expense-Cottages No. 620

Date	Explanation	Ref.	Debit	Credit	Balance

Depreciation Expense - Furniture No. 621

Date	Explanation	Ref.	Debit	Credit	Balance

Repair Expense No. 622

Date	Explanation	Ref.	Debit	Credit	Balance

Supplies Expense No. 631

Date	Explanation	Ref.	Debit	Credit	Balance

Interest Expense No. 718

Date	Explanation	Ref.	Debit	Credit	Balance

Insurance Expense No. 722

Date	Explanation	Ref.	Debit	Credit	Balance

(b) (Continued)

Salaries Expense No. 726

Date	Explanation	Ref.	Debit	Credit	Balance

Utilities Expense No. 732

Date	Explanation	Ref.	Debit	Credit	Balance

(c)

MUDDY RIVER RESORT
Adjusted Trial Balance
August 31, 2002

	Debit	Credit

Name

Section

Date

Problem 3-2A Continued

Muddy River Resort

(d)

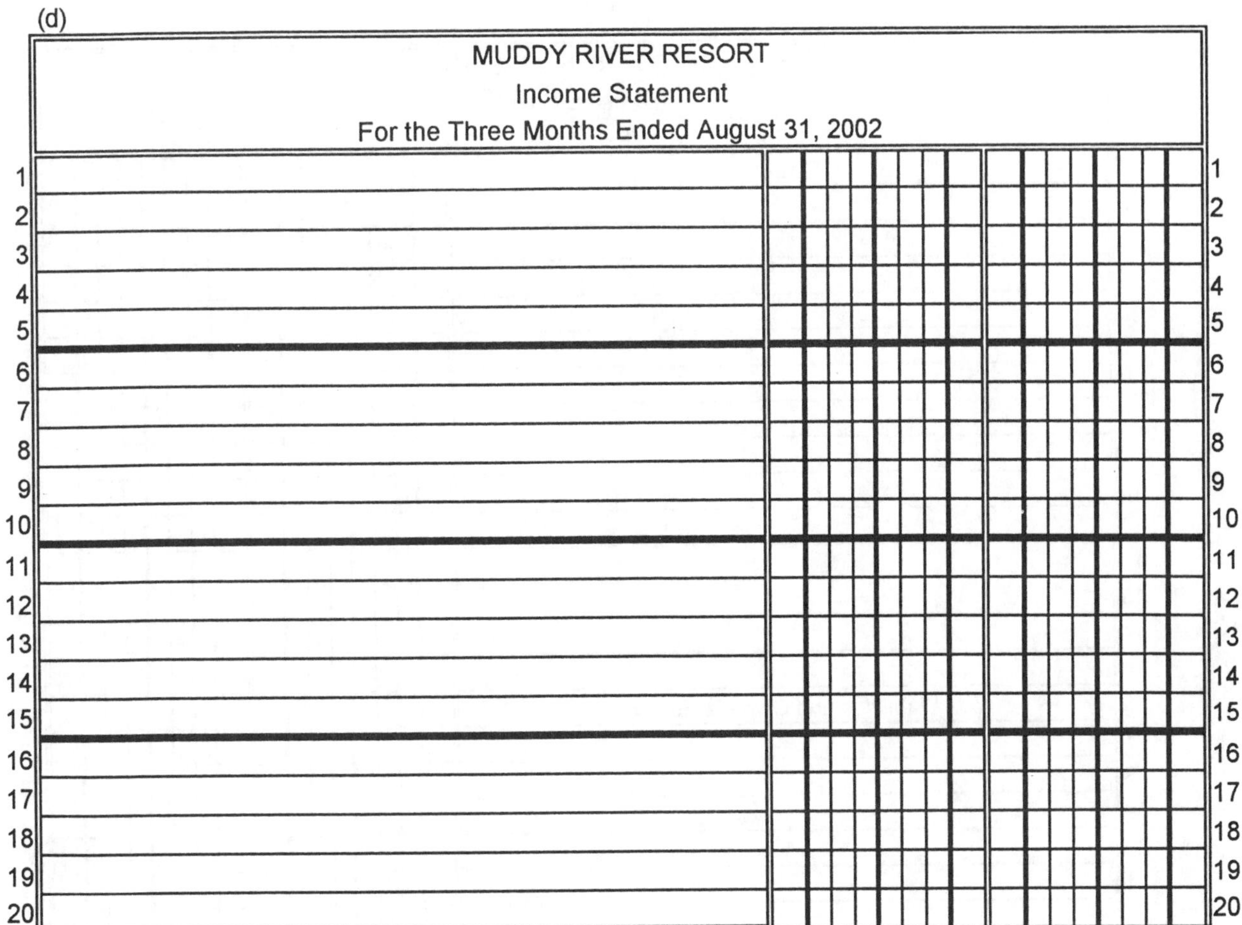

MUDDY RIVER RESORT

Income Statement

For the Three Months Ended August 31, 2002

MUDDY RIVER RESORT

Owner's Equity Statement

For the Three Months Ended August 31, 2002

Name
Section
Date

(d) (Continued)

MUDDY RIVER RESORT
Balance Sheet
August 31, 2002

Assets

Liabilities and Owner's Equity

Name Problem 3-3A

Section

Date Grant Advertising Agency

(a) General Journal

Date	Accounts Titles and Explanation	Ref.	Debit	Credit

(b)

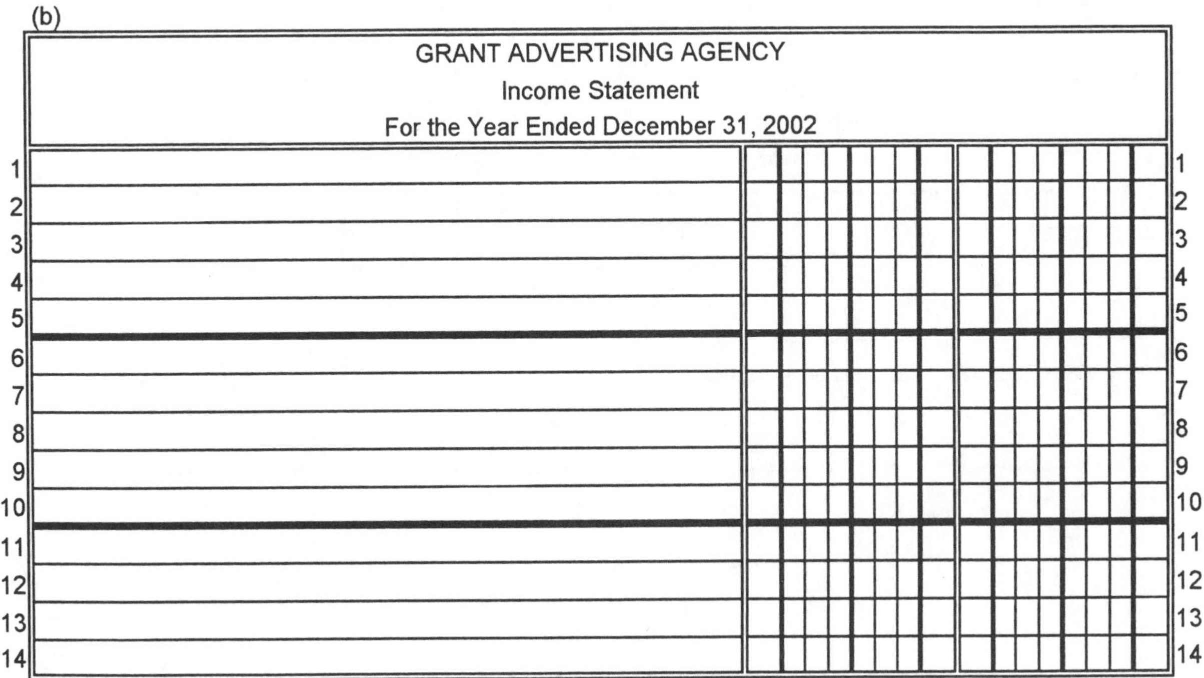

GRANT ADVERTISING AGENCY
Income Statement
For the Year Ended December 31, 2002

(b) (Continued)

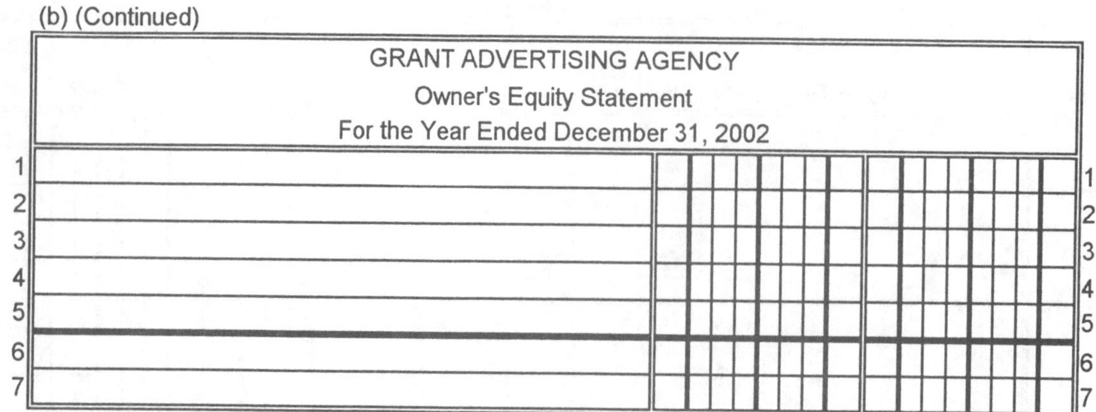

GRANT ADVERTISING AGENCY
Owner's Equity Statement
For the Year Ended December 31, 2002

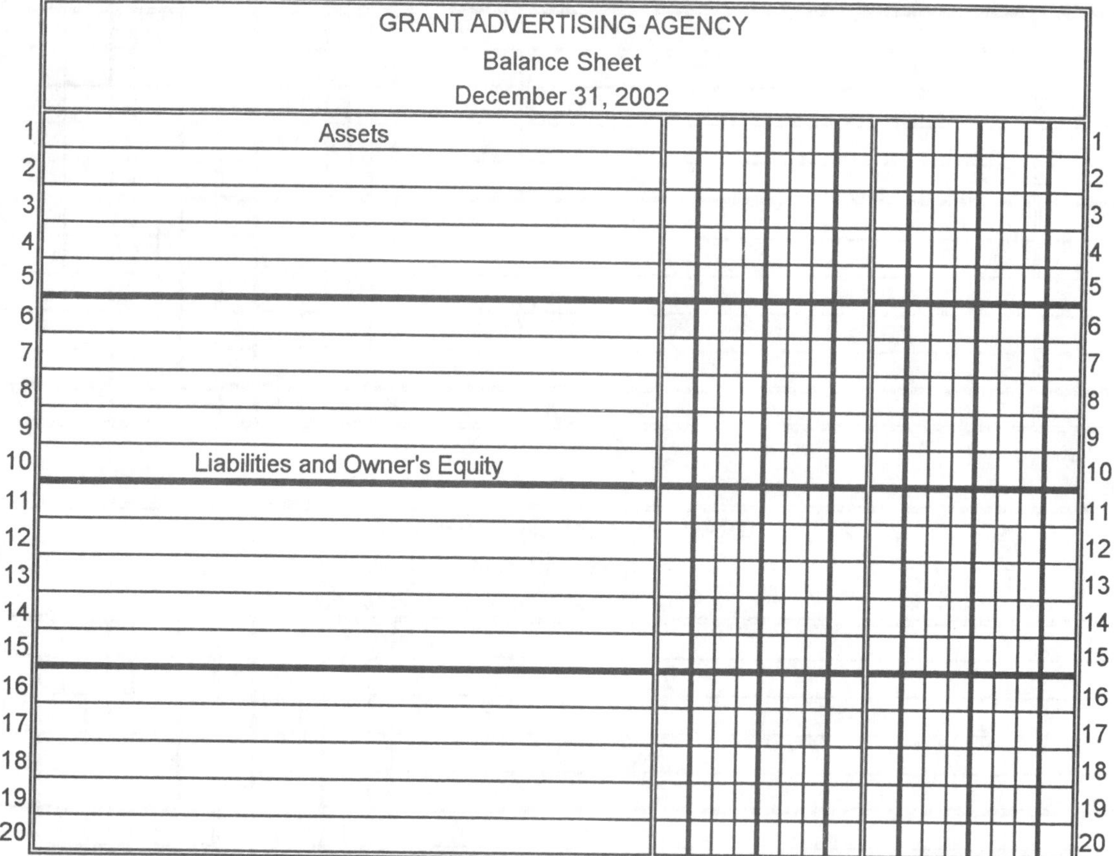

GRANT ADVERTISING AGENCY
Balance Sheet
December 31, 2002

Assets

Liabilities and Owner's Equity

(c)

Name Problem 3-4A

Section

Date Greenberg Company

General Journal

Date	Accounts Titles and Explanation	Ref.	Debit	Credit

Name Problem 3-5A

Section

Date Rijo Equipment Repair

(a), (c) and (e)

Cash No. 101

Date	Explanation	Ref.	Debit	Credit	Balance

Accounts Receivable No. 112

Date	Explanation	Ref.	Debit	Credit	Balance

Supplies No. 126

Date	Explanation	Ref.	Debit	Credit	Balance

Store Equipment No. 153

Date	Explanation	Ref.	Debit	Credit	Balance

Accumulated Depreciation-Store Equipment No. 154

Date	Explanation	Ref.	Debit	Credit	Balance

Name Problem 3-5A

Section

Date Rijo Equipment Repair

(a), (c) and (e) (Continued)

Account Payable No. 201

Date	Explanation	Ref.	Debit	Credit	Balance

Unearned Service Revenue No. 209

Date	Explanation	Ref.	Debit	Credit	Balance

Salaries Payable No. 212

Date	Explanation	Ref.	Debit	Credit	Balance

J. Rijo, Capital No. 301

Date	Explanation	Ref.	Debit	Credit	Balance

Service Revenue No. 407

Date	Explanation	Ref.	Debit	Credit	Balance

Depreciation Expense No. 615

Date	Explanation	Ref.	Debit	Credit	Balance

Name
Section
Date

Problem 3-5A Continued

Rijo Equipment Repair

(a), (c) and (e) (Continued)

Supplies Expense — No. 631

Date	Explanation	Ref.	Debit	Credit	Balance

Salaries Expense — No. 726

Date	Explanation	Ref.	Debit	Credit	Balance

Rent Expense — No. 729

Date	Explanation	Ref.	Debit	Credit	Balance

(b)

General Journal — J1

Date	Account Titles and Explanation	Ref.	Debit	Credit

(b)(Cont General Journal J1

Date	Account Titles and Explanation	Ref.	Debit	Credit

(e) General Journal J2

Date	Account Titles and Explanation	Ref.	Debit	Credit

Name — Problem 3-5A Continued

Section

Date — Rijo Equipment Repair

(d) and (f)

RIJO EQUIPMENT REPAIR
Trial Balances
September 30, 2002

	Before Adjustment		After Adjustment	
	Dr.	Cr.	Dr.	Cr.

(g)

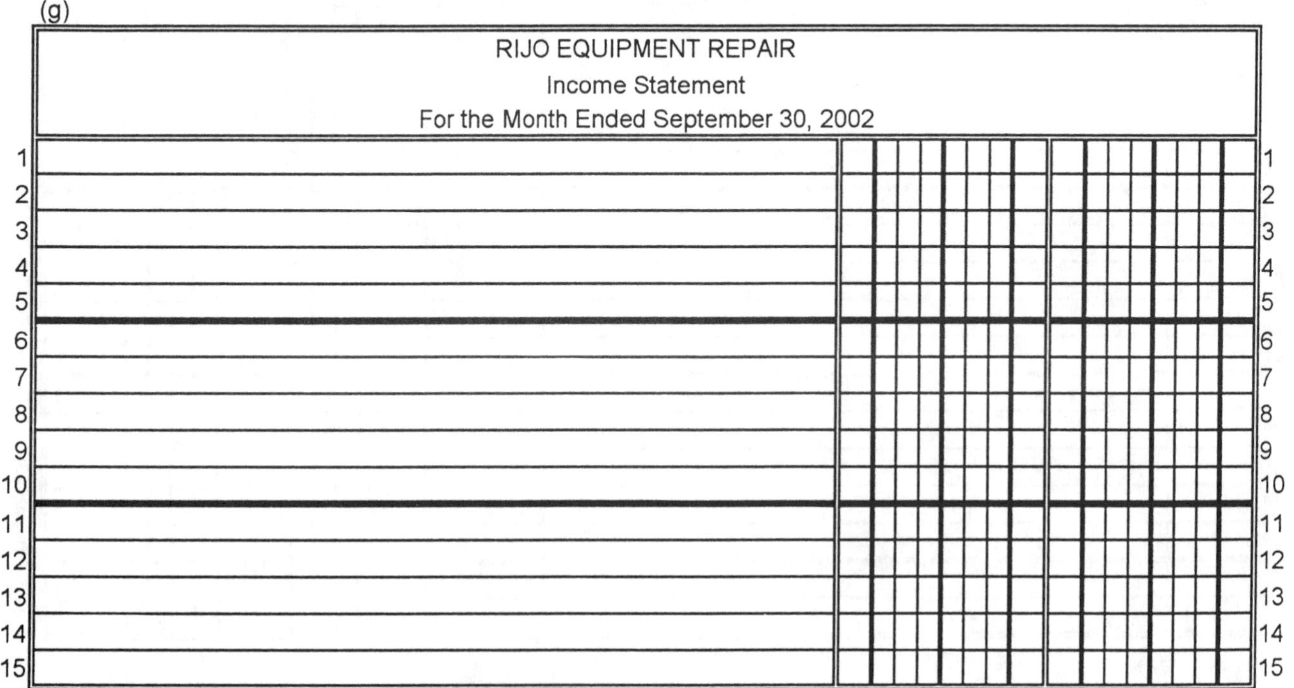

RIJO EQUIPMENT REPAIR
Income Statement
For the Month Ended September 30, 2002

(g) (Continued)

RIJO EQUIPMENT REPAIR
Owner's Equity Statement
For the Month Ended September 30, 2002

RIJO EQUIPEMENT REPAIR
Balance Sheet
September 30, 2002

Assets

Liabilities and Owner's Equity

Name Problem 3-6A

Section

Date Global Graphics Company

(a) General Journal

Date	Account Titles and Explanations	Ref.	Debit	Credit

Name

Section

Date

Problem 3-6A Continued

Global Graphics Company

(b)

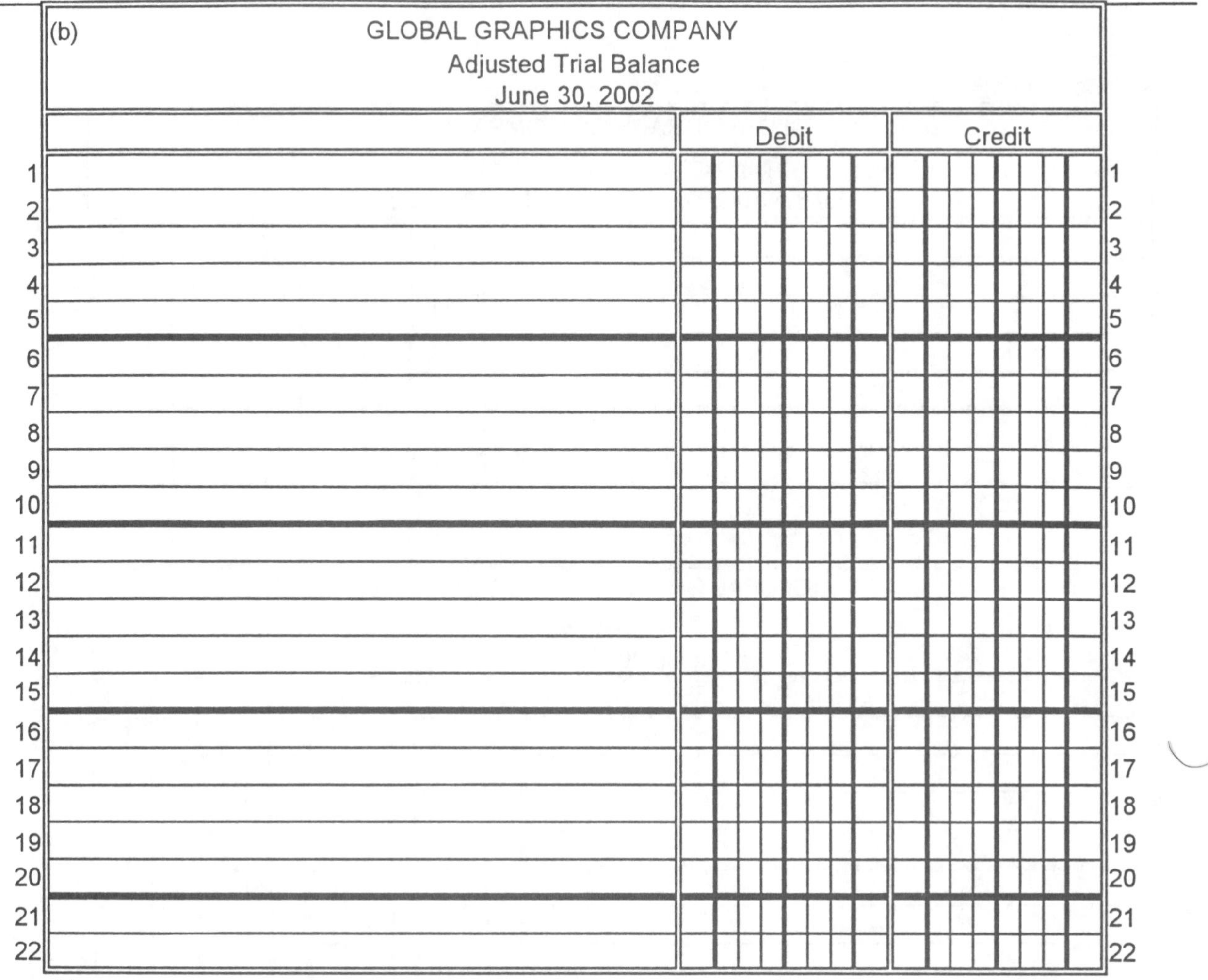

GLOBAL GRAPHICS COMPANY
Adjusted Trial Balance
June 30, 2002

	Debit	Credit

(c)

GLOBAL GRAPHICS COMPANY
Income Statement
For the Six Months Ended June 30, 2002

(c) (Continued)

GLOBAL GRAPHICS COMPANY
Owner's Equity Statement
For the Six Months Ended June 30, 2002

GLOBAL GRAPHICS COMPANY
Balance Sheet
June 30, 2002

Assets

Liabilities and Owner's Equity

Name Problem 3-1B

Section

Date Astromech Consulting

(a) General Journal J4

Date	Account Titles and Explanations	Ref.	Debit	Credit

Name Problem 3-1B

Section

Date Astromech Consulting

(b)

Cash No. 100

Date	Explanation	Ref.	Debit	Credit	Balance

Accounts Receivable No. 110

Date	Explanation	Ref.	Debit	Credit	Balance

Prepaid Insurance No.120

Date	Explanation	Ref.	Debit	Credit	Balance

Supplies No. 130

Date	Explanation	Ref.	Debit	Credit	Balance

Office Furniture No. 135

Date	Explanation	Ref.	Debit	Credit	Balance

Accumulated Depreciation - Office Furniture No. 136

Date	Explanation	Ref.	Debit	Credit	Balance

Accounts Payable No. 200

Date	Explanation	Ref.	Debit	Credit	Balance

(b) (Continued)

Travel Payable — No. 210

Date	Explanation	Ref.	Debit	Credit	Balance

Salaries Payable — No. 220

Date	Explanation	Ref.	Debit	Credit	Balance

Unearned Service Revenue — No. 230

Date	Explanation	Ref.	Debit	Credit	Balance

J. Brown, Capital — No. 300

Date	Explanation	Ref.	Debit	Credit	Balance

Service Revenue — No. 400

Date	Explanation	Ref.	Debit	Credit	Balance

Salaries Expense — No. 510

Date	Explanation	Ref.	Debit	Credit	Balance

(b) (Continued)

Rent Expense No. 520

Date	Explanation	Ref.	Debit	Credit	Balance

Depreciation Expense No. 530

Date	Explanation	Ref.	Debit	Credit	Balance

Insurance Expense No. 540

Date	Explanation	Ref.	Debit	Credit	Balance

Travel Expense No. 550

Date	Explanation	Ref.	Debit	Credit	Balance

Supplies Expense No. 560

Date	Explanation	Ref.	Debit	Credit	Balance

Name

Section

Date

(c)

ASTROMECH CONSULTING
Adjusted Trial Balance
May 31, 2002

	Debit	Credit

Name Problem 3-2B

Section

Date Roach Motel

(a) General Journal

Date	Account Titles and Explanations	Ref.	Debit	Credit

(b)

Cash No. 100

Date	Explanation	Ref.	Debit	Credit	Balance

Supplies No. 126

Date	Explanation	Ref.	Debit	Credit	Balance

Prepaid Insurance No. 130

Date	Explanation	Ref.	Debit	Credit	Balance

Land No. 140

Date	Explanation	Ref.	Debit	Credit	Balance

Lodge No. 141

Date	Explanation	Ref.	Debit	Credit	Balance

Accumulated Depreciation-Lodge No. 142

Date	Explanation	Ref.	Debit	Credit	Balance

Furniture No. 149

Date	Explanation	Ref.	Debit	Credit	Balance

Name

Section

Date

Problem 3-2B Continued

Roach Motel

(b) (Continued)

Accumulated Depreciation-Furniture — No. 150

Date	Explanation	Ref.	Debit	Credit	Balance

Accounts Payable — No. 201

Date	Explanation	Ref.	Debit	Credit	Balance

Unearned Rent — No. 208

Date	Explanation	Ref.	Debit	Credit	Balance

Salaries Payable — No. 212

Date	Explanation	Ref.	Debit	Credit	Balance

Interest Payable — No. 290

Date	Explanation	Ref.	Debit	Credit	Balance

Mortgage Payable — No. 275

Date	Explanation	Ref.	Debit	Credit	Balance

Sara Sutton, Capital — No. 301

Date	Explanation	Ref.	Debit	Credit	Balance

Name

Section

Date

Problem 3-2B Continued

Roach Motel

(b) (Continued)

Rent Revenue — No. 429

Date	Explanation	Ref.	Debit	Credit	Balance

Advertising Expense — No. 610

Date	Explanation	Ref.	Debit	Credit	Balance

Depreciation Expense-Lodge — No. 619

Date	Explanation	Ref.	Debit	Credit	Balance

Depreciation Expense - Furniture — No. 621

Date	Explanation	Ref.	Debit	Credit	Balance

Supplies Expense — No. 631

Date	Explanation	Ref.	Debit	Credit	Balance

Interest Expense — No. 718

Date	Explanation	Ref.	Debit	Credit	Balance

Insurance Expense — No. 722

Date	Explanation	Ref.	Debit	Credit	Balance

(b) (Continued)

Salaries Expense — No. 726

Date	Explanation	Ref.	Debit	Credit	Balance

Utilities Expense — No. 732

Date	Explanation	Ref.	Debit	Credit	Balance

Name

Section

Date

(c)

ROACH MOTEL
Adjusted Trial Balance
May 31, 2002

	Debit	Credit

Name

Section

Date

Problem 3-2B Continued

Roach Motel

(d)

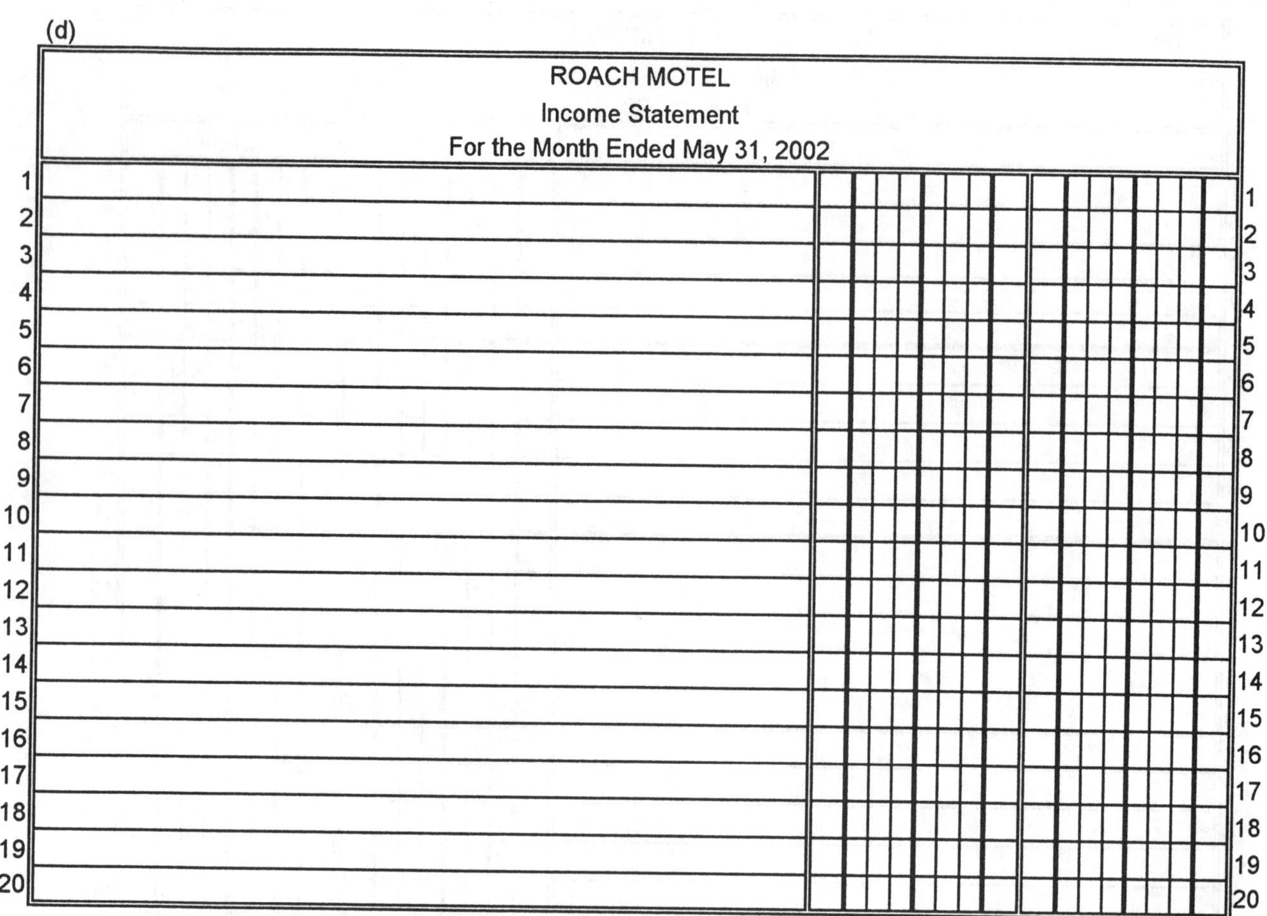

ROACH MOTEL

Income Statement

For the Month Ended May 31, 2002

ROACH MOTEL

Owner's Equity Statement

For the Month Ended May 31, 2002

Name

Section

Date

(d) (Continued)

ROACH MOTEL
Balance Sheet
May 31, 2002

Assets

Liabilities and Owner's Equity

Name

Section

Date

Problem 3-3B

Otaki Company

(a)

General Journal

Date	Accounts Titles and Explanation	Ref.	Debit	Credit

(b)

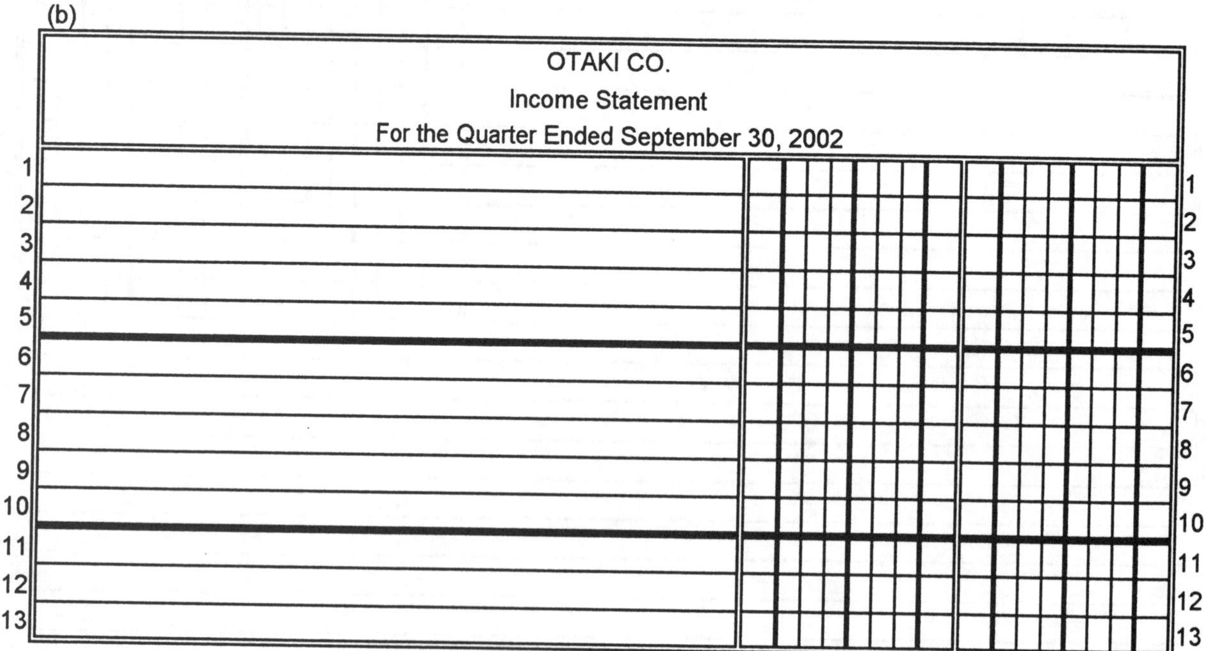

OTAKI CO.

Income Statement

For the Quarter Ended September 30, 2002

Name

Section

Date

Otaki Company

(b) (Continued)

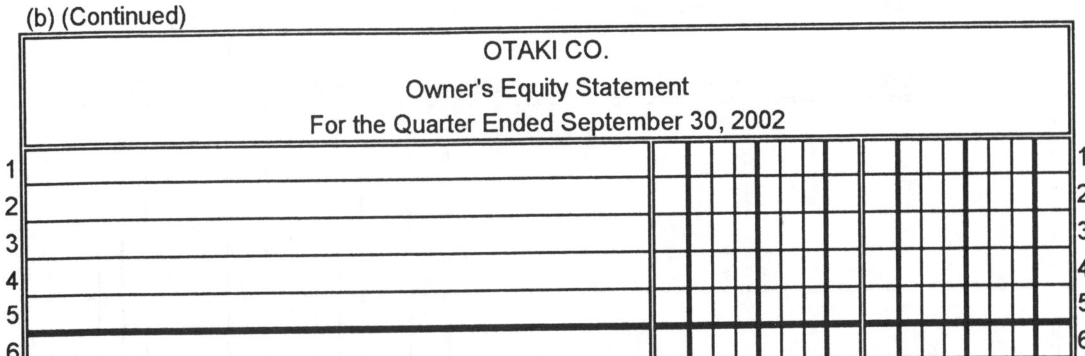

OTAKI CO.

Owner's Equity Statement

For the Quarter Ended September 30, 2002

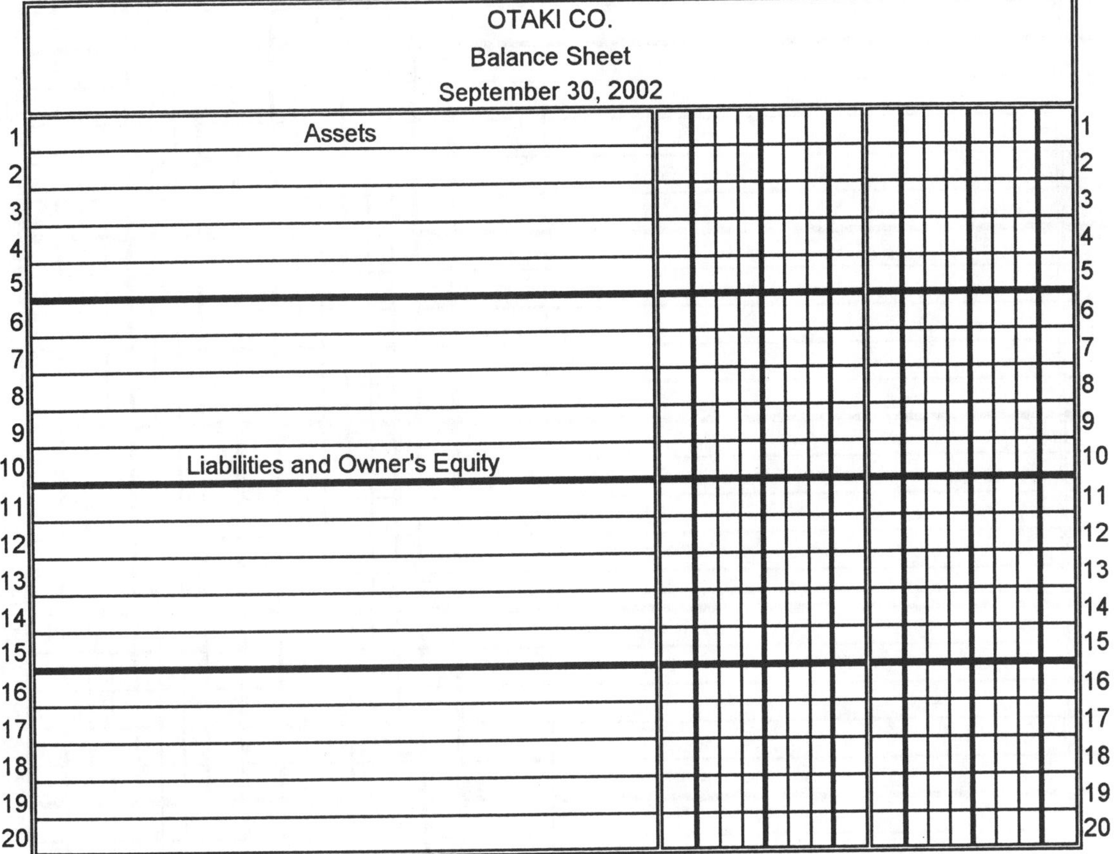

OTAKI CO.

Balance Sheet

September 30, 2002

Assets

Liabilities and Owner's Equity

(c)

(1)

(2)

Name

Section

Date

Problem 3-4B

Zieger Company

General Journal

Date	Accounts Titles and Explanation	Ref.	Debit	Credit

Name

Section

Date

Problem 3-5B

Thao Equipment Repair

(a), (c) and (e)

Cash — No. 101

Date	Explanation	Ref.	Debit	Credit	Balance

Accounts Receivable — No. 112

Date	Explanation	Ref.	Debit	Credit	Balance

Supplies — No. 126

Date	Explanation	Ref.	Debit	Credit	Balance

Store Equipment — No. 153

Date	Explanation	Ref.	Debit	Credit	Balance

Accumulated Depreciation-Store Equipment — No. 154

Date	Explanation	Ref.	Debit	Credit	Balance

Name

Section

Date

Problem 3-5B Continued

Thao Equipment Repair

(a), (c) and (e) (Continued)

Accounts Payable — No. 201

Date	Explanation	Ref.	Debit	Credit	Balance

Unearned Service Revenue — No. 209

Date	Explanation	Ref.	Debit	Credit	Balance

Salaries Payable — No. 212

Date	Explanation	Ref.	Debit	Credit	Balance

P. Thao, Capital — No. 301

Date	Explanation	Ref.	Debit	Credit	Balance

Service Revenue — No. 407

Date	Explanation	Ref.	Debit	Credit	Balance

Depreciation Expense — No. 615

Date	Explanation	Ref.	Debit	Credit	Balance

Name

Section

Date

Problem 3-5B Continued

Thao Equipment Repair

(a), (c) and (e) (Continued)

Supplies Expense No. 615

Date	Explanation	Ref.	Debit	Credit	Balance

Salaries Expense No. 726

Date	Explanation	Ref.	Debit	Credit	Balance

Rent Expense No. 729

Date	Explanation	Ref.	Debit	Credit	Balance

(b) General Journal J1

Date	Accounts Titles and Explanation	Ref.	Credit	Balance

Name

Section

Date

Problem 3-5B Continued

Thao Equipment Repair

(b)

General Journal J1

Date	Accounts Titles and Explanation	Ref.	Credit	Balance

(e)

General Journal J2

Date	Accounts Titles and Explanation	Ref.	Credit	Balance

(d) and (f)

THAO EQUIPMENT REPAIR

Trial Balances

November 30, 2002

	Before Adjustment		After Adjustment	
	Dr.	Cr.	Dr.	Cr.

(g)

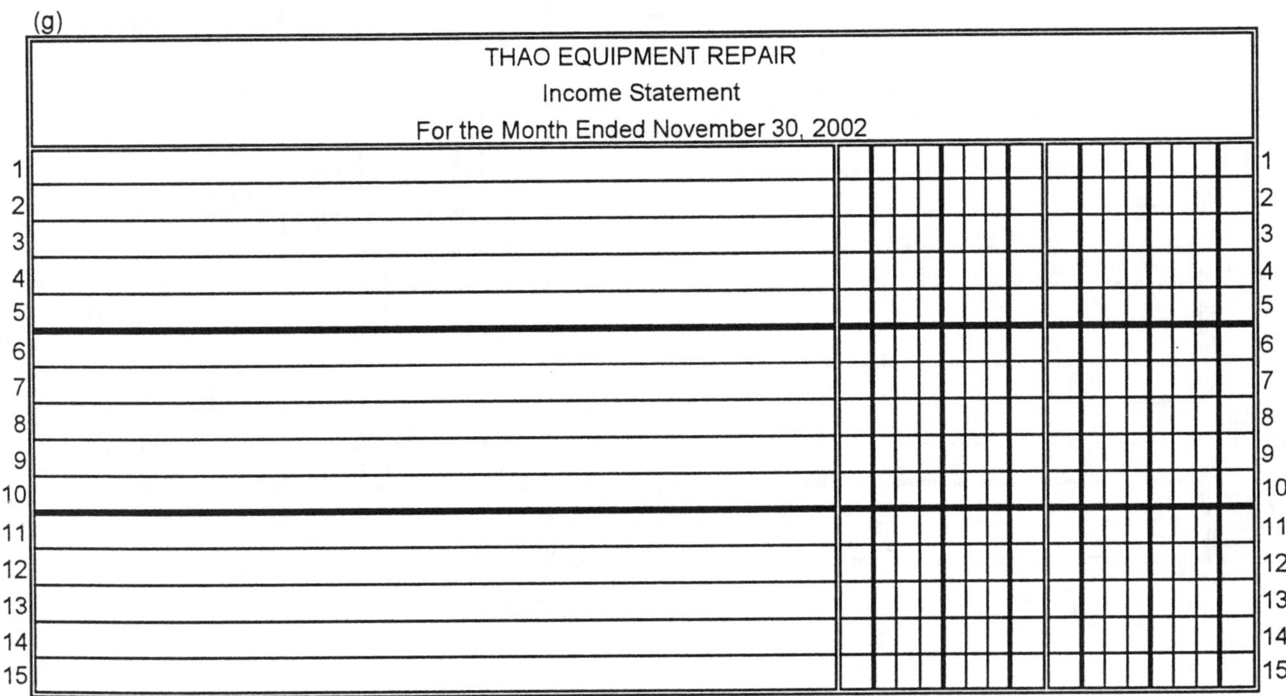

THAO EQUIPMENT REPAIR

Income Statement

For the Month Ended November 30, 2002

Name

Section

Date

Problem 3-5B Concluded

Thao Equipment Repair

(g) (Continued)

THAO EQUIPMENT REPAIR

Owner's Equity Statement

For the Month Ended November 30, 2002

THAO EQUIPEMENT REPAIR

Balance Sheet

November 30, 2002

Assets

Liabilities and Owner's Equity

Name

Section

Date

(a)

(b)

(c)

Name

Section

Date

Lands' End vs Abercrombie & Fitch

	Lands' End	Abercrombie & Fitch
Increase (decrease) from 1999 to 2000 (in thousands) in		
(a) Property, plant, and equipment, net		
(b) Selling, general, and administrative expenses		
(c) Accounts payable		
(d) Net income		
(e) Cash and cash equivalents		

Name

Section

Date

Hoescht Marion Roussel (HMR)

(a)

(b)

Name

Section

Date

Name

Section

Date

(a)

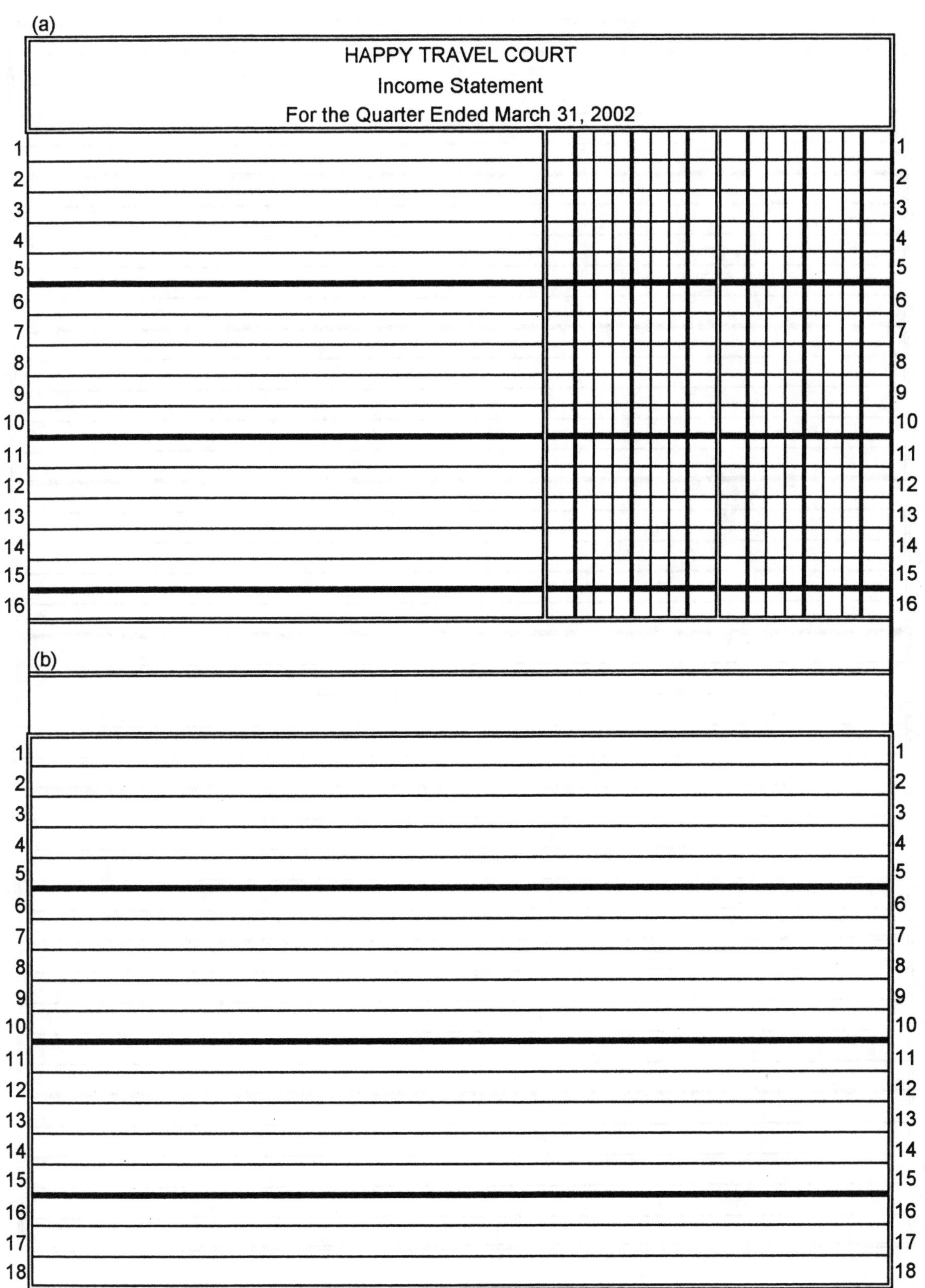

HAPPY TRAVEL COURT

Income Statement

For the Quarter Ended March 31, 2002

(b)

Name

Chapter 3 Communication Activity

Section

Date

Marylee Co.

Name Chapter 3 Ethics Case

Section

Date Die Hard Company

Name

Date

CHAPTER 4 BRIEF EXERCISES CONTINUED

see appendix

Name

Section

Date

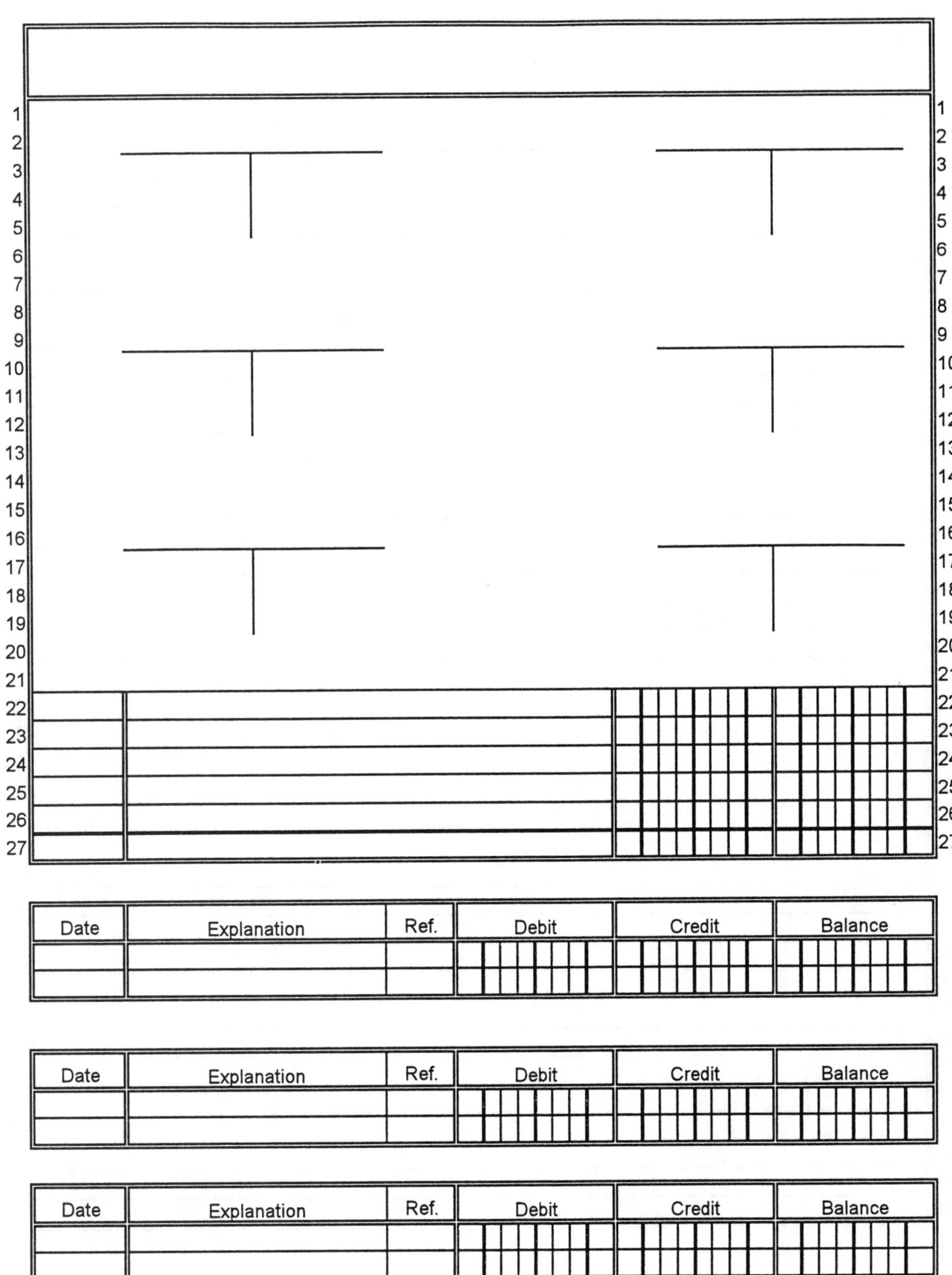

Date	Explanation	Ref.	Debit	Credit	Balance

Date	Explanation	Ref.	Debit	Credit	Balance

Date	Explanation	Ref.	Debit	Credit	Balance

Name

Section

Date

Name

Section

Date

Name

Section

Date

Exercise 4-1

Jose Tortilla Company

JOSE TORTILLA COMPANY

Work Sheet (Partial)

For the Month Ended April 30, 2002

Account Titles	Adjusted Trial Balance		Income Statement		Balance Sheet	
	Dr.	Cr.	Dr.	Cr.	Dr.	Cr.

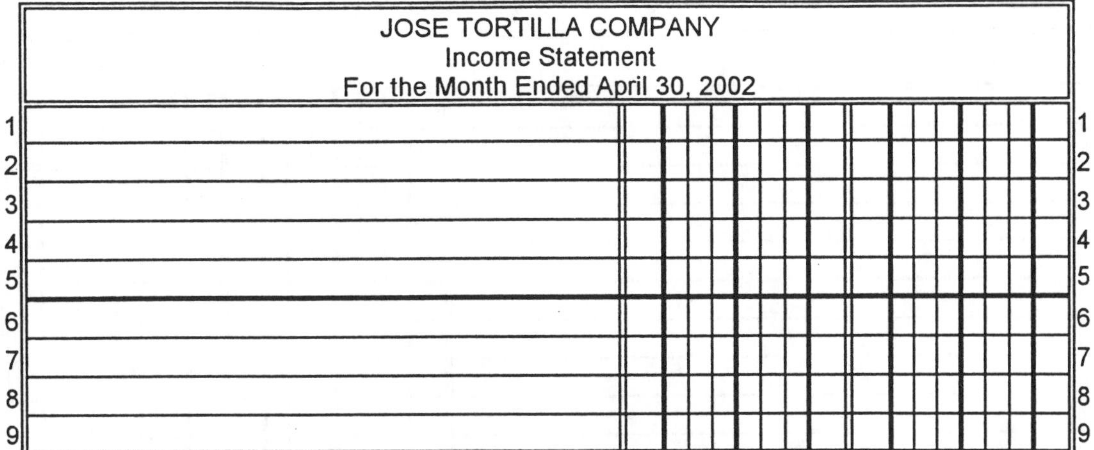
JOSE TORTILLA COMPANY
Income Statement
For the Month Ended April 30, 2002

JOSE TORTILLA COMPANY
Owner's Equity Statement
For the Month Ended April 30, 2002

JOSE NAVARRO COMPANY
Balance Sheet
April 30, 1999

Assets

Liabilities and Owner's Equity

Name

Section

Date

Exercise 4-3

Jose Tortilla Company

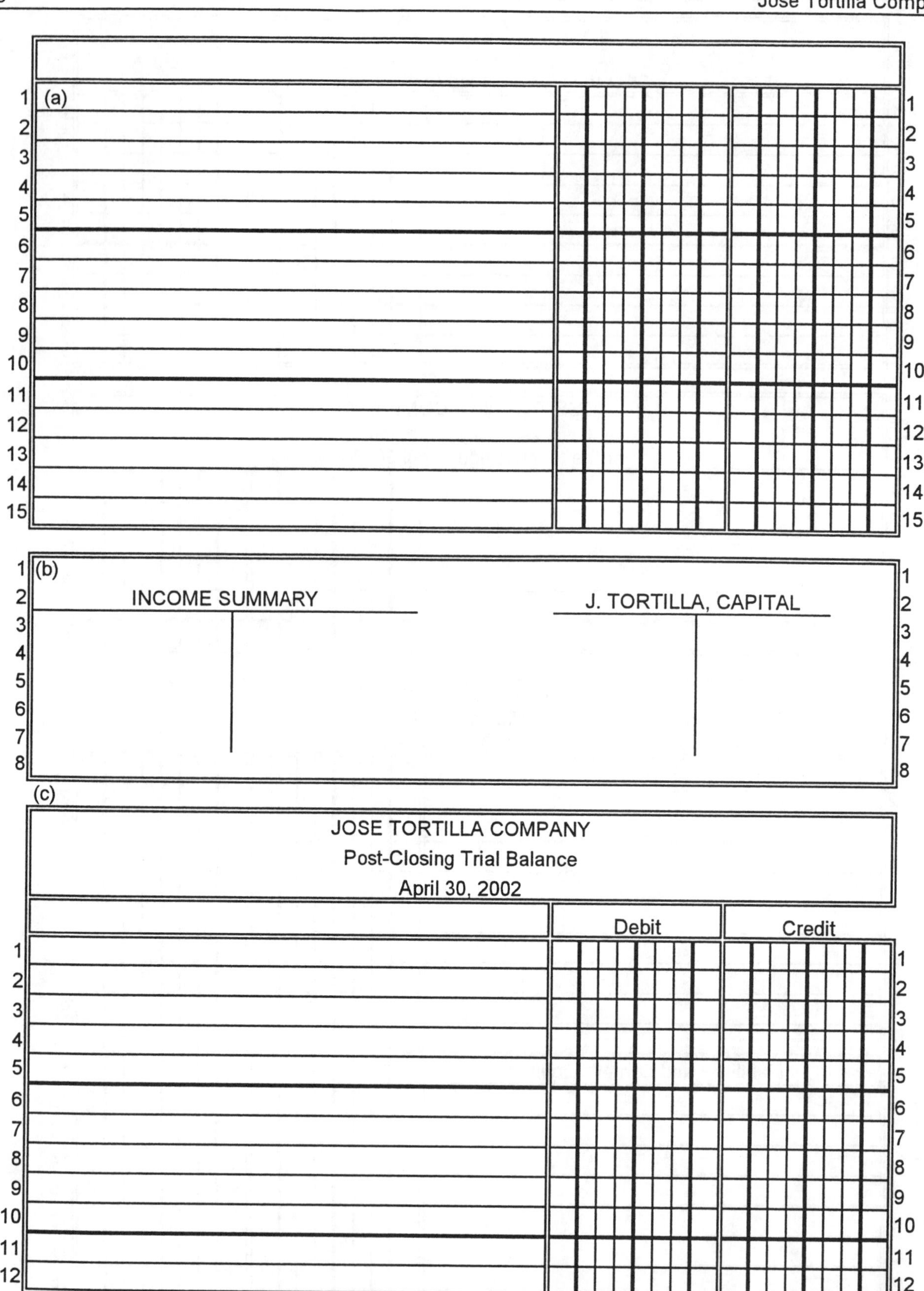

(a)

(b)

INCOME SUMMARY

J. TORTILLA, CAPITAL

(c)

JOSE TORTILLA COMPANY
Post-Closing Trial Balance
April 30, 2002

	Debit	Credit

Name | Exercises 4-4 to 4-5

Section

Date

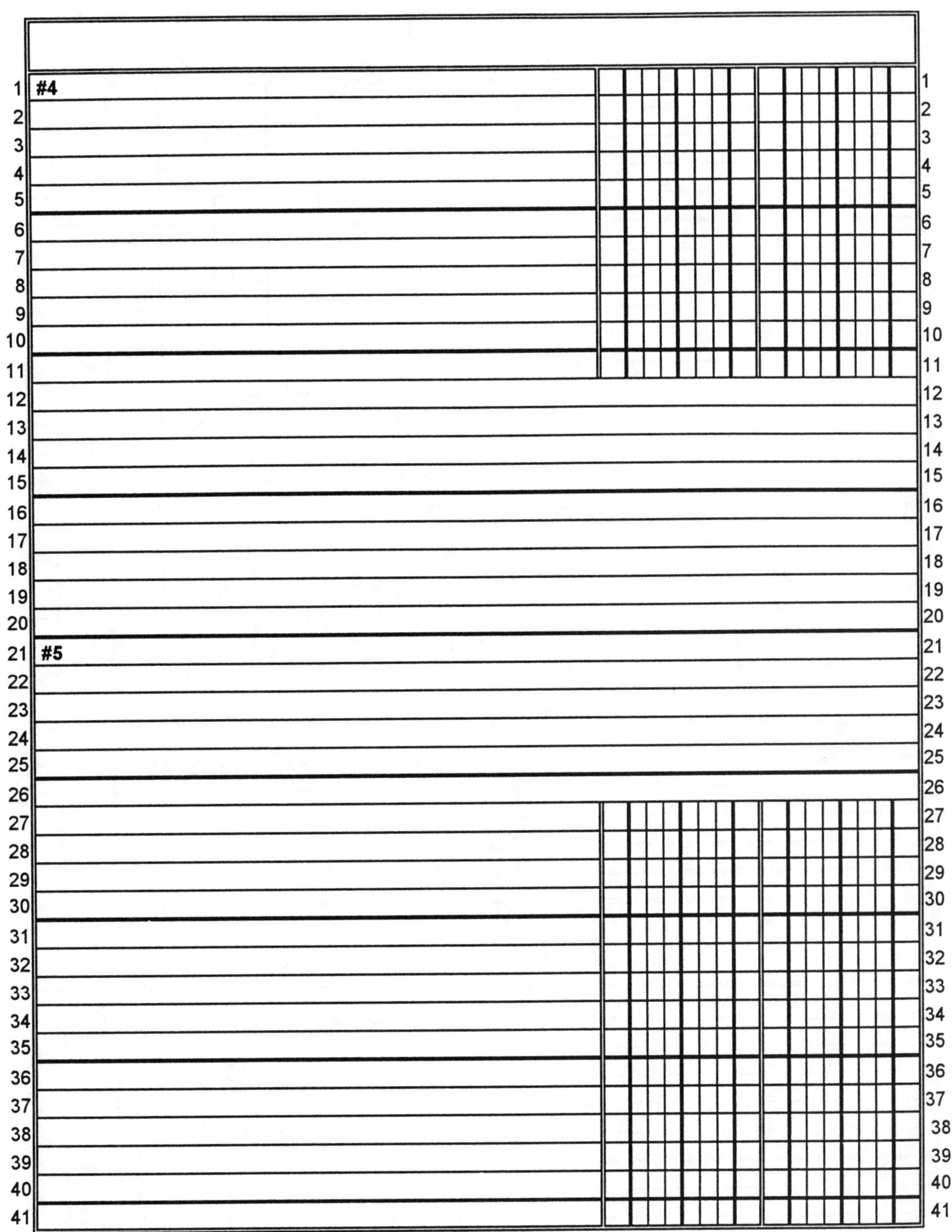

#4

#5

Name

Section

Date

Exercise 4-6

Mozart Company

(a)

General Journal

Date	Account Titles and Explanations	Ref.	Debit	Credit

(b)

W. A. Mozart, Capital — No. 301

Date	Explanation	Ref.	Debit	Credit	Balance

Income Summary — No. 350

Date	Explanation	Ref.	Debit	Credit	Balance

(c)

MOZART COMPANY
Post-Closing Trial Balance
July 31, 2002

	Debit	Credit

Name

Section

Date

Exercise 4-7

Mozart Company

MOZART COMPANY

Income Statement

For The Year Ended July 31, 2002

MOZART COMPANY

Owner's Equity Statement

For the Year Ended July 31, 2002

Name

Section

Date

MOZART COMPANY
Balance Sheet
July 31, 2002

Assets		
Liabilities and Owner's Equity		

Name

Section

Date

#8

(a)

(b)

INCOME SUMMARY

#9

Name

Section

Date

Exercises 4-10

Bristol Bowling Alley

(a)

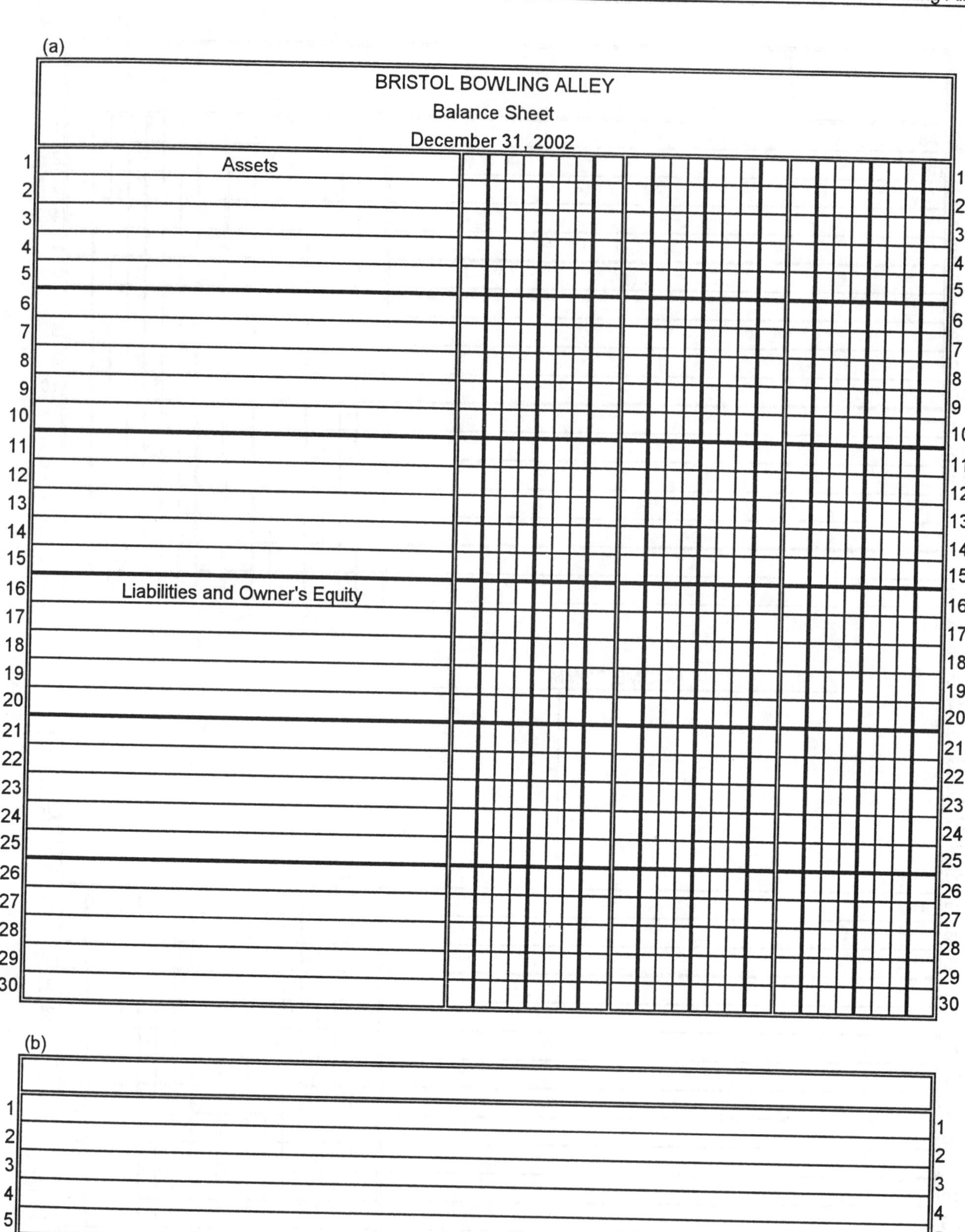

BRISTOL BOWLING ALLEY
Balance Sheet
December 31, 2002

Assets

Liabilities and Owner's Equity

(b)

Name

Section

Date

Exercises 4-11

Becky Employment Agency

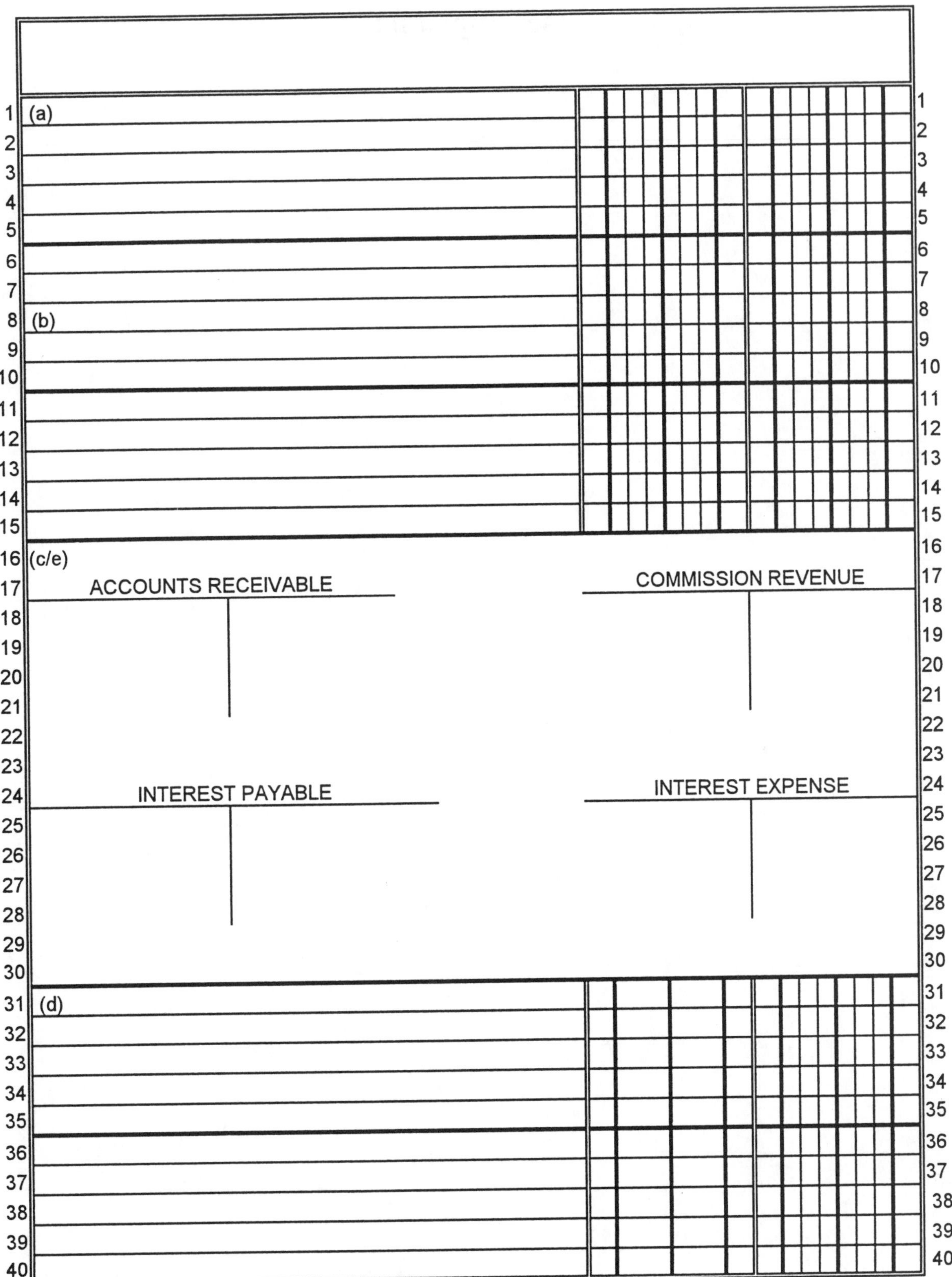

PROBLEM 4-1A

see appendix

Name

Section

Date

Problem 4-1A Con tinued

Darth Vader P. I.

(b)

DARTH VADER P.I.

Income Statement

For the Quarter Ended March 31, 2002

DARTH VADER P.I.

Owner's Equity Statement

For the Quarter Ended March 31, 2002

Name

Section

Date

(b) (Continued)

DARTH VADER P.I.

Balance Sheet

March 31, 2002

Assets		

Name

Section

Date

(c)

General Journal

Date	Account Titles and Explanations	Ref.	Debit	Credit
	Adjusting Entries			

(d)

General Journal

Date	Account Titles and Explanations	Ref.	Debit	Credit
	Closing Entries			

Name

Section

Date

Problem 4-2A

Shmi Skywalker Company

SHMI SKYWALKER COMPANY

Work Sheet (Partial)

For the Year Ended December 31, 2002

(a)

Account		Adjusted Trial Balance		Income Statement		Balance Sheet	
No.	Title	Dr.	Cr.	Dr.	Cr.	Dr.	Cr.

(b)

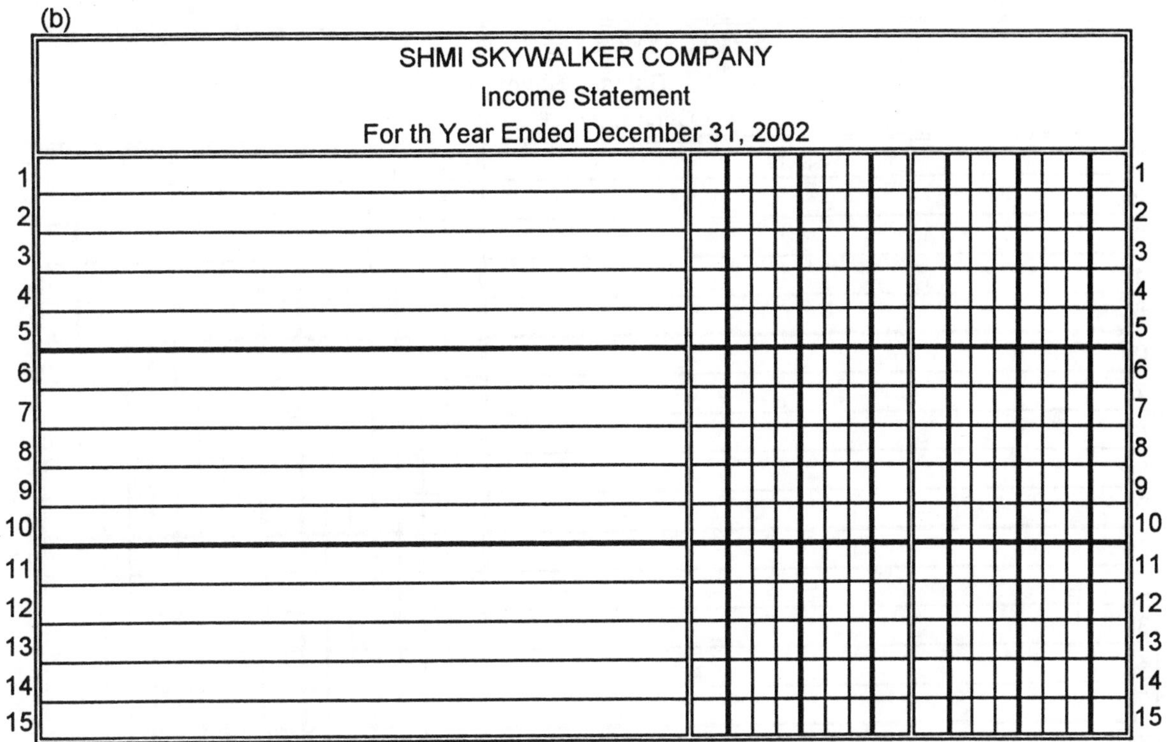

SHMI SKYWALKER COMPANY
Income Statement
For th Year Ended December 31, 2002

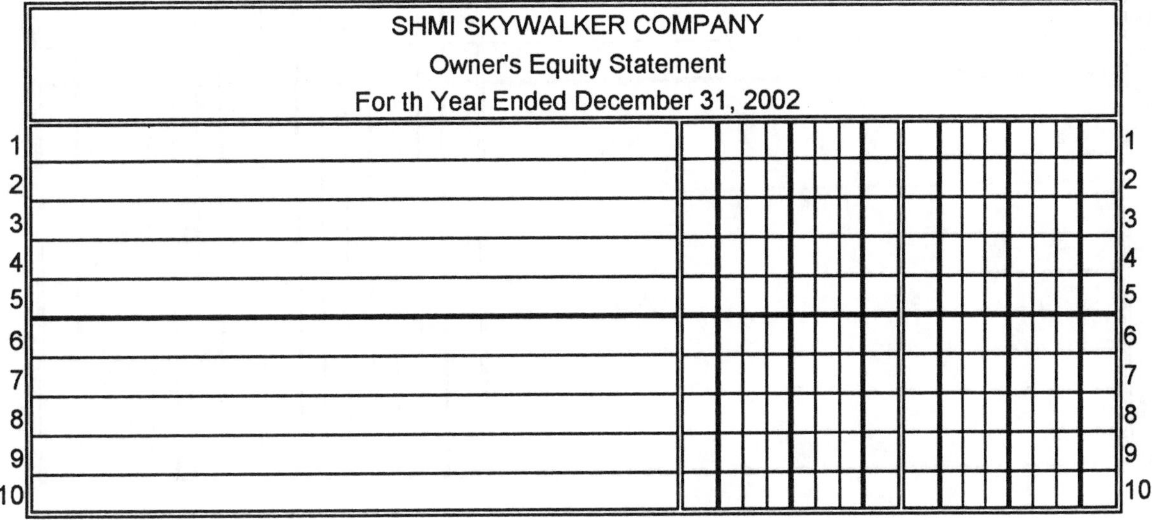

SHMI SKYWALKER COMPANY
Owner's Equity Statement
For th Year Ended December 31, 2002

Name

Section

Date

Problem 4-2 A Continued

Shmi Skywalker Company

(b) (Continued)

SHMI SKYWALKER COMPANY
Balance Sheet
December 31, 2002

Assets

Liabilities and Owner's Equity

Name

Section

Date

Problem 4-2A Continued

Shmi Skywalker Company

(b) General Journal J14

Date	Account Titles and Explanation	Ref.	Debit	Credit

(d) S. Skywalker, Capital No. 301

Date	Explanation	Ref.	Debit	Credit	Balance

S. Skywalker, Drawing No. 306

Date	Explanation	Ref.	Debit	Credit	Balance

Income Summary No. 350

Date	Explanation	Ref.	Debit	Credit	Balance

(d) (Continued)

Service Revenue — No. 400

Date	Explanation	Ref.	Debit	Credit	Balance

Advertising Expense — No. 610

Date	Explanation	Ref.	Debit	Credit	Balance

Supplies Expense — No. 631

Date	Explanation	Ref.	Debit	Credit	Balance

Depreciation Expense — No. 711

Date	Explanation	Ref.	Debit	Credit	Balance

Insurance Expense — No. 722

Date	Explanation	Ref.	Debit	Credit	Balance

Salaries Expense — No. 726

Date	Explanation	Ref.	Debit	Credit	Balance

(d) (Continued)

Interest Expense — No. 905

Date	Explanation	Ref.	Debit	Credit	Balance

(e)

SHMI SKYWALKER COMPANY
Post-Closing Trial Balance
December 31, 2002

	Debit	Credit

Name

Section

Date

Problem 4-3A

Panaka Company

(a)

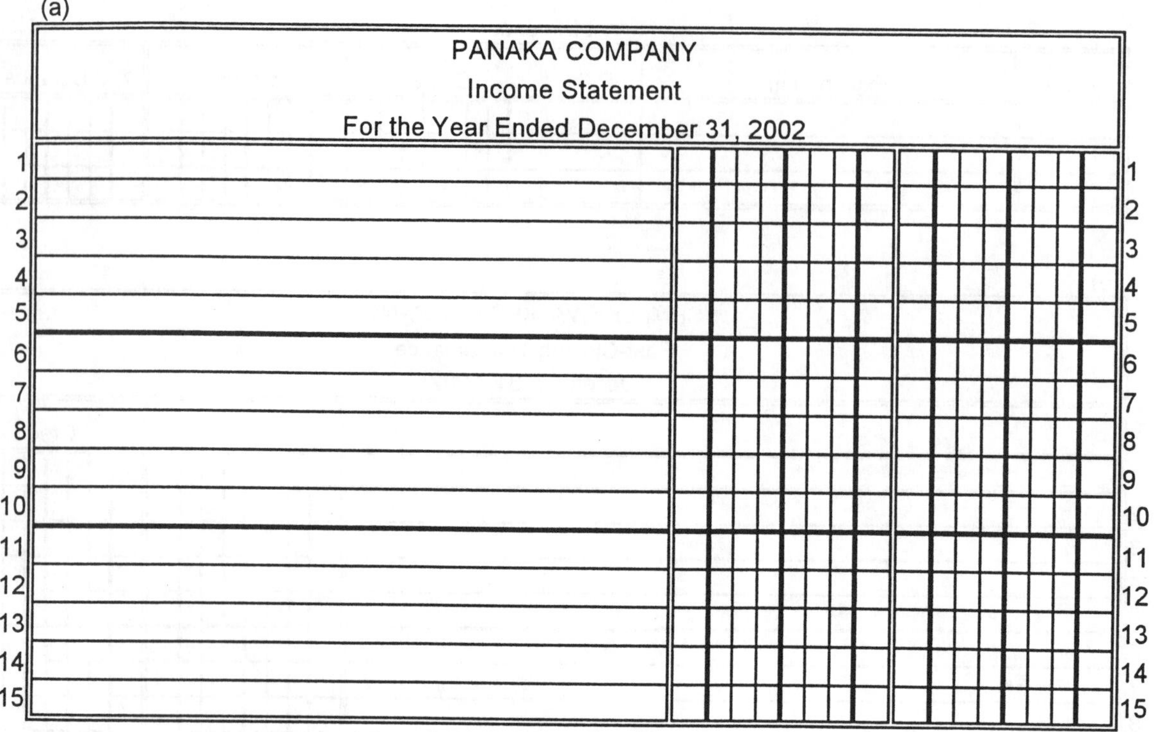

PANAKA COMPANY

Income Statement

For the Year Ended December 31, 2002

PANAKA COMPANY

Balance Sheet

December 31, 2002

Assets

Liabilities and Owner's Equity

Name

Section

Date

Problem 4-3A Continued

Panaka Company

(a) (Continued)

PANAKA COMPANY

Owner's Equity Statement

For the Year Ended December 31, 2002

(b)

General Journal

Date	Accounts Titles	Ref.	Credit	Balance
	Closing Entries			

Name

Section

Date

(c) General Ledger Accounts

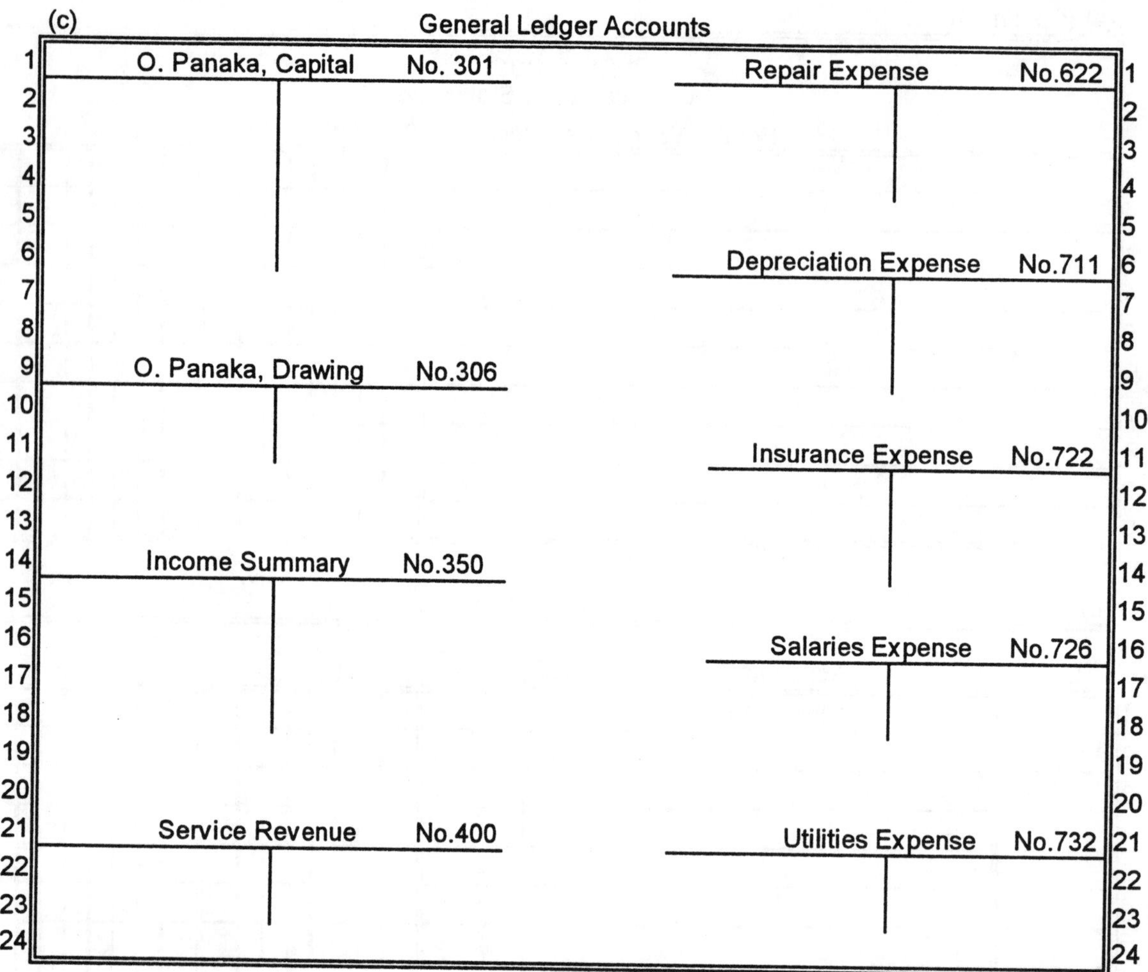

(d)

PANAKA COMPANY
Post-Closing Trial Balance
December 31, 2002

	Debit	Credit

PROBLEM 4-4A

see appendix

Name

Section

Date

Problem 4-4A Continued

Wookie Amusement Park

(b)

WOOKIE AMUSEMENT PARK

Balance Sheet

September 30, 2002

Assets

Liabilities and Owner's Equity

Name | Problem 4-4A Continued

Section

Date | Wookie Amusement Park

(c) and (d)

General Journal

Date	Accounts Titles and Explanation	Ref.	Debit	Credit
(c)	Adjusting Entries			
(d)	Closing Entries			

(e)

WOOKIE AMUSEMENT PARK
Post-Closing Trial Balance
September 30, 2002

	Debit	Credit

Name Problem 4-5A

Section

Date Ewok's Carpet Cleaners

(a) General Journal

Date	Accounts Titles and Explanation	Ref.	Debit	Credit

Name ________ Problem 4-5A Continued

Section ________

Date ________ Ewok's Carpet Cleaners

(a), (e) and (f)

Cash — No. 101

Date	Explanation	Ref.	Debit	Credit	Balance

Accounts Receivable — No. 112

Date	Explanation	Ref.	Debit	Credit	Balance

Cleaning Supplies — No. 128

Date	Explanation	Ref.	Debit	Credit	Balance

Prepaid Insurance — No. 130

Date	Explanation	Ref.	Debit	Credit	Balance

Equipment — No. 157

Date	Explanation	Ref.	Debit	Credit	Balance

Name Problem 4-5 Continued

Section

Date Ewok's Carpet Cleaners

(a), (e) and (f) (Continued)

Accumulated Depreciation-Equipment No. 158

Date	Explanation	Ref.	Debit	Credit	Balance

Accounts Payable No. 201

Date	Explanation	Ref.	Debit	Credit	Balance

Salaries Payable No. 212

Date	Explanation	Ref.	Debit	Credit	Balance

A. Ewok, Capital No. 301

Date	Explanation	Ref.	Debit	Credit	Balance

A. Ewok, Drawing No. 306

Date	Explanation	Ref.	Debit	Credit	Balance

Income Summary No. 350

Date	Explanation	Ref.	Debit	Credit	Balance

Name

Section

Date

Problem 4-5A Continued

Ewok's Carpet Cleaners

(a), (e) and (f) (Continued)

Service Revenue — No. 400

Date	Explanation	Ref.	Debit	Credit	Balance

Gas & Oil Expense — No. 633

Date	Explanation	Ref.	Debit	Credit	Balance

Cleaning Supplies Expense — No. 634

Date	Explanation	Ref.	Debit	Credit	Balance

Depreciation Expense — No. 711

Date	Explanation	Ref.	Debit	Credit	Balance

Insurance Expense — No. 722

Date	Explanation	Ref.	Debit	Credit	Balance

Salaries Expense — No. 726

Date	Explanation	Ref.	Debit	Credit	Balance

PROBLEM 4-5A CONTINUED

see appendix

Name Problem 4-5A Continued

Section

Date Ewok's Carpet Cleaners

(d)

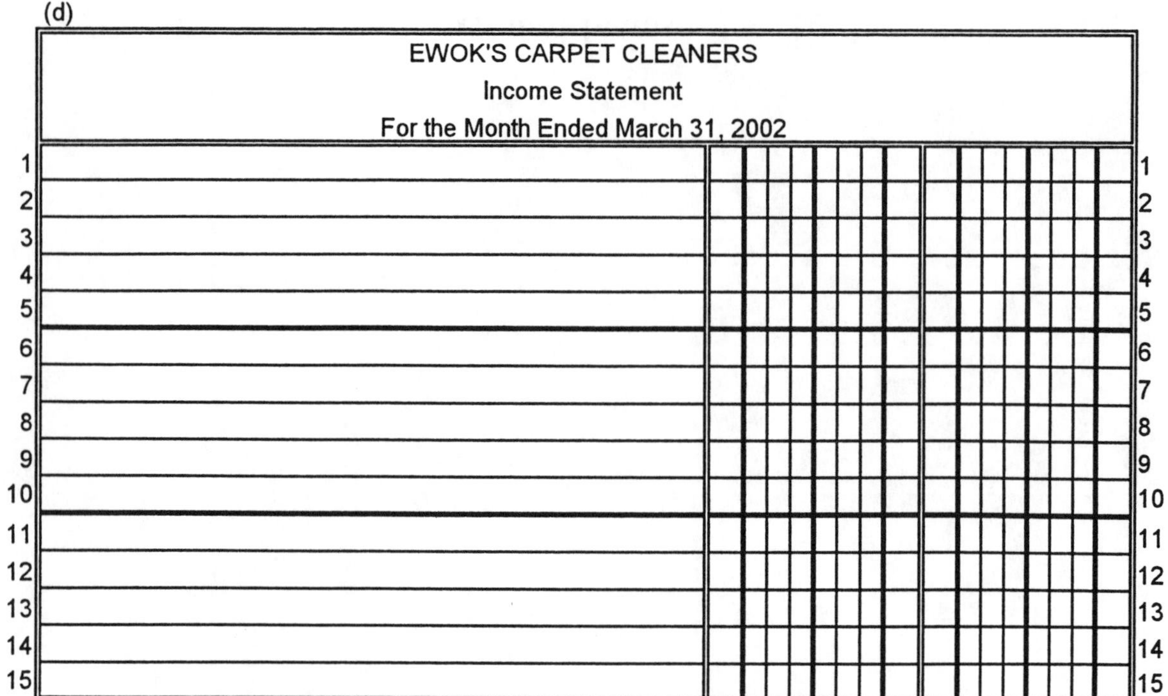

EWOK'S CARPET CLEANERS

Income Statement

For the Month Ended March 31, 2002

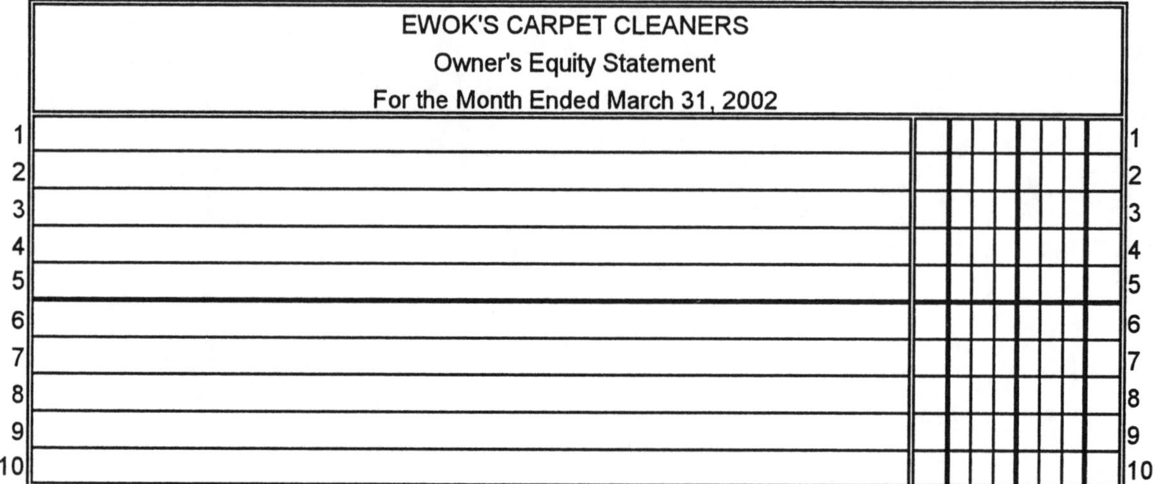

EWOK'S CARPET CLEANERS

Owner's Equity Statement

For the Month Ended March 31, 2002

(d) (Continued)

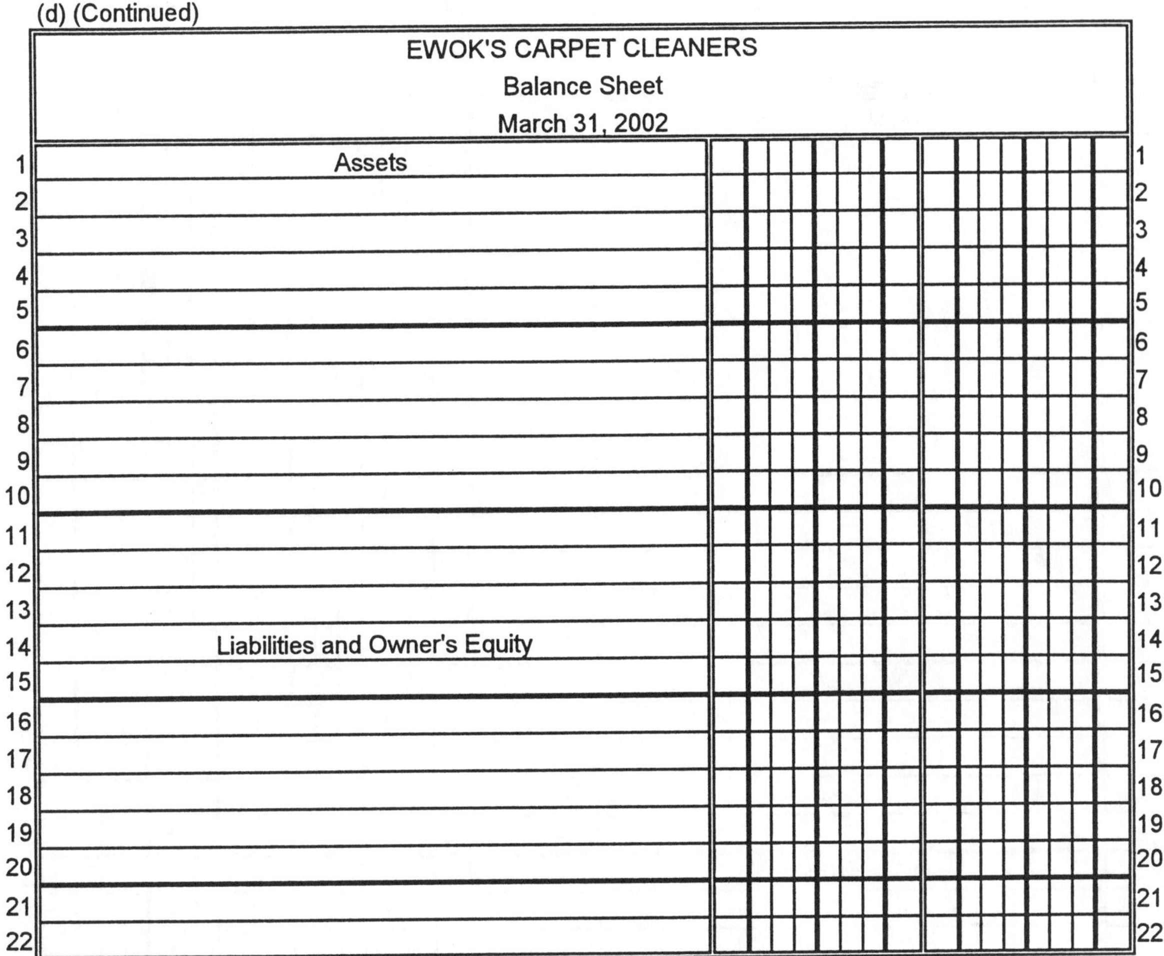
EWOK'S CARPET CLEANERS
Balance Sheet
March 31, 2002

Assets

Liabilities and Owner's Equity

(g)

EWOK'S CARPET CLEANERS
Post-Closing Trial Balance
March 31, 2002

	Debit	Credit

Name Problem 4-5 A Concluded

Section

Date Ewok's Carpet Cleaners

(e) and (f) General Journal J2-J3

Date	Accounts Titles and Explanation	Ref.	Debit	Credit
(e)	Adjusting Entries			
(f)	Closing Entries			

Problem 4-6 A

Name

Section

Date

Doneright TV Repair

DONERIGHT TV REPAIR

Incorrect Entry			Correct Entry			Correcting Entry		
Account Titles	Dr.	Cr.	Account Titles	Dr.	Cr.	Account Titles	Dr.	Cr.

Name

Section

Date

(b)

DONERIGHT TV REPAIR

Trial Balance

April 30, 2002

	Debit	Credit

PROBLEM 4-1B

see appendix

Name

Section

Date

Problem 4-1B Continued

Phantom Roofing

(b)

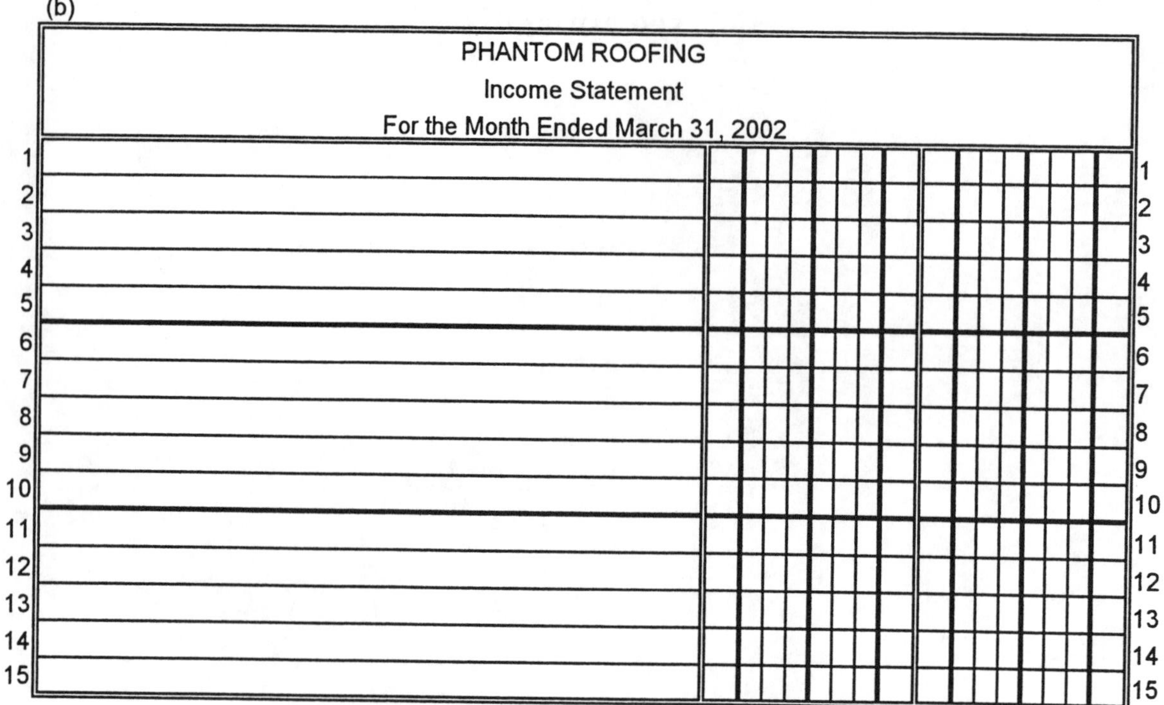

PHANTOM ROOFING
Income Statement
For the Month Ended March 31, 2002

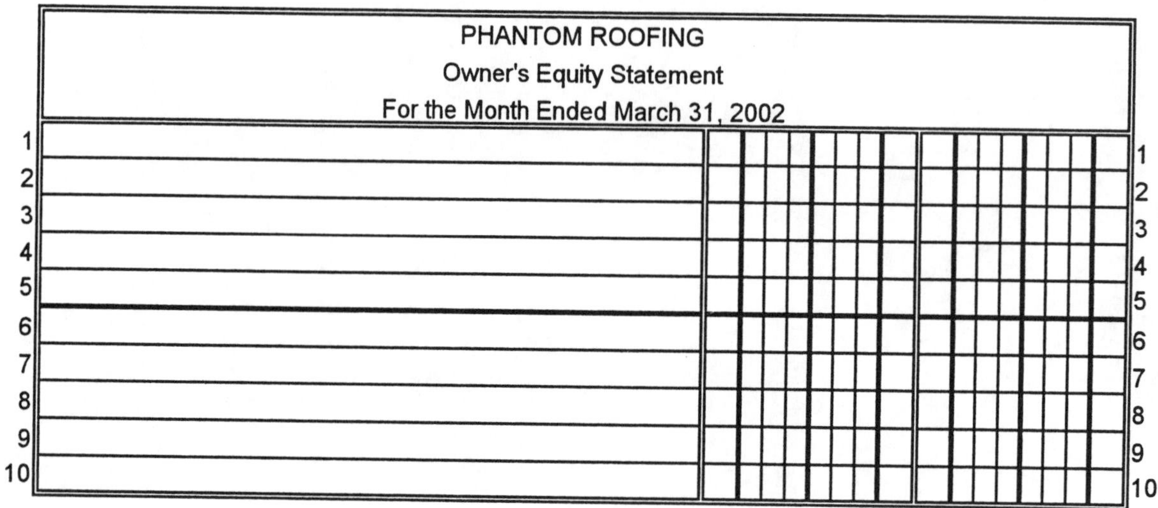

PHANTOM ROOFING
Owner's Equity Statement
For the Month Ended March 31, 2002

(b) (Continued)

PHANTOM ROOFING
Balance Sheet
March 31, 2002

Assets

Liabilities and Owner's Equity

Name

Section

Date

Problem 4-1B Concluded

Phantom Roofing

(c)

General Journal

Date	Account Titles and Explanation	Ref.	Debit	Credit
	Adjusting Entries			

(d)

General Journal

Date	Account Titles and Explanation	Ref.	Debit	Credit
	Closing Entries			

Name

Section

Date

Boss Nass Company

BOSS NASS COMPANY
Work Sheet (Partial)
For the Year Ended December 31, 2002

(a)

	Account		Adjusted Trial Balance		Income Statement		Balance Sheet		
	No.	Titles	Dr.	Cr.	Dr.	Cr.	Dr.	Cr.	
1									1
2									2
3									3
4									4
5									5
6									6
7									7
8									8
9									9
10									10
11									11
12									12
13									13
14									14
15									15
16									16
17									17
18									18
19									19
20									20
21									21
22									22
23									23
24									24
25									25
26									26
27									27
28									28

Name

Section

Date

Problem 4-2 B Continued

Boss Nass Company

(b)

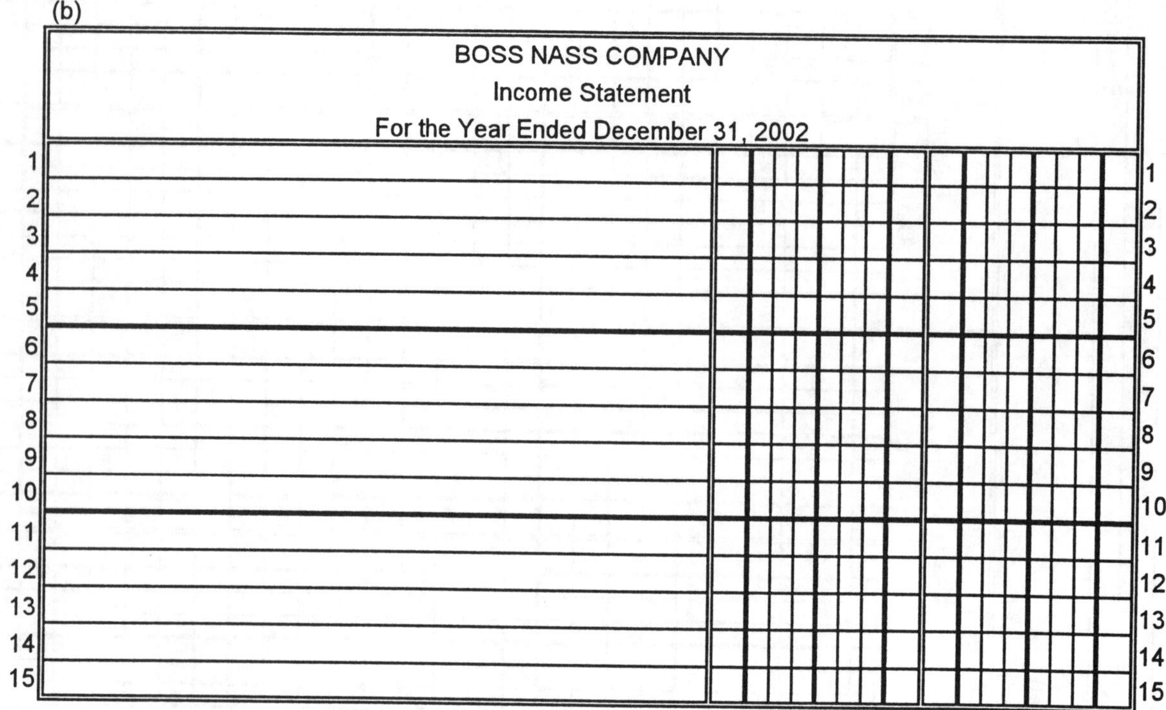

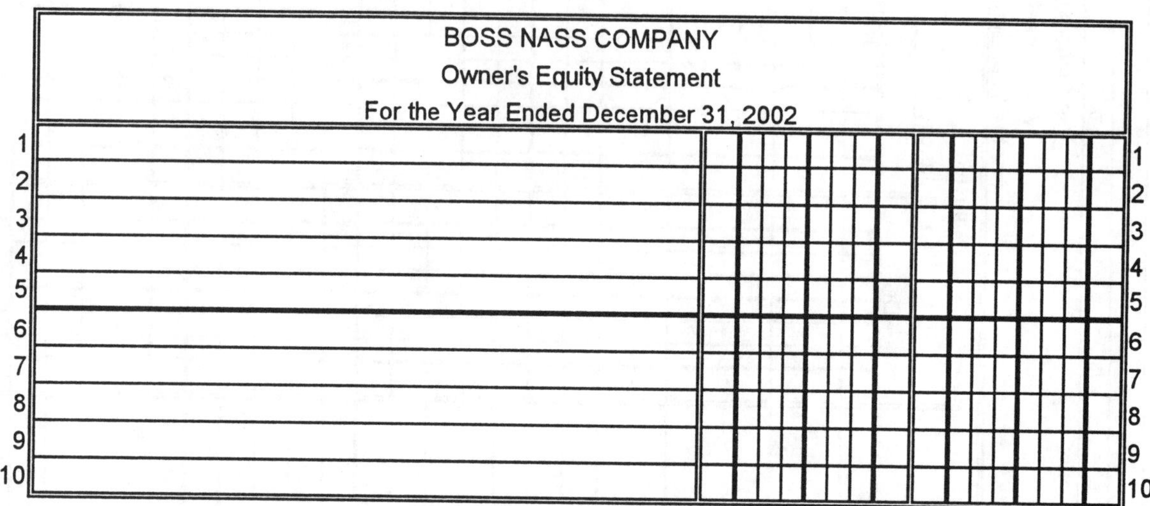

Name | Problem 4-2B Continued
Section
Date | Boss Nass Company

(b) (Continued)

BOSS NASS COMPANY
Balance Sheet
December 31, 2002

Assets

Liabilities and Owner's Equity

Name

Section

Date

Problem 4-2B Continued

Boss Nass Company

(c)

General Journal

J14

Date	Accounts Titles and Explanation	Ref.	Debit	Credit
	Closing Entries			

Name

Section

Date

(d)

Boss Nass, Capital — No. 301

Date	Explanation	Ref.	Debit	Credit	Balance

Boss Nass, Drawing — No. 306

Date	Explanation	Ref.	Debit	Credit	Balance

Income Summary — No. 350

Date	Explanation	Ref.	Debit	Credit	Balance

Service Revenue — No. 400

Date	Explanation	Ref.	Debit	Credit	Balance

Advertising Expense — No. 610

Date	Explanation	Ref.	Debit	Credit	Balance

Supplies Expense — No. 631

Date	Explanation	Ref.	Debit	Credit	Balance

Depreciation Expense — No. 711

Date	Explanation	Ref.	Debit	Credit	Balance

Insurance Expense — No. 722

Date	Explanation	Ref.	Debit	Credit	Balance

Name

Section

Date

Problem 4-2 B Concluded

Boss Nass Company

(d) (Continued)

Salaries Expense — No. 726

Date	Explanation	Ref.	Debit	Credit	Balance

Interest Expense — No. 905

Date	Explanation	Ref.	Debit	Credit	Balance

(e)

BOSS NASS COMPANY
Post-Closing Trial Balance
December 31, 2002

		Debit	Credit	
1				1
2				2
3				3
4				4
5				5
6				6
7				7
8				8
9				9
10				10
11				11
12				12
13				13
14				14

Name | Problem 4-3B

Section

Date | Nute Gunray Company

(a)

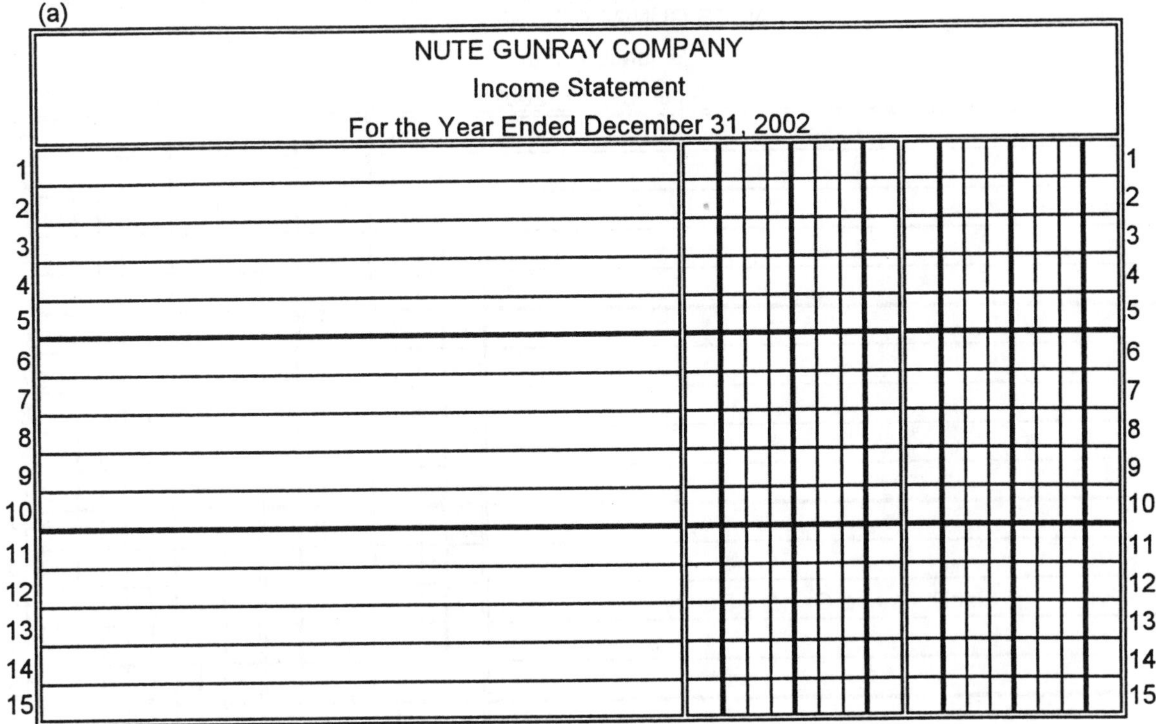

NUTE GUNRAY COMPANY

Owner's Equity Statement

For the Year Ended December 31, 2002

Name

Section

Date

Problem 4-3B Continued

Nute Gunray Company

(a) (Continued)

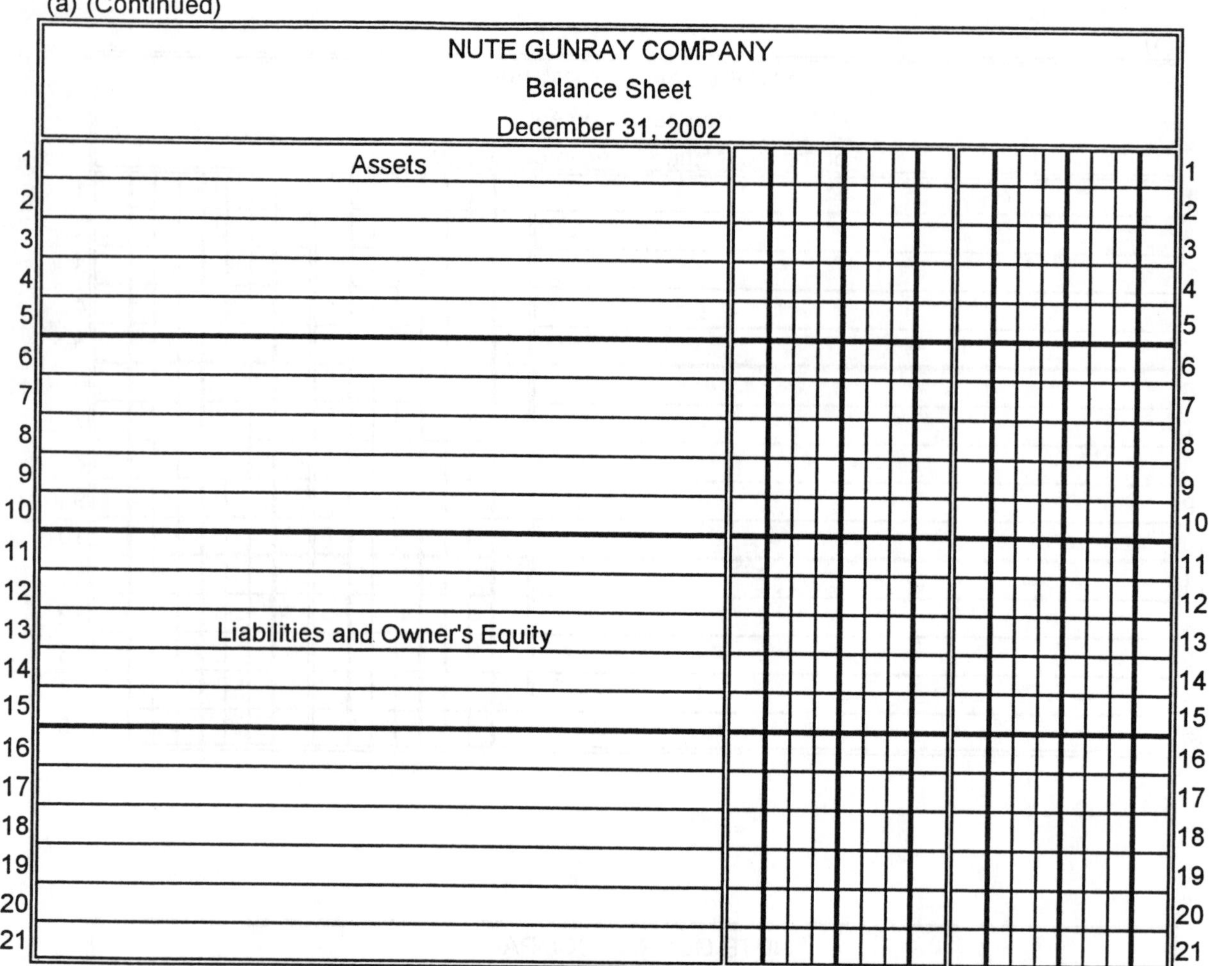

NUTE GUNRAY COMPANY

Balance Sheet

December 31, 2002

Assets

Liabilities and Owner's Equity

(b)

General Journal

Date	Accounts Titles	Ref.	Debit	Credit

Name	Problem 4-3B Concluded
Section	
Date	Nute Gunray Company

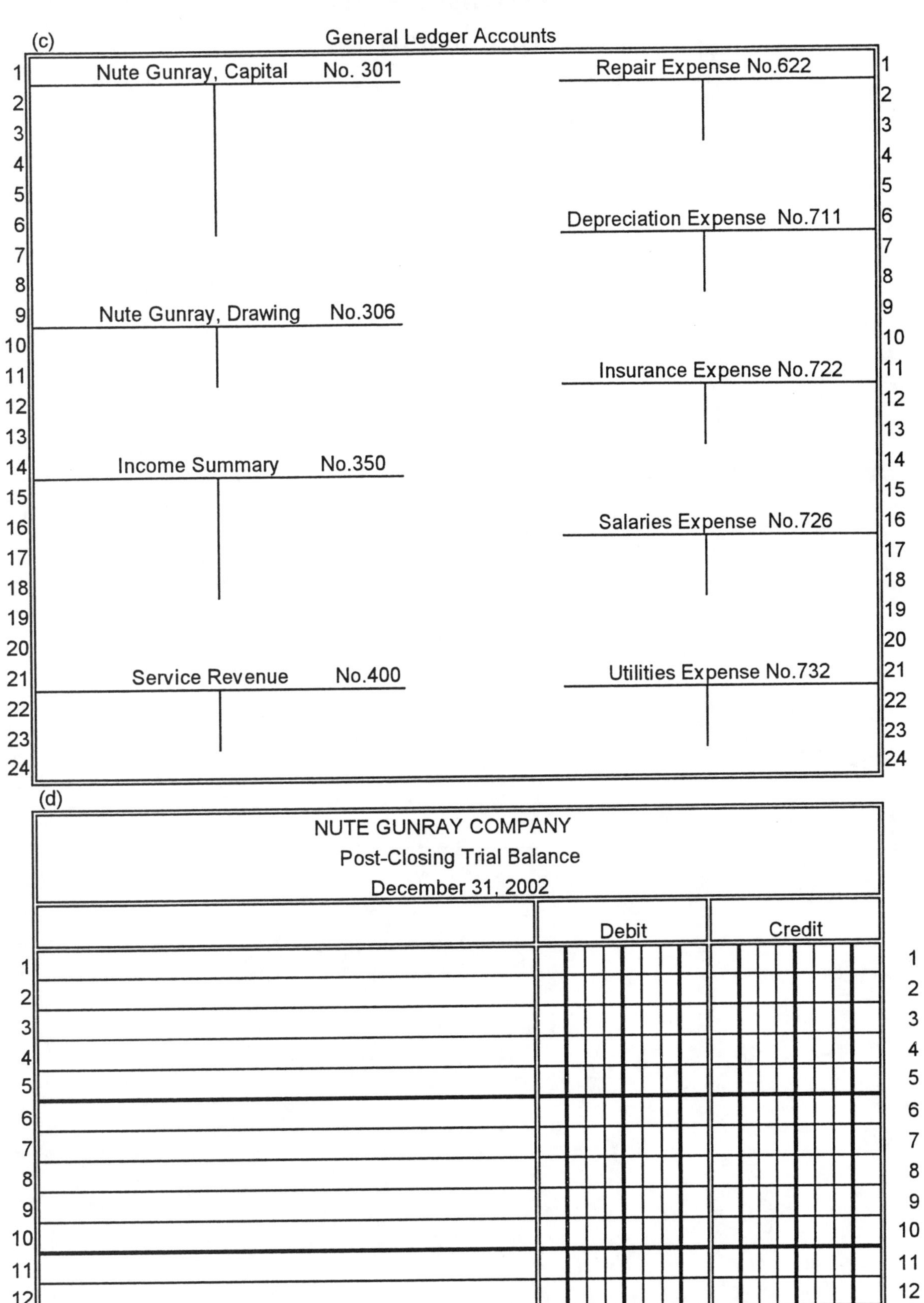

(c) General Ledger Accounts

Nute Gunray, Capital	No. 301
Nute Gunray, Drawing	No.306
Income Summary	No.350
Service Revenue	No.400
Repair Expense	No.622
Depreciation Expense	No.711
Insurance Expense	No.722
Salaries Expense	No.726
Utilities Expense	No.732

(d)

NUTE GUNRAY COMPANY
Post-Closing Trial Balance
December 31, 2002

	Debit	Credit

PROBLEM 4-4B
see appendix

Name

Section

Date

Problem 4-4 B Continued

Rebecca Sherrick Management Services

(b)

REBECCA SHERRICK MANAGEMENT SERVICES

Balance Sheet

December 31, 2002

Assets

Liabilities and Owner's Equity

Name

Section

Date

Problem 4-4B Continued

Rebecca Sherrick Management Services

(c) and (d)

General Journal

Date	Accounts Titles and Explanation	Ref.	Debit	Credit
(c)	Adjusting Entries			
(d)	Closing Entries			

Name

Section

Date

Problem 4-4B Concluded

Rebecca Sherrick Management Services

(e)

REBECCA SHERRICK MANAGEMENT SERVICES

Post-Closing Trial Balance

December 31, 2002

	Debit	Credit

Name Problem 4-5B

Section

Date Terry's Window Washing

(a)

General Journal

Date	Accounts Titles and Explanation	Ref.	Debit	Credit

PROBLEM 4-5B

see appendix

Name | Problem 4-5B Continued
Section
Date | Terry's Window Washing

(a), (e) and (f)

Cash | No. 101

Date	Explanation	Ref.	Debit	Credit	Balance

Accounts Receivable | No. 112

Date	Explanation	Ref.	Debit	Credit	Balance

Cleaning Supplies | No. 128

Date	Explanation	Ref.	Debit	Credit	Balance

Prepaid Insurance | No. 130

Date	Explanation	Ref.	Debit	Credit	Balance

Equipment | No. 157

Date	Explanation	Ref.	Debit	Credit	Balance

Accumulated Depreciation - Equipment | No. 158

Date	Explanation	Ref.	Debit	Credit	Balance

Name | Problem 4-5 B Continued
Section
Date | Terry's Window Washing

(a), (e) and (f) (Continued)

Accounts Payable — No. 201

Date	Explanation	Ref.	Debit	Credit	Balance

Salaries Payable — No. 212

Date	Explanation	Ref.	Debit	Credit	Balance

Terry Duffy, Capital — No. 301

Date	Explanation	Ref.	Debit	Credit	Balance

Terry Duffy, Drawing — No. 306

Date	Explanation	Ref.	Debit	Credit	Balance

Income Summary — No. 350

Date	Explanation	Ref.	Debit	Credit	Balance

Service Revenue — No. 400

Date	Explanation	Ref.	Debit	Credit	Balance

Name | Problem 4-5B Continued

Section

Date | Terry's Window Washing

(a), (e) and (f) (Continued)

Gas & Oil Expense — No. 633

Date	Explanation	Ref.	Debit	Credit	Balance

Cleaning Supplies Expense — No. 634

Date	Explanation	Ref.	Debit	Credit	Balance

Depreciation Expense — No. 711

Date	Explanation	Ref.	Debit	Credit	Balance

Insurance Expense — No. 722

Date	Explanation	Ref.	Debit	Credit	Balance

Salaries Expense — No. 726

Date	Explanation	Ref.	Debit	Credit	Balance

Name

Section

Date

Problem 4-5B Continued

Terry's Window Washing

(d)

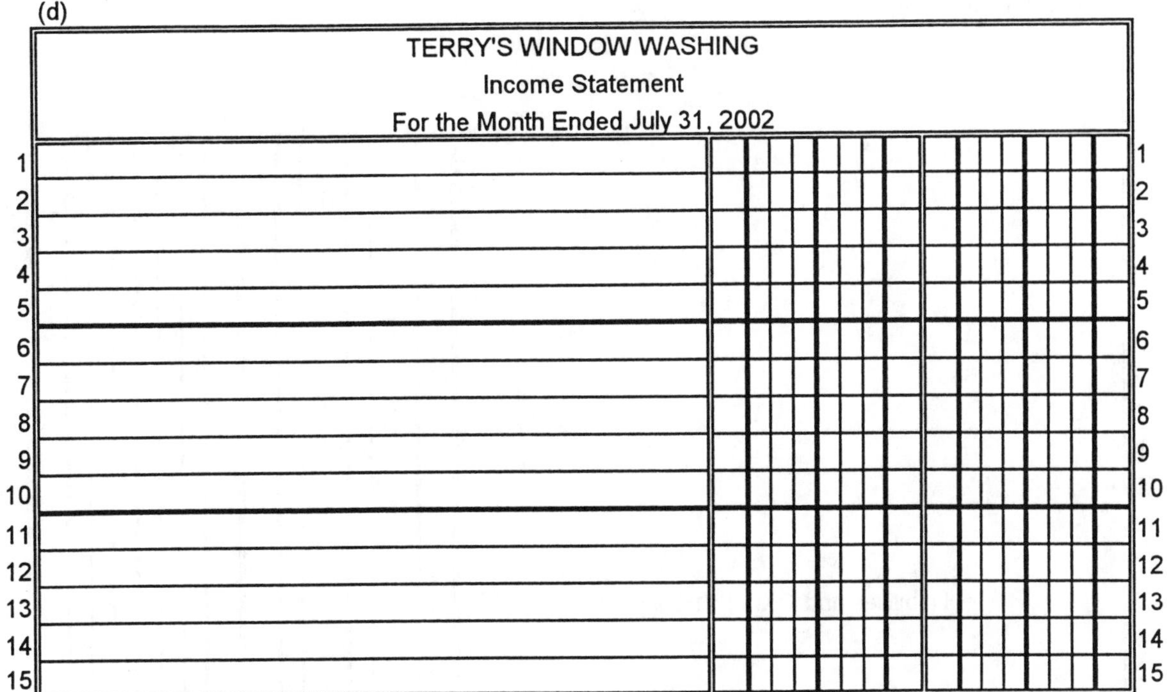

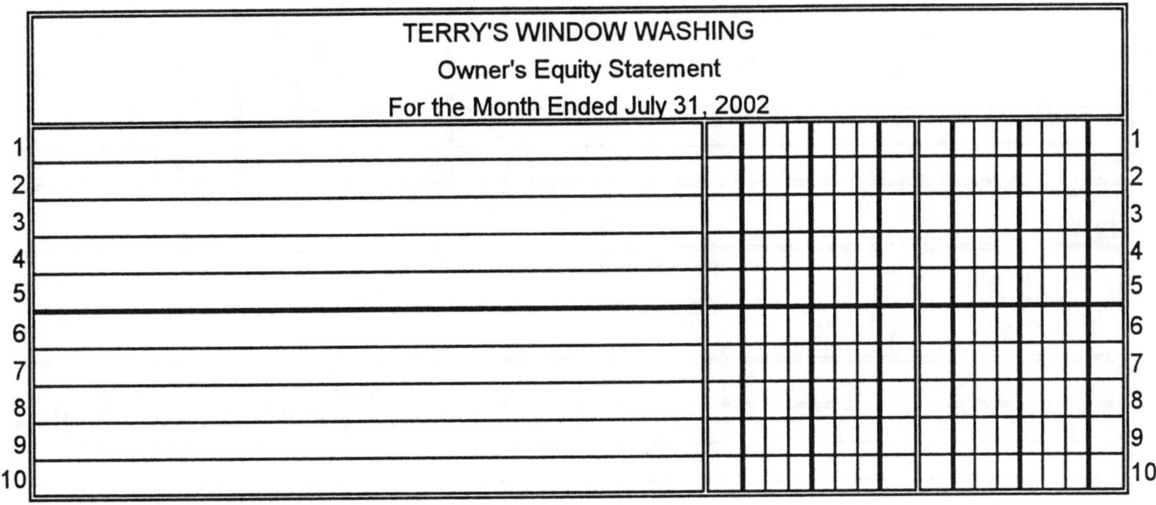

(d) (Continued)

TERRY'S WINDOW WASHING
Balance Sheet
July 31, 2002

Assets		
Liabilities and Owner's Equity		

(g)

TERRY'S WINDOW WASHING
Post-Closing Trial Balance
July 31, 2002

	Debit	Credit

Name | Problem 4-5 B Concluded

Section

Date | Terry's Window Washing

(e) and (f) General Journal J2-J3

Date	Accounts Titles and Explanation	Ref.	Debit	Credit
(e)	Adjusting Entries			
(f)	Closing Entries			

Name Comprehensive Problem Chapters 2-4

Section

Date Bill's Window Washing

(a)

General Journal

Date	Accounts Titles and Explanation	Ref.	Debit	Credit

Name

Section

Date

(b) & (c)

BILL'S WINDOW WASHING
Work Sheet
For the Month Ended July 31, 2002

	Account Titles	Trial Balance		Adjustments		Adjusted Trial Balance		Income Statement		Balance Sheet		
		Dr.	Cr.	Dr.	Cr.	Dr.	Cr	Dr.	Cr	Dr.	Cr.	
1	Cash											1
2	Accounts Receivable											2
3	Cleaning Supplies											3
4	Prepaid Insurance											4
5	Equipment											5
6	Accounts Payable											6
7	B. Murphy, Capital											7
8	B. Murphy, Drawing											8
9	Service Revenue											9
10	Gas and Oil Expense											10
11	Salaries Expense											11
12	Totals											12
13												13
14	Depreciation Expense											14
15	Accumulated Depreciation - Equipment											15
16	Insurance Expense											16
17	Cleaning Supplies Expense											17
18	Salaries Payable											18
19	Totals											19
20												20
21	Net Income											21
22	Totals											22
23												23
24												24
25												25
26												26
27												27
28												28
29												29
30												30
31												31
32												32
33												33
34												34
35												35
36												36
37												37
38												38
39												39
40												40

Name
Section
Date

Comprehensive Problem Chapters 2-4 Continued

Bill's Window Washing

(a), (e) and (f)

Cash — No. 101

Date	Explanation	Ref.	Debit	Credit	Balance

Accounts Receivable — No. 112

Date	Explanation	Ref.	Debit	Credit	Balance

Cleaning Supplies — No. 128

Date	Explanation	Ref.	Debit	Credit	Balance

Prepaid Insurance — No. 130

Date	Explanation	Ref.	Debit	Credit	Balance

Equipment — No. 157

Date	Explanation	Ref.	Debit	Credit	Balance

Accumulated Depreciation - Equipment — No. 158

Date	Explanation	Ref.	Debit	Credit	Balance

(a), (e) and (f) (Continued)

Accounts Payable No. 201

Date	Explanation	Ref.	Debit	Credit	Balance

Salaries Payable No. 212

Date	Explanation	Ref.	Debit	Credit	Balance

Bill Murphy, Capital No. 301

Date	Explanation	Ref.	Debit	Credit	Balance

Bill Murphy, Drawing No. 306

Date	Explanation	Ref.	Debit	Credit	Balance

Income Summary No. 350

Date	Explanation	Ref.	Debit	Credit	Balance

Service Revenue No. 400

Date	Explanation	Ref.	Debit	Credit	Balance

(a), (e) and (f) (Continued)

Gas & Oil Expense No. 633

Date	Explanation	Ref.	Debit	Credit	Balance

Cleaning Supplies Expense No. 634

Date	Explanation	Ref.	Debit	Credit	Balance

Depreciation Expense No. 711

Date	Explanation	Ref.	Debit	Credit	Balance

Insurance Expense No. 722

Date	Explanation	Ref.	Debit	Credit	Balance

Salaries Expense No. 726

Date	Explanation	Ref.	Debit	Credit	Balance

(d)

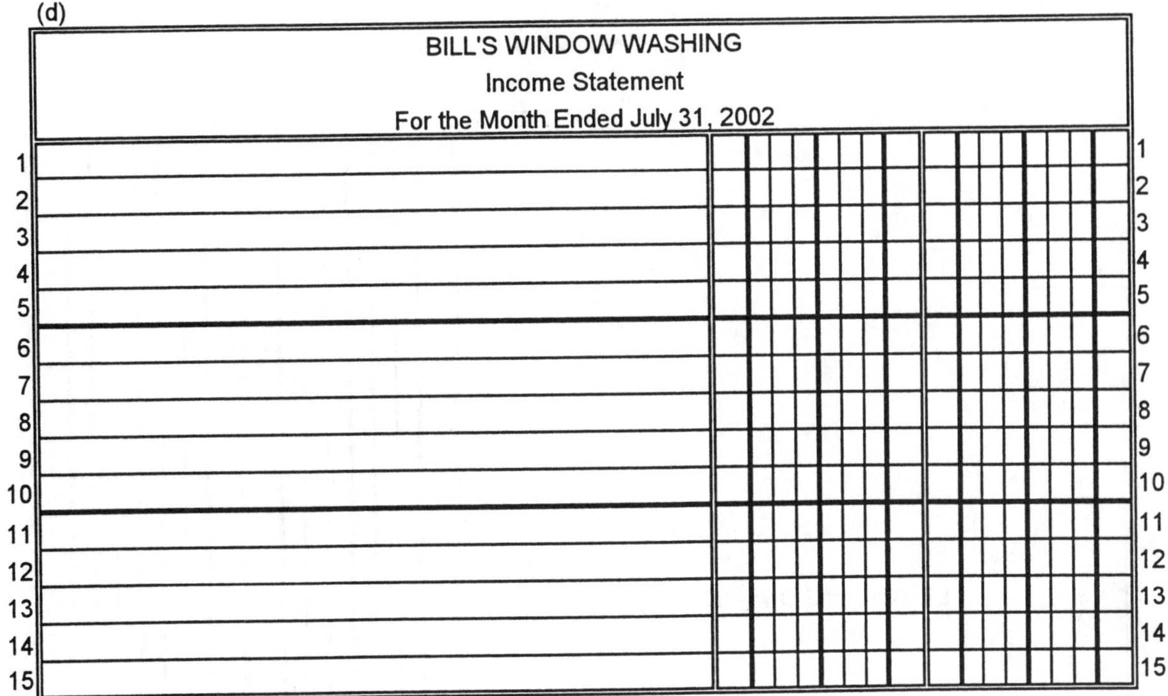
BILL'S WINDOW WASHING
Income Statement
For the Month Ended July 31, 2002

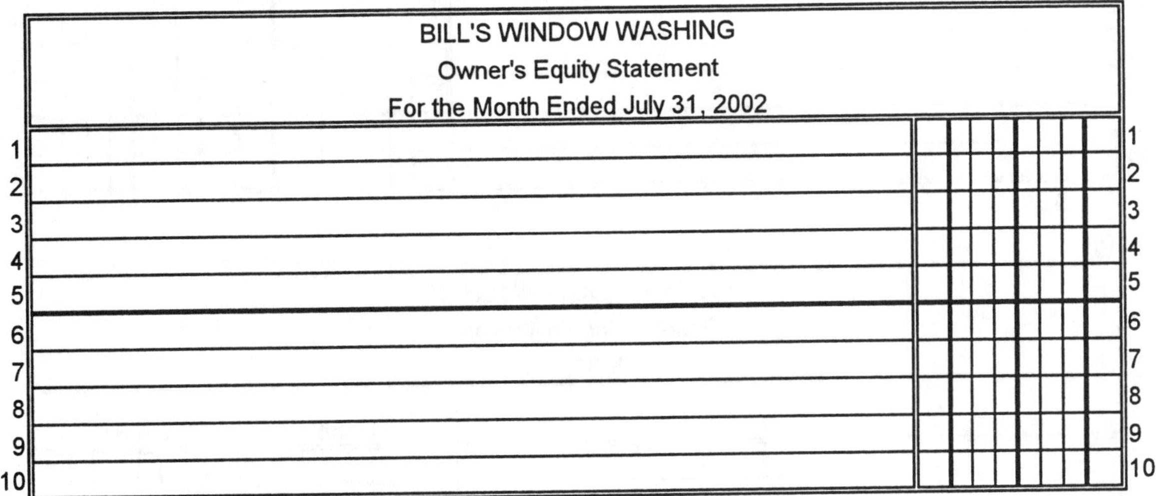
BILL'S WINDOW WASHING
Owner's Equity Statement
For the Month Ended July 31, 2002

(d) (Continued)

BILL'S WINDOW WASHING
Balance Sheet
July 31, 2002

Assets		
Liabilities and Owner's Equity		

(g)

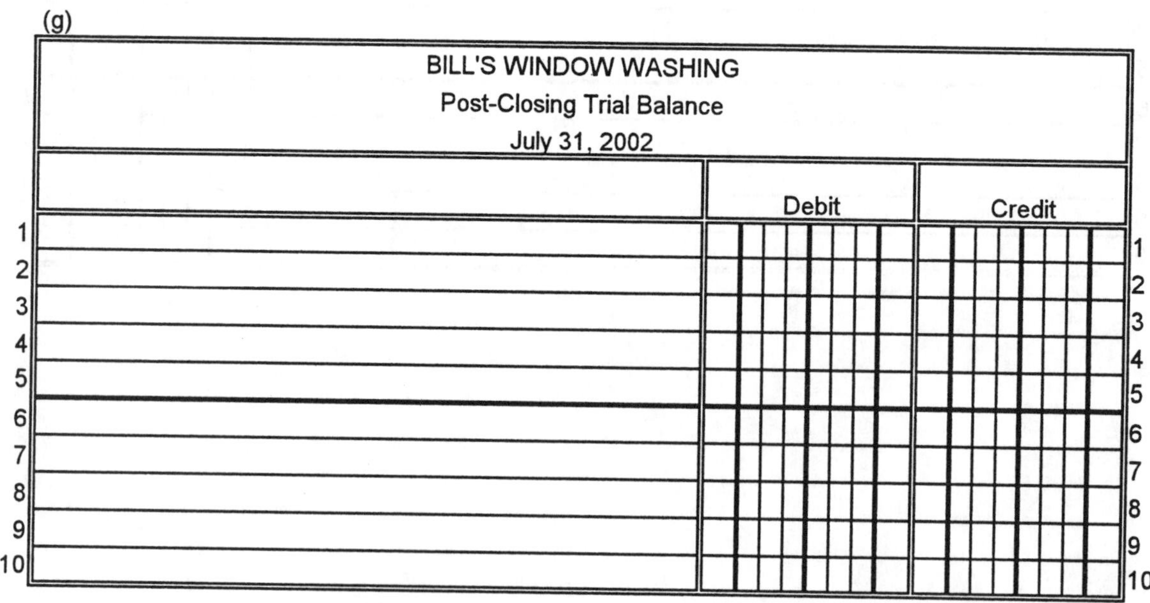

BILL'S WINDOW WASHING
Post-Closing Trial Balance
July 31, 2002

	Debit	Credit

Name

Section

Date

Bill's Window Washing

(e) and (f) General Journal J2-J3

Date	Accounts Titles and Explanation	Ref.	Debit	Credit
(e)	Adjusting Entries			
(f)	Closing Entries			

Name

Section

Date

Land's End, Inc.

(a)

(b)

(c)

(d)

(e)

Name

Section

Date

Land's End vs. Abercrombie & Fitch

(a) In millions	Lands' End	Abercrombie & Fitch
1. Total current assets		
2. Net property, plant, and equipment		
3. Total current liabilities		
4. Total stockholders' (shareholders')equity		

(b)

Name

Section

Date

Mo och Comsjo AB (MoDo)

Name

Section

Date

Company Home Pages

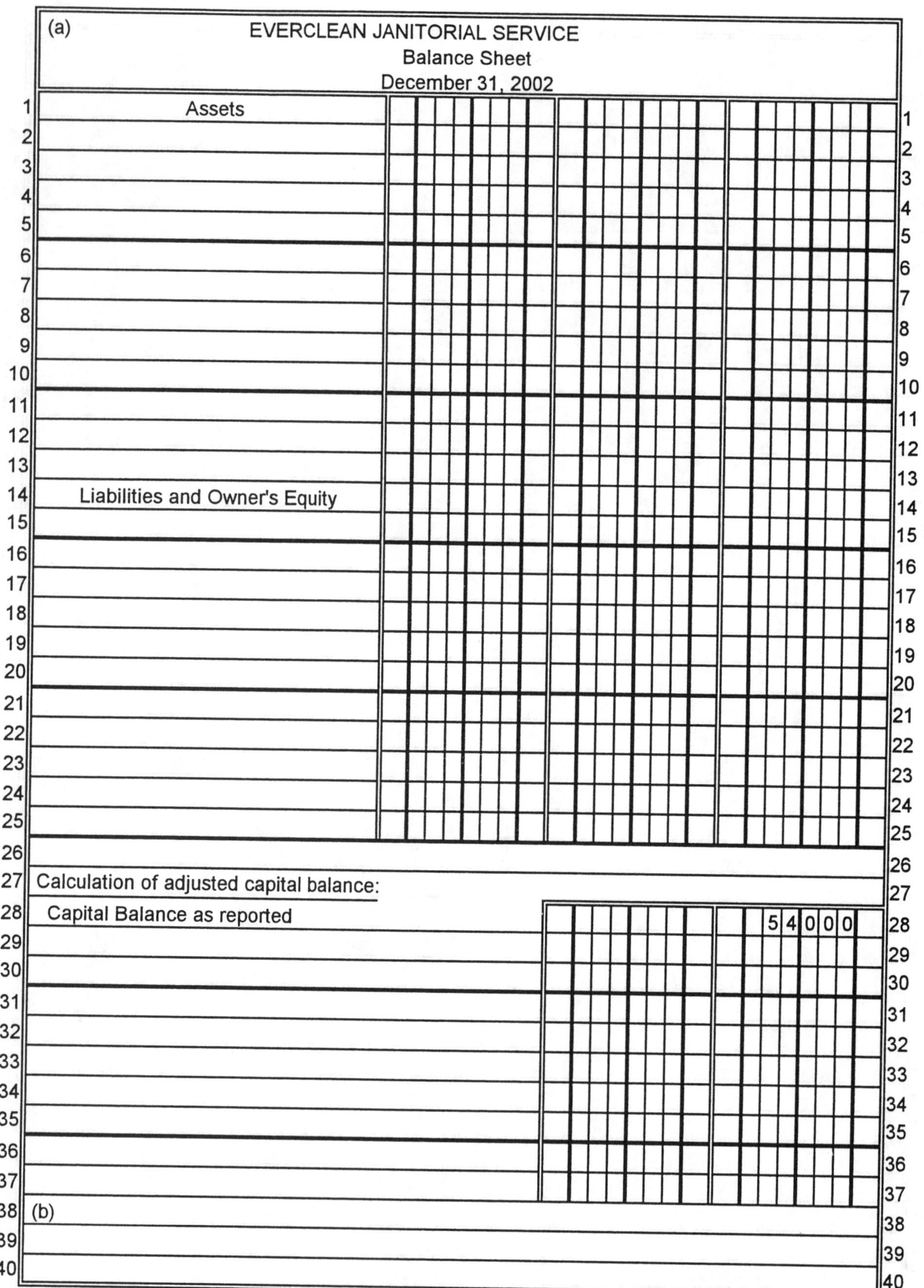

(a)

EVERCLEAN JANITORIAL SERVICE
Balance Sheet
December 31, 2002

Assets

Liabilities and Owner's Equity

Calculation of adjusted capital balance:

Capital Balance as reported		54000

(b)

Name

Section

Date

Name

Section

Date

Chapter 4 Ethics Case

TellTale Perfume Company

(a)

(b)

(c)

Name

Section

Date

Name

Section

Date

Name

Section

Date

Name

Section

Date

Exercises 5-1 and 5-2

General Journal

Date	Account Titles and Explanation	Debit	Credit

Name Exercises 5-3

Section

Date Kogan Company and Rego Company

General Journal

Date	Account Titles and Explanation	Ref.	Debit	Credit
(a)				
(b)				

Name
Section
Date

Exercises 5-4

R. Garg Company

General Journal

Date	Account Titles and Explanation	Ref.	Debit	Credit
(a)				
(b)				

Name | Exercises 5-5 and 5-6

Section

Date | Dimitry Company and Croce Co.

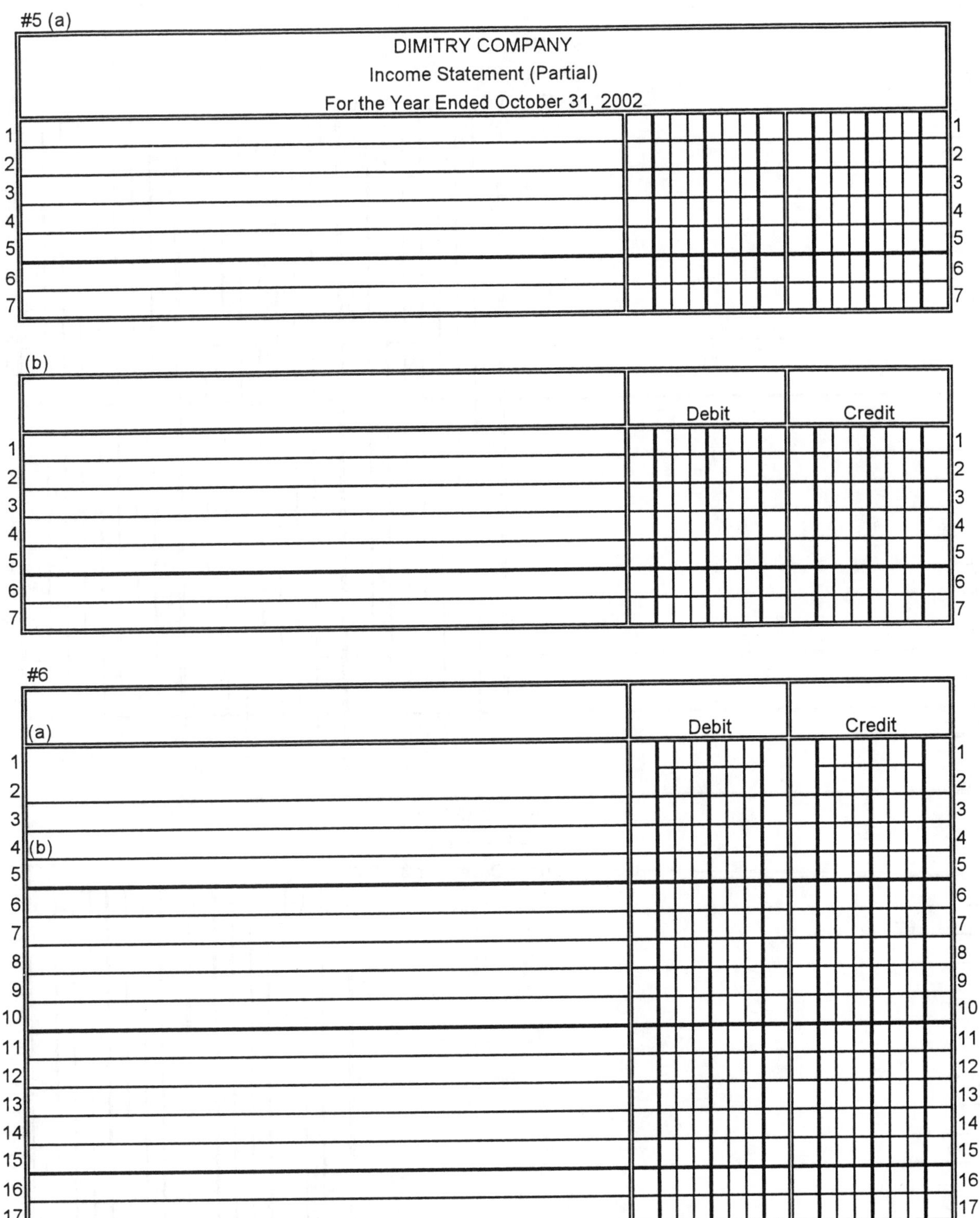

#5 (a)

DIMITRY COMPANY

Income Statement (Partial)

For the Year Ended October 31, 2002

(b)

	Debit	Credit

#6

(a)	Debit	Credit
(b)		

Name

Section

Date

Exercises 5-7

Berman Company

(a)

BERMAN COMPANY

Income Statement

For the Year Ended December 31, 2002

(b)

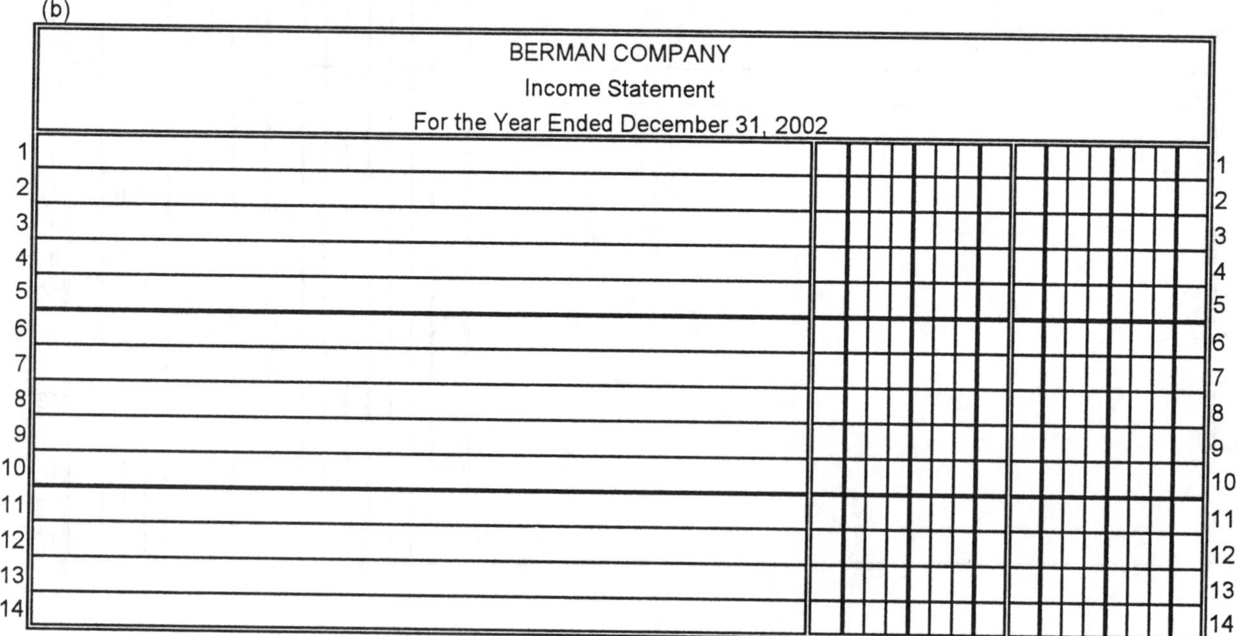

BERMAN COMPANY

Income Statement

For the Year Ended December 31, 2002

Name

Section

Date

8

9

Name

Section

Date

Exercise 5-10

Garland Company

GARLAND COMPANY

Work Sheet (Partial)

For the Period Ended May 31, 2002

	Account Titles	Adjusted Trial Balance		Income Statement		Balance Sheet		
		Dr.	Cr.	Dr.	Cr.	Dr.	Cr.	
1								1
2								2
3								3
4								4
5								5
6								6
7								7
8								8
9								9
10								10
11								11
12								12
13								13
14								14
15								15
16								16
17								17
18								18
19								19
20								20

Name | Problem 5-1A

Section

Date | Travel Warehouse

General Journal

Date	Account Titles and Explanation	Ref.	Debit	Credit

Name Problem 5-1A Concluded

Section

Date Travel Warehouse

General Journal

Date	Account Titles and Explanation	Ref.	Debit	Credit

Name | Problem 5-2A
Section
Date | Hubbs Distributing Company

General Journal

Date	Account Titles and Explanation	Ref.	Debit	Credit

Name

Section

Date

Problem 5-2A Continued

Hubbs Distributing Company

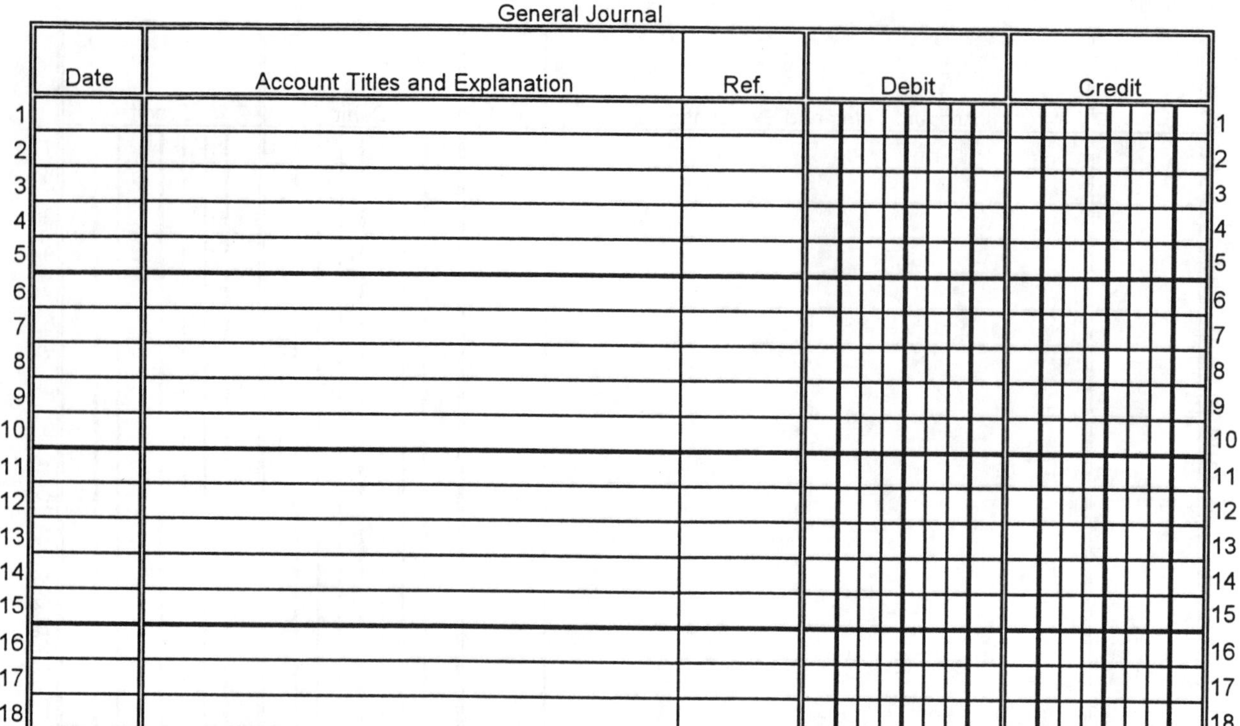

General Journal

Date	Account Titles and Explanation	Ref.	Debit	Credit

(b)

Cash No. 101

Date	Explanation	Ref.	Debit	Credit	Balance

Accounts Receivable No. 112

Date	Explanation	Ref.	Debit	Credit	Balance

(b) (Continued)

Merchandise Inventory No. 120

Date	Explanation	Ref.	Debit	Credit	Balance

Accounts Payable No. 201

Date	Explanation	Ref.	Debit	Credit	Balance

J. Carlos, Capital No. 301

Date	Explanation	Ref.	Debit	Credit	Balance

Sales No. 401

Date	Explanation	Ref.	Debit	Credit	Balance

(b) (Continued)

Sales Returns and Allowances — No. 412

Date	Explanation	Ref.	Debit	Credit	Balance

Sales Discounts — No. 414

Date	Explanation	Ref.	Debit	Credit	Balance

Cost of Goods Sold — No. 505

Date	Explanation	Ref.	Debit	Credit	Balance

Freight-Out — No. 644

Date	Explanation	Ref.	Debit	Credit	Balance

(c)

HUBBS DISTRIBUTING COMPANY
Income Statement (Partial)
For the Month Ended April 30, 2002

Name Problem 5-3A

Section

Date Gitler Departament Store

(a)

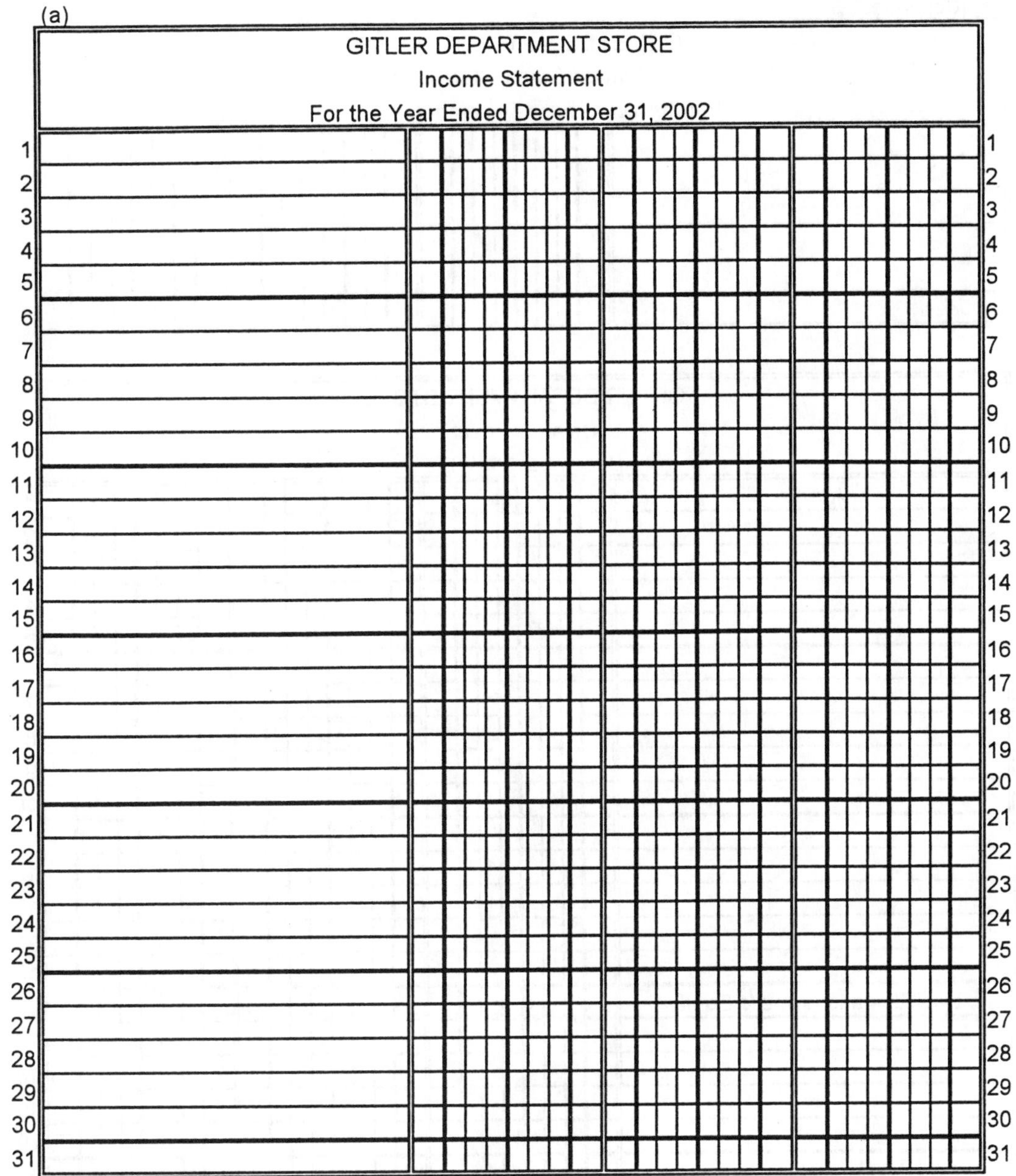

Name Section Date

Problem 5-3A Continued

Gitler Department Store

(a) (Continued)

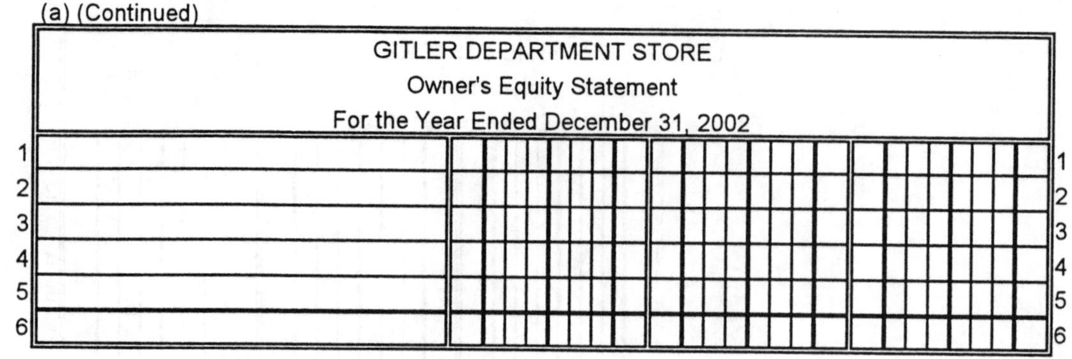
GITLER DEPARTMENT STORE

Owner's Equity Statement

For the Year Ended December 31, 2002

GITLER DEPARTMENT STORE

Balance Sheet

December 31, 2002

Assets

Liabilities and Owner's Equity

Name Problem 5-3S Continued

Section

Date Gitler Department Store

(b) and (c) General Journal

Date	Account Titles and Explanation	Ref.	Debit	Credit
(b)	Adjusting Entries			
(d)	Closing Entries			

(c) continued

General Journal

Date	Account Titles and Explanation	Ref.	Debit	Credit

Name — Problem 5-4A

Section

Date — Mike's Tennis Shop

(a) General Journal

Date	Account Titles and Explanation	Ref.	Debit	Credit

Name

Section

Date

Problem 5-4A Continued

Mike's Tennis Shop

(a) Continued

General Journal

Date	Account Titles and Explanation	Ref.	Debit	Credit

(b)

Cash No. 101

Date	Explanation	Ref.	Debit	Credit	Balance

Accounts Receivable No. 112

Date	Explanation	Ref.	Debit	Credit	Balance

Merchandise Inventory No. 120

Date	Explanation	Ref.	Debit	Credit	Balance

Accounts Payable No. 201

Date	Explanation	Ref.	Debit	Credit	Balance

(b) (Continued)

M. Young, Capital — No. 301

Date	Explanation	Ref.	Debit	Credit	Balance

Sales — No. 401

Date	Explanation	Ref.	Debit	Credit	Balance

Sales Returns and Allowances — No. 412

Date	Explanation	Ref.	Debit	Credit	Balance

Cost of Goods Sold — No. 505

Date	Explanation	Ref.	Debit	Credit	Balance

(c)

MIKE'S TENNIS SHOP
Trial Balance
April 30, 2002

		Debit	Credit	
1				1
2				2
3				3
4				4
5				5
6				6
7				7
8				8
9				9
10				10
11				11
12				12

Name
Section
Date

Brennan Fashion Center

(a)

BRENNAN FASHION CENTER
Work Sheet
For the Year Ended November 30, 2002

	Account Titles	Trial Balance		Adjustments		Adjusted Trial Balance		Income Statement		Balance Sheet		
		Dr.	Cr.	Dr.	Cr.	Dr.	Cr	Dr.	Cr	Dr.	Cr.	
1	Cash	23,400										1
2	Accounts Receivable	37,600										2
3	Merchandise Inventory	90,000										3
4	Land	92,000										4
5	Buildings	197,000										5
6	Accumulated Depreciation - Building		54,000									6
7	Equipment	83,500										7
8	Accumulated Depreciation - Equipment		42,400									8
9	Notes Payable		50,000									9
10	Accounts Payable		37,500									10
11	M. Zuma, Capital		267,800									11
12	M. Zuma, Drawing	10,000										12
13	Sales		902,100									13
14	Sales Discounts	4,600										14
15	Cost of Goods Sold	709,900										15
16	Salaries Expense	69,800										16
17	Utilities Expense	19,400										17
18	Repair Expense	5,900										18
19	Gas and Oil Expense	7,200										19
20	Insurance Expense	3,500										20
21	Totals	1,353,800	1,353,800									21
22	Totals											22
23												23
24												24
25												25
26												26
27												27

Name

Section

Date

Problem 5-5A Continued

Brennan Fashion Center

(b)

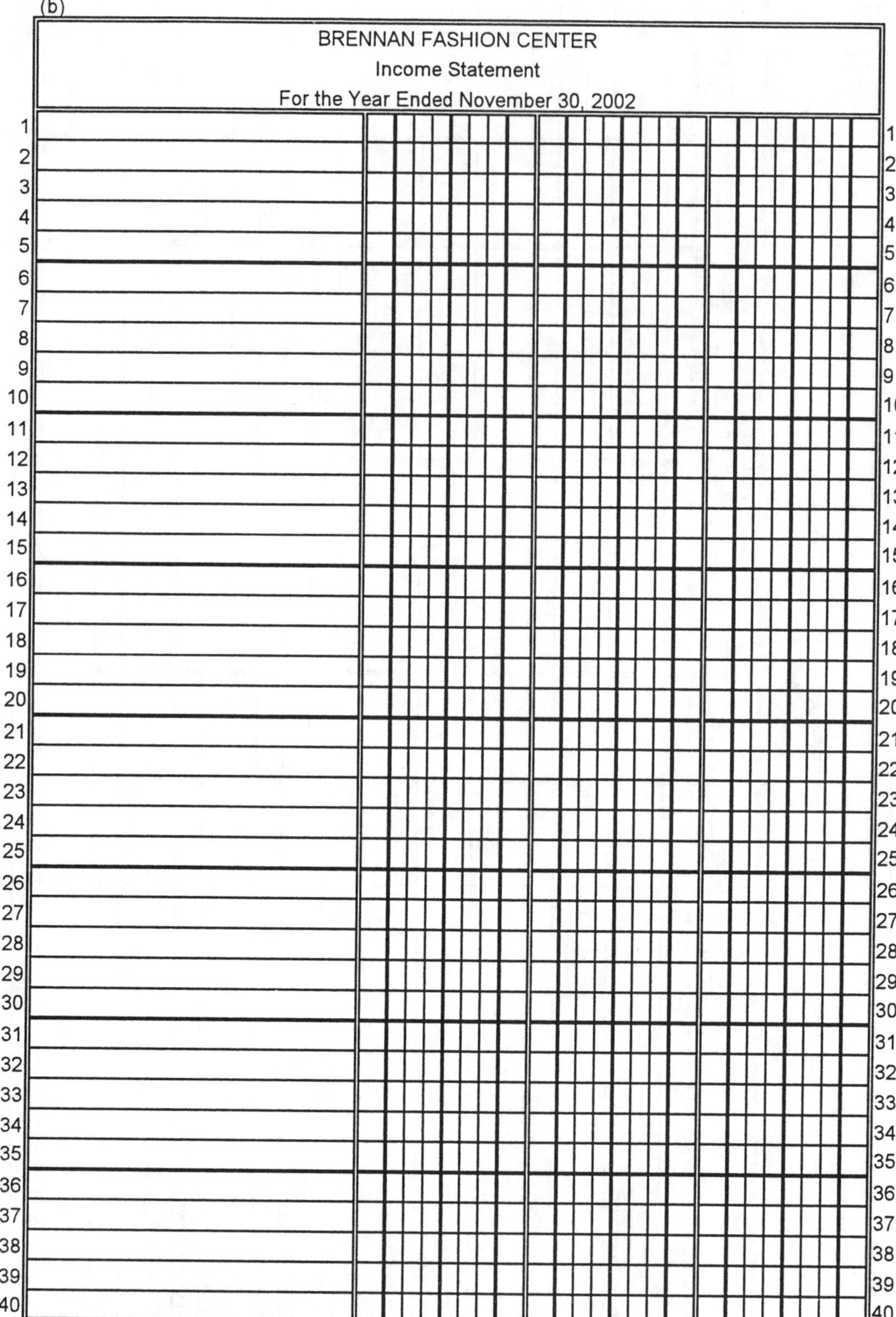

BRENNAN FASHION CENTER

Income Statement

For the Year Ended November 30, 2002

Name
Section
Date

Problem 5-5A Continued

Brennan Fashion Center

(b) (Continued)

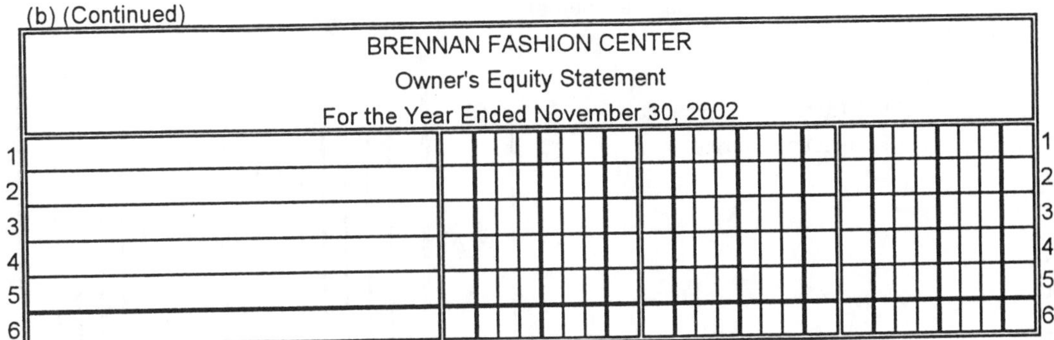

BRENNAN FASHION CENTER
Owner's Equity Statement
For the Year Ended November 30, 2002

BRENNAN FASHION CENTER
Balance Sheet
November 30, 2002

Assets

Liabilities and Owner's Equity

Name

Section

Date

Problem 5-5A Continued

Brennan Fashion Center

(c) and (d)

General Journal

	Date	Account Titles and Explanation	Ref.	Debit	Credit	
1	(c)	Adjusting Entries				1
2						2
3						3
4						4
5						5
6						6
7						7
8						8
9						9
10						10
11						11
12						12
13						13
14						14
15						15
16						16
17						17
18						18
19						19
20						20
21	(d)	Closing Entries				21
22						22
23						23
24						24
25						25
26						26
27						27
28						28
29						29
30						30
31						31
32						32
33						33
34						34
35						35
36						36
37						37
38						38
39						39
40						40

Problem 5-5A Concluded

Name

Section

Brennan Fashion Center

Date

(d) (Continued)

General Journal

Date	Account Titles and Explanation	Ref.	Debit	Credit

(e)

BRENNAN FASHION CENTER

Post-Closing Trial Balance

November 30, 2002

Name

Section

Date

Problem 5-1B

Dazzle Book Warehouse

General Journal

Date	Account Titles and Explanation	Ref.	Debit	Credit

Name

Section

Date

Problem 5-1B Concluded

Dazzle Book Warehouse

General Journal

Date	Account Titles and Explanation	Ref.	Debit	Credit

Name

Section

Date

Problem 5-2B

Eagle Hardware Store

(a)

General Journal

Date	Account Titles and Explanation	Ref.	Debit	Credit

Name
Section
Date

Problem 5-2B Continued

Eagle Hardware Store

(a) (Continued)

General Journal

Date	Account Titles and Explanation	Ref.	Debit	Credit

(b)

Cash — No. 101

Date	Explanation	Ref.	Debit	Credit	Balance

Accounts Receivable — No. 112

Date	Explanation	Ref.	Debit	Credit	Balance

(b) (Continued)

Merchandise Inventory No. 120

Date	Explanation	Ref.	Debit	Credit	Balance

Supplies No. 126

Date	Explanation	Ref.	Debit	Credit	Balance

Accounts Payable No. 201

Date	Explanation	Ref.	Debit	Credit	Balance

J. Eagle, Capital No. 301

Date	Explanation	Ref.	Debit	Credit	Balance

Sales No. 401

Date	Explanation	Ref.	Debit	Credit	Balance

(b) (Continued)

Sales Returns and Allowances — No.412

Date	Explanation	Ref.	Debit	Credit	Balance

Sales Discounts — No. 414

Date	Explanation	Ref.	Debit	Credit	Balance

Cost of Goods Sold — No. 505

Date	Explanation	Ref.	Debit	Credit	Balance

(c)

EAGLE HARDWARE STORE
Income Statement (Partial)
For the Month Ended May 31, 2002

1				1
2				2
3				3
4				4
5				5
6				6
7				7
8				8
9				9
10				10

Name — Problem 5-3B

Section

Date — Forcina Department Store

(a)

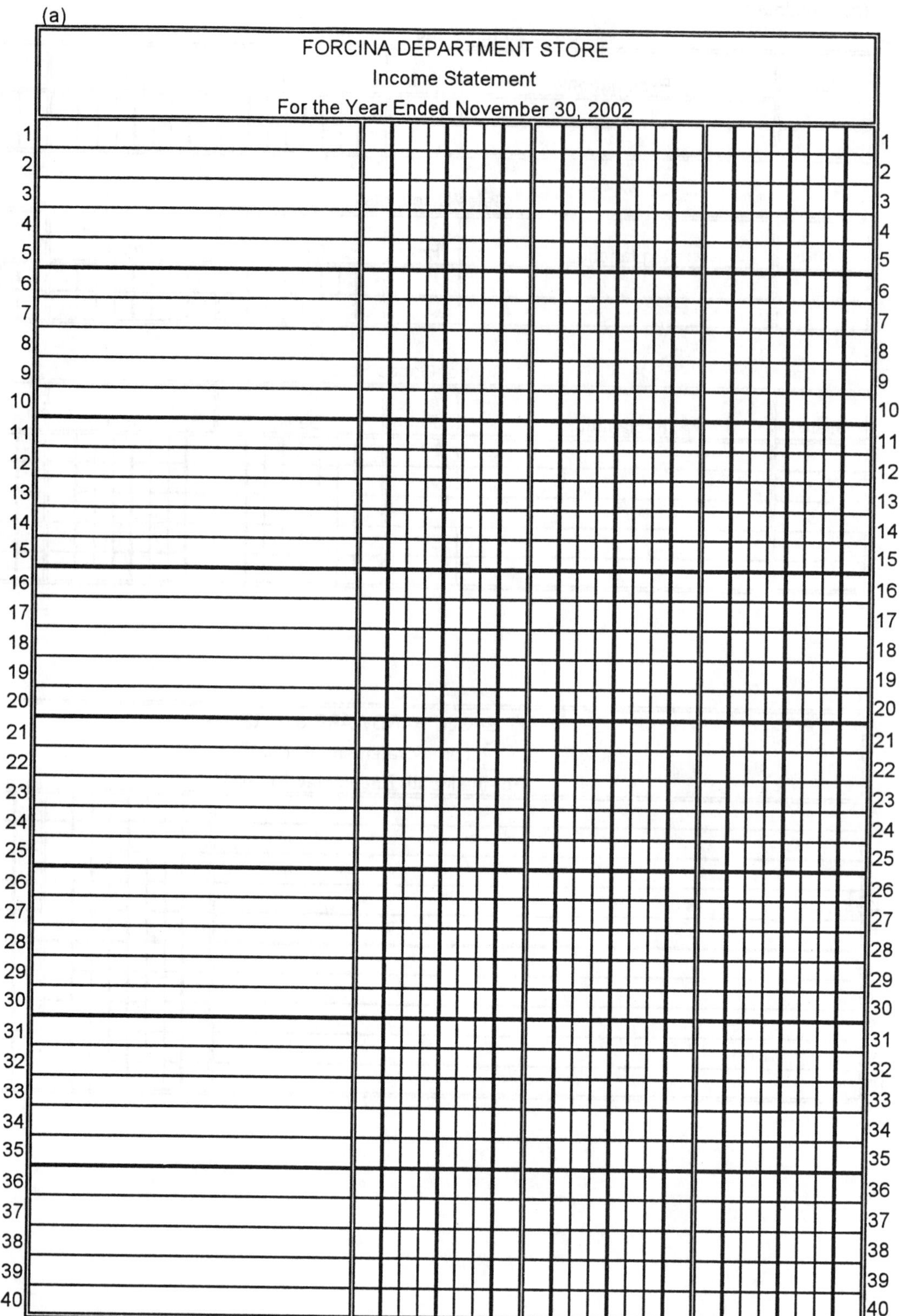

FORCINA DEPARTMENT STORE

Income Statement

For the Year Ended November 30, 2002

(a) (Continued)

FORCINA DEPARTMENT STORE
Owner's Equity Statement
For the Year Ended November 30, 2002

1			1
2			2
3			3
4			4
5			5
6			6

(b) General Journal

	Date	Accounts Titles and Explanation	Ref.	Debit	Credit	
1		Adjusting Entries				1
2						2
3						3
4						4
5						5
6						6
7						7
8						8
9						9
10						10
11						11
12						12
13						13
14						14
15						15
16						16
17						17
18						18
19						19
20						20

Name

Section

Date

(a) (Continued)

FORCINA DEPARTMENT STORE

Balance Sheet

November 30, 2002

Assets

Liabilities and Owner's Equity

Name Problem 5-3B Concluded

Section

Date Forcina Department Store

(c) General Journal

Date	Accounts Titles and Explanation	Ref.	Debit	Credit
	Closing Entries			

Name

Section

Date

Problem 5-4B

Greg's Pro Shop

(a)

General Journal

J1

Date	Account Titles and Explanation	Ref.	Debit	Credit

Name

Section

Date

Problem 5-4B Continued

Greg's Pro Shop

(b)

Cash — No. 101

Date	Explanation	Ref.	Debit	Credit	Balance

Accounts Receivable — No. 112

Date	Explanation	Ref.	Debit	Credit	Balance

Merchandise Inventory — No. 120

Date	Explanation	Ref.	Debit	Credit	Balance

Accounts Payable — No. 201

Date	Explanation	Ref.	Debit	Credit	Balance

Name

Section

Date

Problem 5-4B Continued

Greg's Pro Shop

(b) (Continued)

G. Scott, Capital — No. 301

Date	Explanation	Ref.	Debit	Credit	Balance

Sales — No. 401

Date	Explanation	Ref.	Debit	Credit	Balance

Sales Return and Allowances — No. 412

Date	Explanation	Ref.	Debit	Credit	Balance

Cost of Goods Sold — No. 505

Date	Explanation	Ref.	Debit	Credit	Balance

(c)

GREG'S PRO SHOP
Trial Balance
April 30, 2002

		Debit	Credit
1			
2			
3			
4			
5			
6			
7			
8			
9			
10			
11			
12			
13			
14			

Name

Section

Date

Problem 5-5B

Graham Wholesale Company

(a)

GRAHAM WHOLESALE COMPANY

Work Sheet

For the Year Ended December 31, 2002

	Account Titles	Trial Balance		Adjustments		Adjusted Trial Balance		Income Statement		Balance Sheet		
		Dr.	Cr.	Dr.	Cr.	Dr.	Cr	Dr.	Cr	Dr.	Cr.	
1	Cash	25,400										1
2	Accounts Receivable	37,600										2
3	Merchandise Inventory	90,000										3
4	Land	92,000										4
5	Buildings	197,000										5
6	Accumulated Depreciation - Buildings		54,000									6
7	Equipment	83,500										7
8	Accumulated Depreciation - Equipment		42,400									8
9	Notes Payable		50,000									9
10	Accounts Payable		37,500									10
11	M. Graham, Capital		267,800									11
12	M. Graham, Drawing	10,000										12
13	Sales		904,100									13
14	Sales Discounts	4,600										14
15	Cost of Goods Sold	709,900										15
16	Salaries Expense	69,800										16
17	Utilities Expense	19,400										17
18	Repair Expense	5,900										18
19	Gas and Oil Expense	7,200										19
20	Insurance Expense	3,500										20
21	Totals	1,355,800	1,355,800									21
22												22
23												23
24												24
25												25

Name

Section

Date

Problem 5-5B Continued

Graham Wholesale Company

(b)

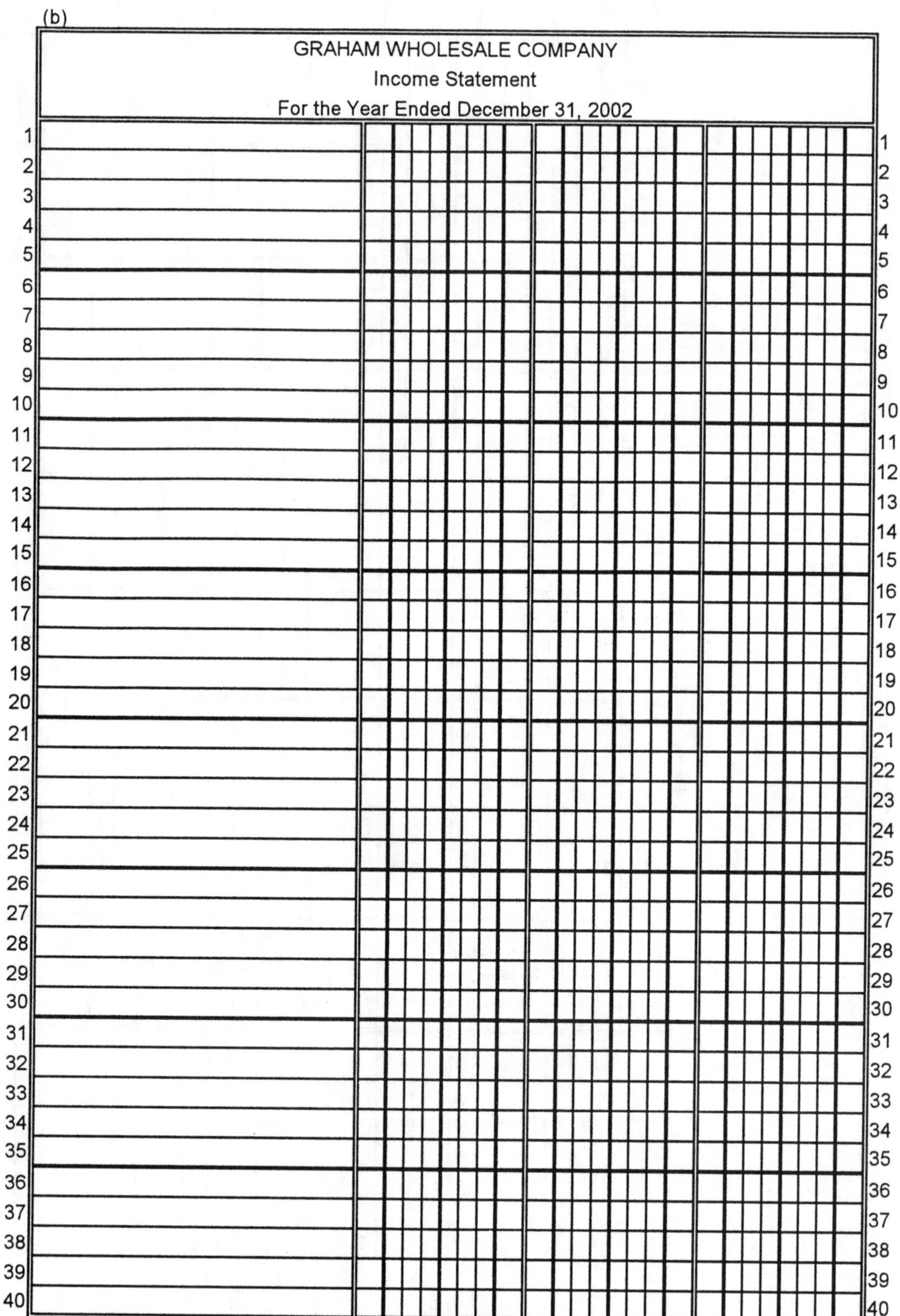

GRAHAM WHOLESALE COMPANY

Income Statement

For the Year Ended December 31, 2002

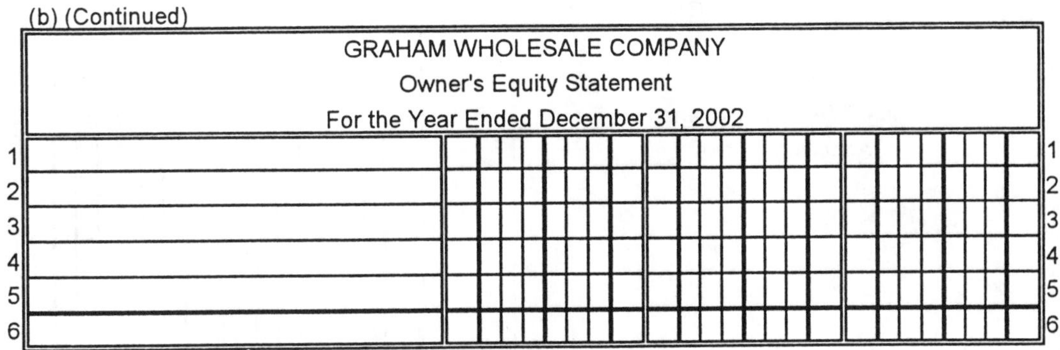

(b) (Continued)

GRAHAM WHOLESALE COMPANY

Owner's Equity Statement

For the Year Ended December 31, 2002

GRAHAM WHOLESALE COMPANY

Balance Sheet

December 31, 2002

Assets

Liabilities and Owner's Equity

Name

Section

Date

Problem 5-5B Continued

Graham Wholesale Company

(c) and (d)

General Journal

	Date	Account Titles and Explanation	Ref.	Debit	Credit	
1	(c)	Adjusting Entries				1
2						2
3						3
4						4
5						5
6						6
7						7
8						8
9						9
10						10
11						11
12						12
13						13
14						14
15	(d)	Closing Entries				15
16						16
17						17
18						18
19						19
20						20
21						21
22						22
23						23
24						24
25						25
26						26
27						27
28						28
29						29
30						30
31						31
32						32
33						33
34						34
35						35
36						36
37						37
38						38
39						39
40						40

Name

Section

Date

Problem 5-5B Concluded

Graham Wholesale Company

(e)

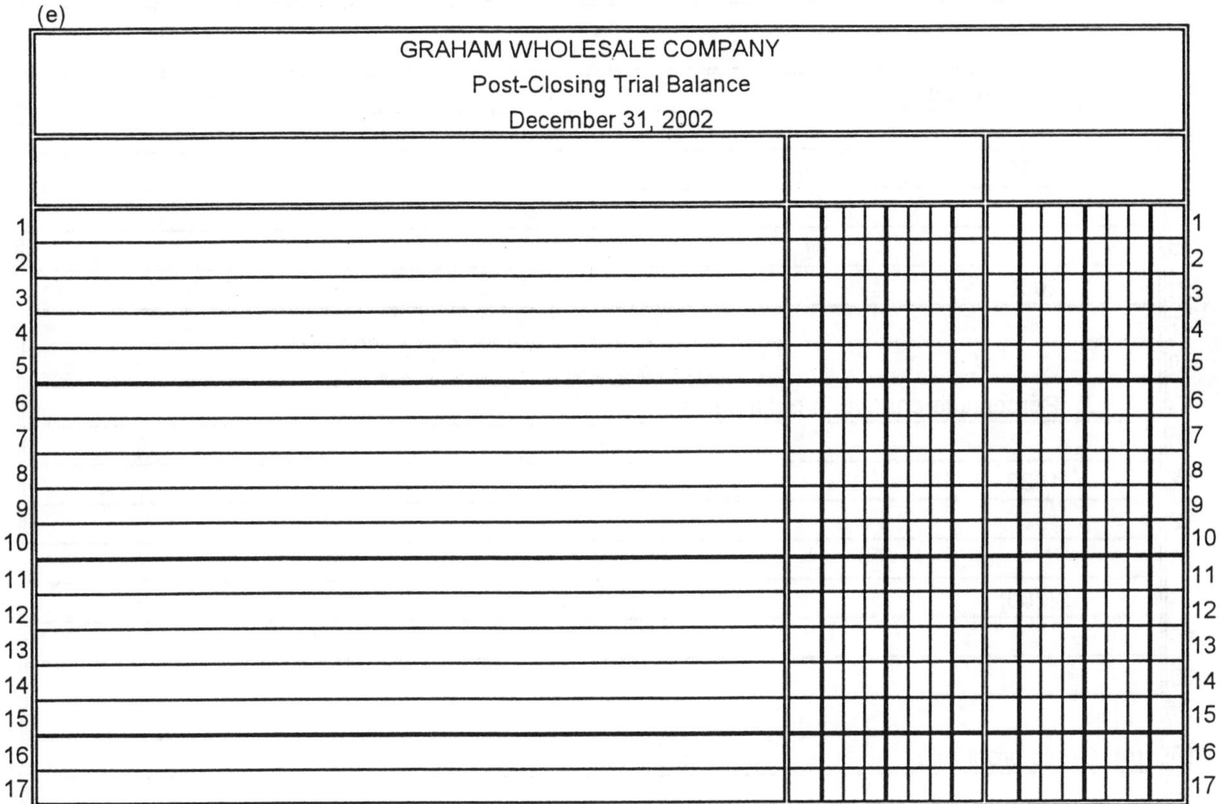

GRAHAM WHOLESALE COMPANY

Post-Closing Trial Balance

December 31, 2002

(a) (1) Percentage change in sales -

1999:

2000:

(2) Percentage change in net income -

1999:

2000:

(b) Gross profit rate-

1998:

1999:

2000:

(c) Percentage of net income to sales -

1998:

1999:

2000:

	Lands' End	Abercrombie & Fitch
(a)		
(1) 2000 Gross profit		
(2) 2000 Gross profit rate		
(3) 2000 Operating Income		
(4) Percentage change in operating income, 1999 to 2000		

(b)

(a)

(b)

(c)

Name | Chapter Exploring The Web

Section

Date | Lands' End or Abercrombie & Fitch

(a)

(b)

(a) (1)

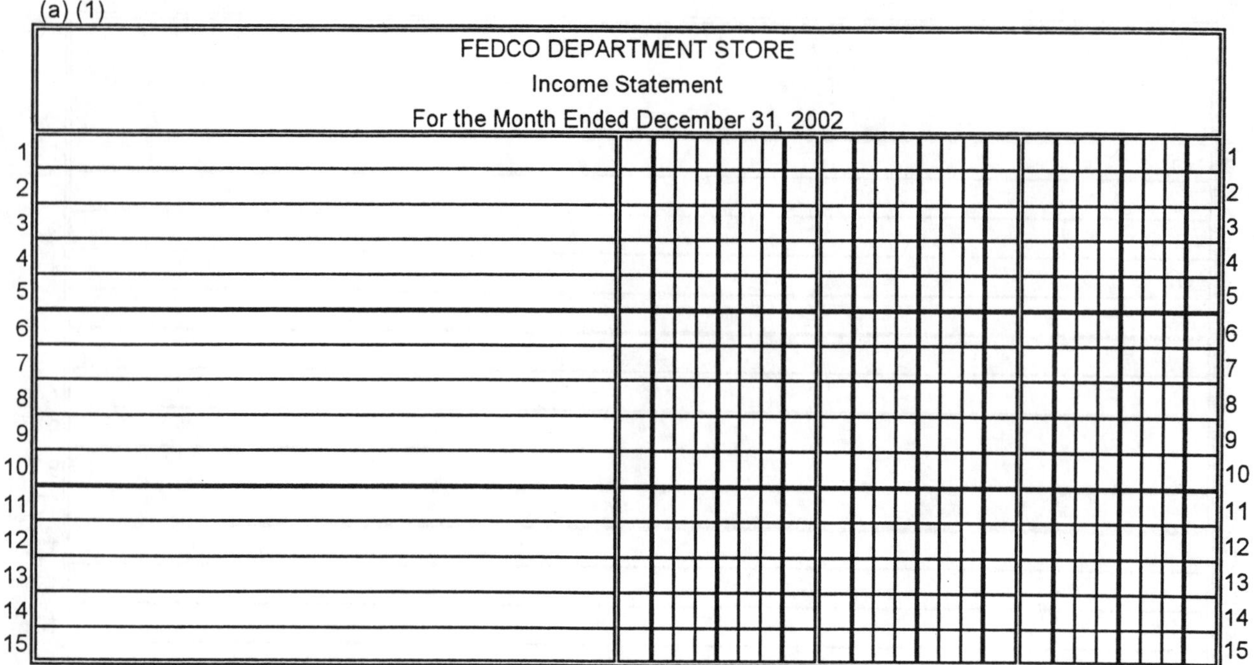
FEDCO DEPARTMENT STORE
Income Statement
For the Month Ended December 31, 2002

(2)

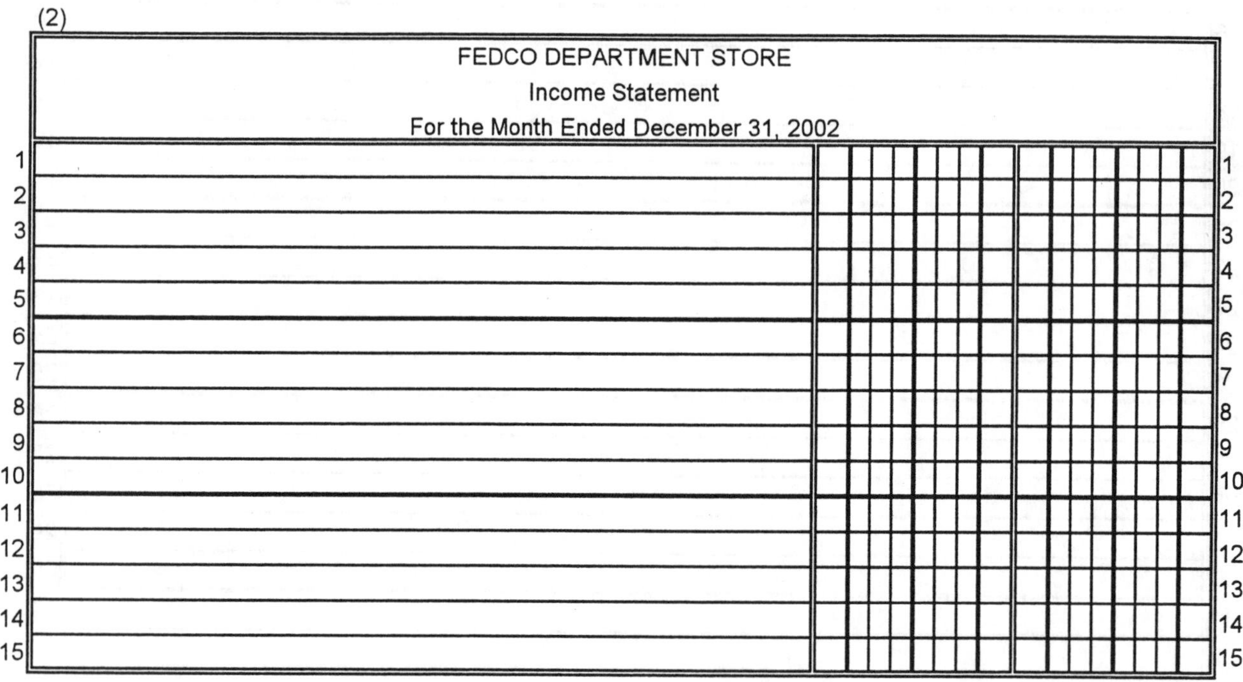
FEDCO DEPARTMENT STORE
Income Statement
For the Month Ended December 31, 2002

(b)

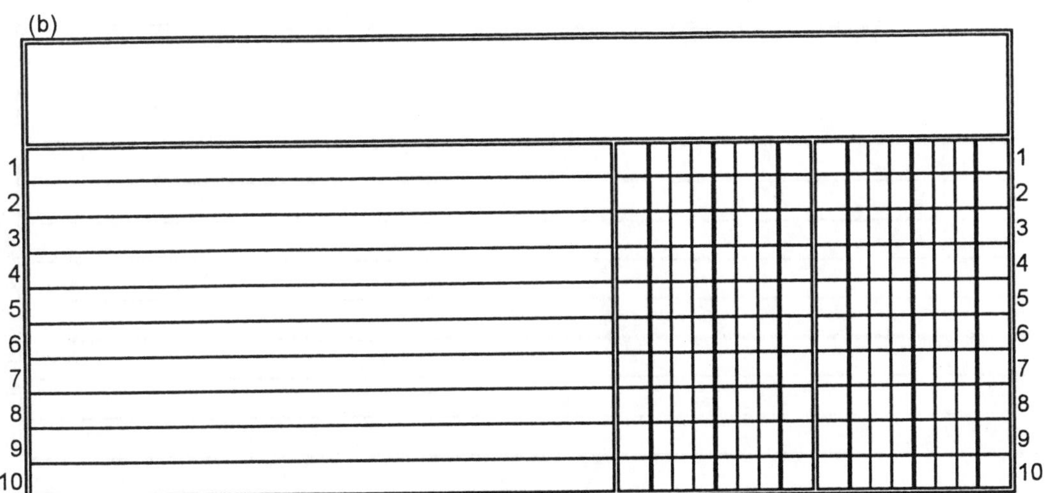

(c)

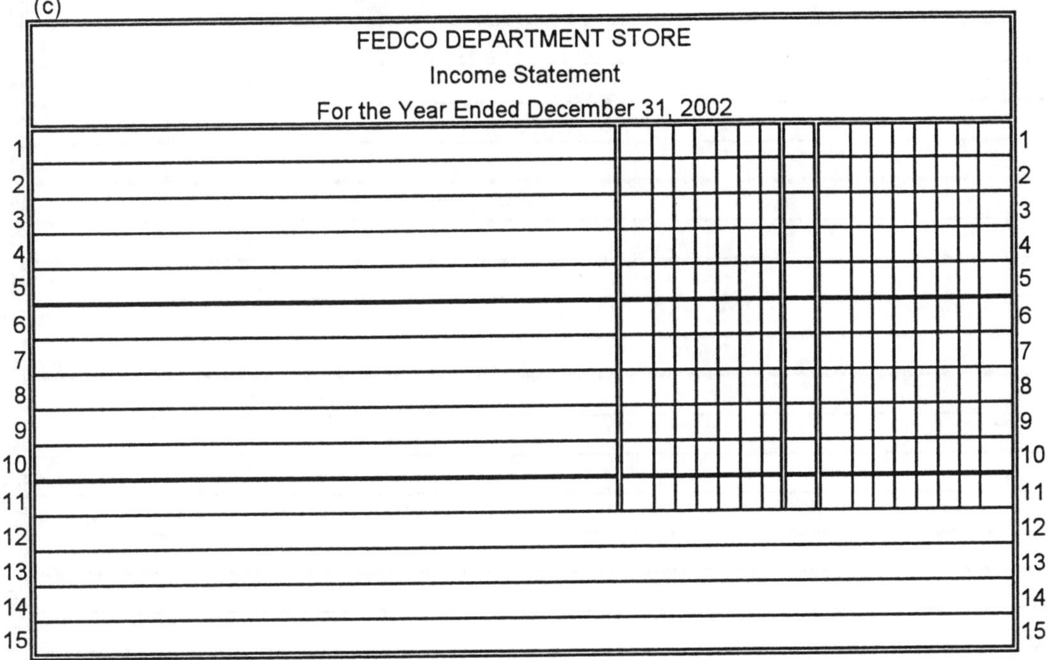
FEDCO DEPARTMENT STORE
Income Statement
For the Year Ended December 31, 2002

Name

Section

Date

Surfing USA Co.

(a) & (b)

Name | Chapter 5 Ethics Case
Section
Date | Yorkshire Store

(a)

(b)

(c)

Name

Section

Date

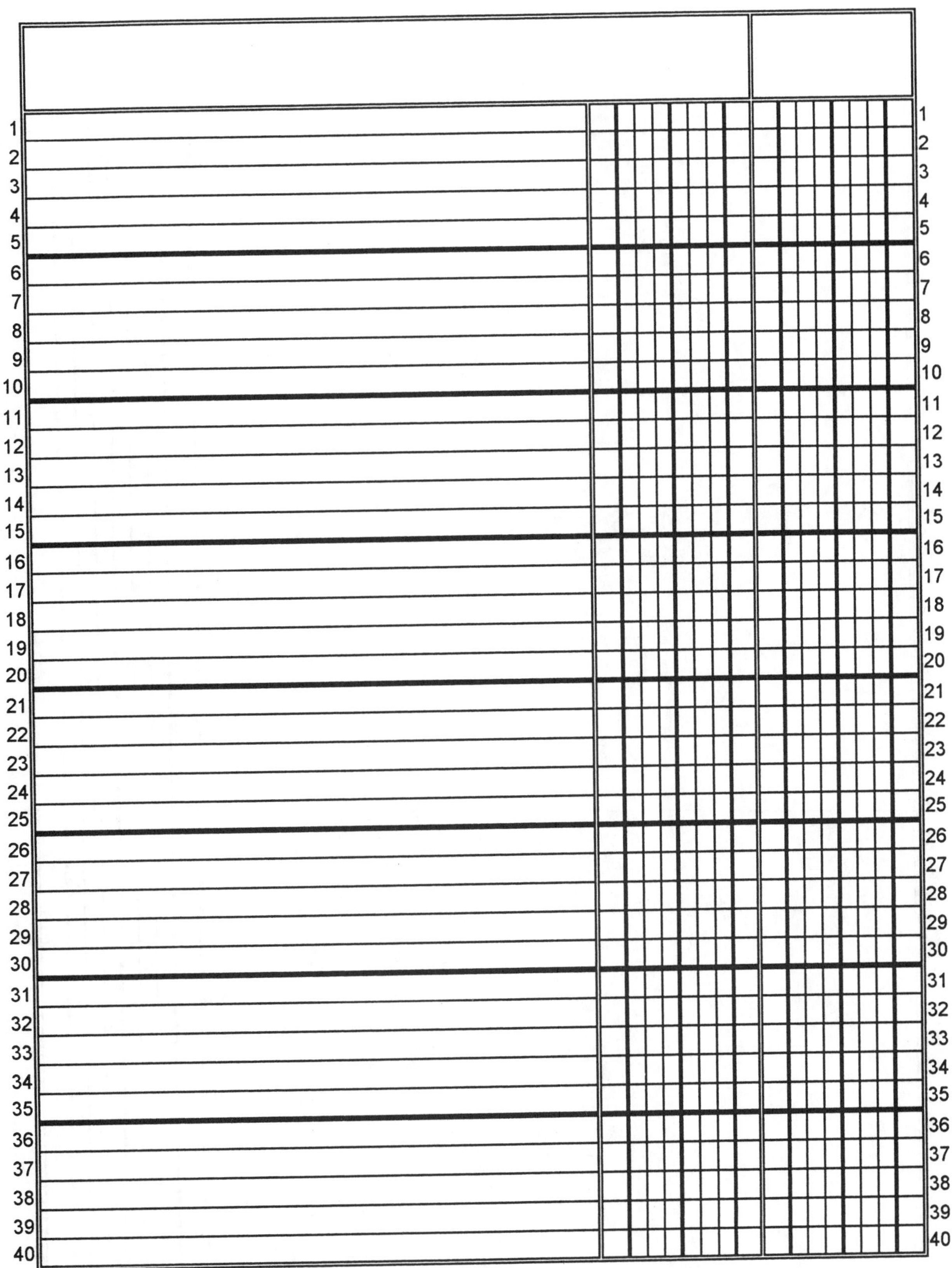

Name

Section

Date

Name ____________________

Section ____________________

Date ____________________

Name

Section

Date

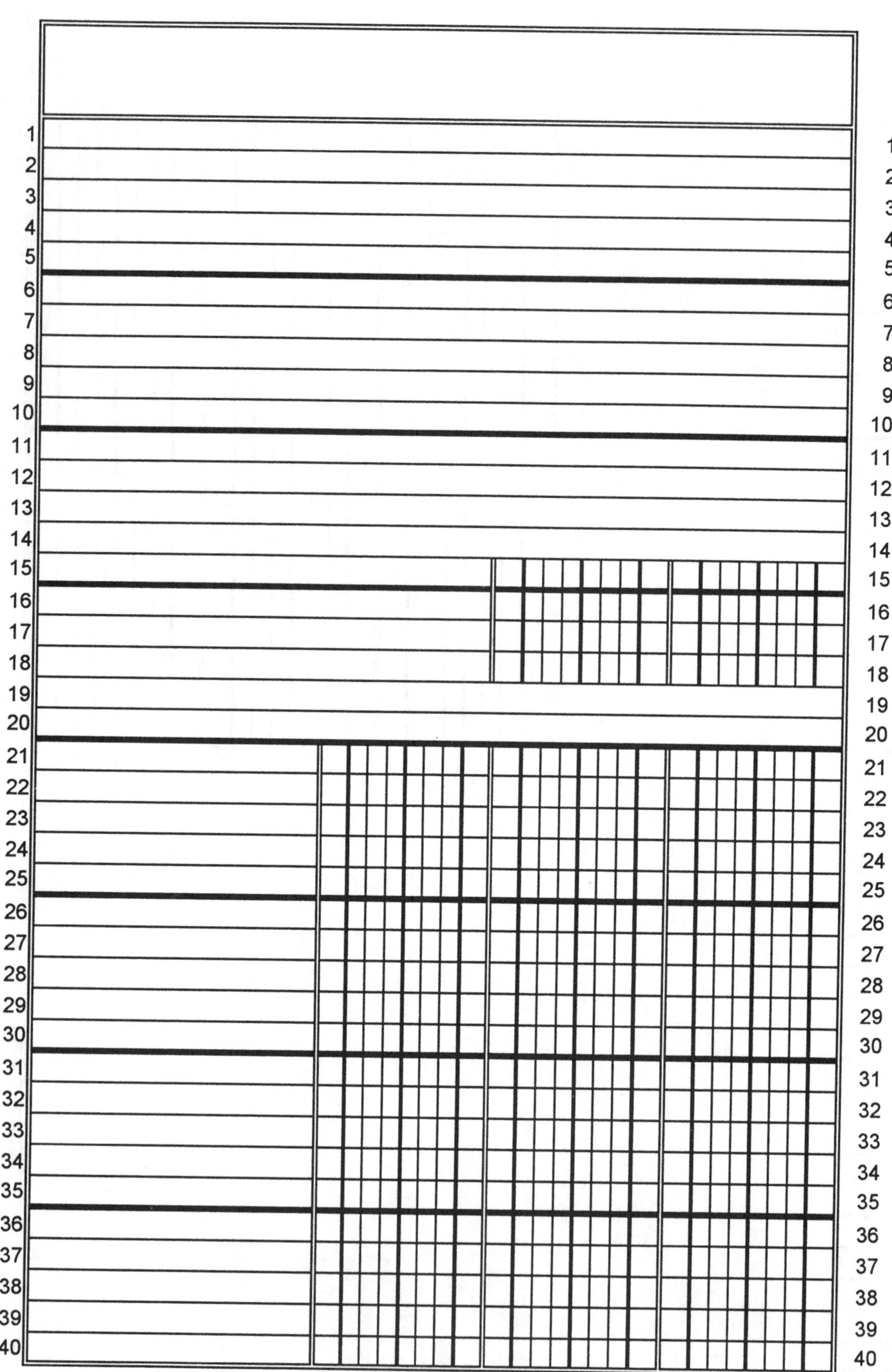

Name

Section

Date

#1

#2

Name
Section
Date

Exercise 6-3

Boliva Company

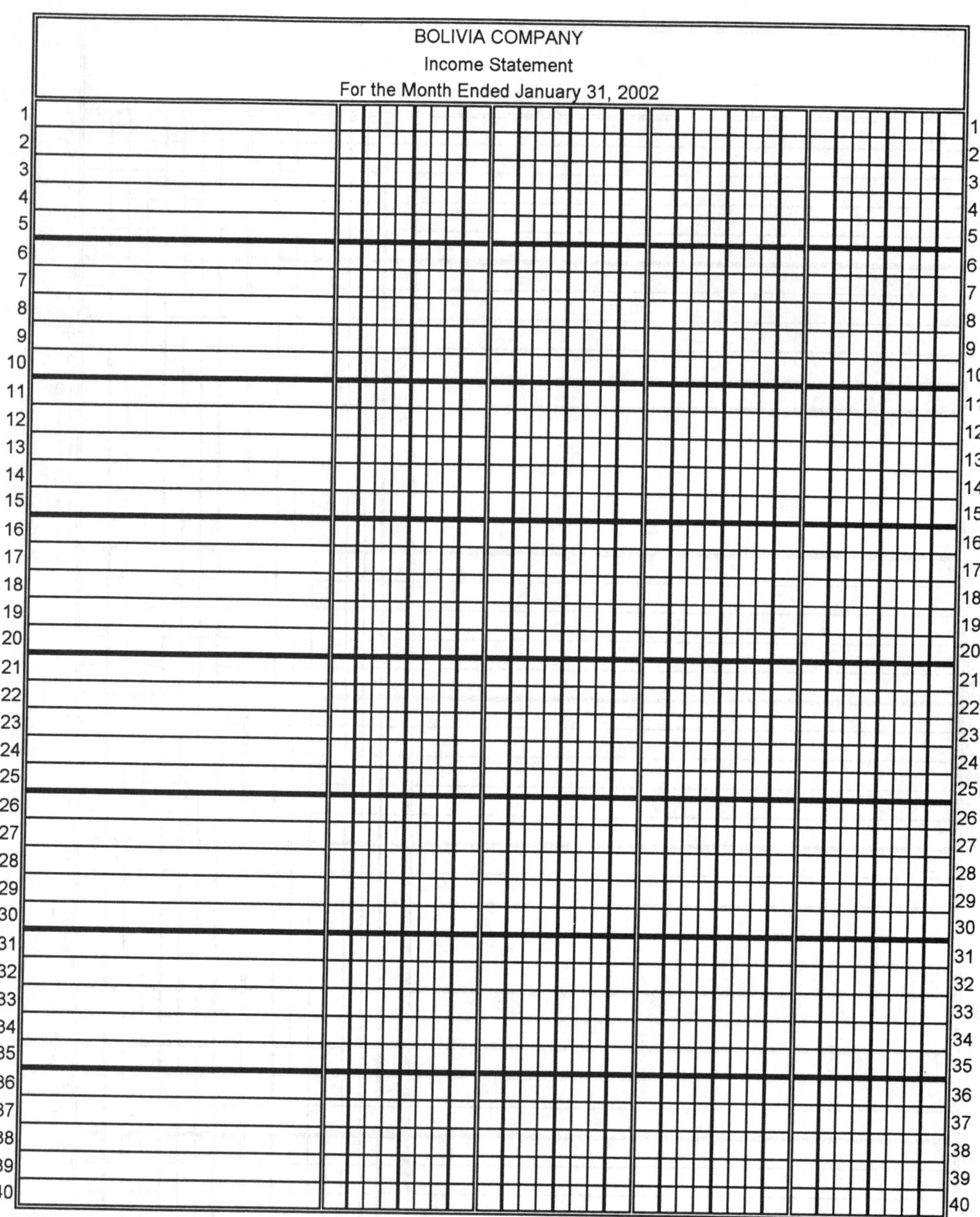
BOLIVIA COMPANY
Income Statement
For the Month Ended January 31, 2002

Name

Section

Date

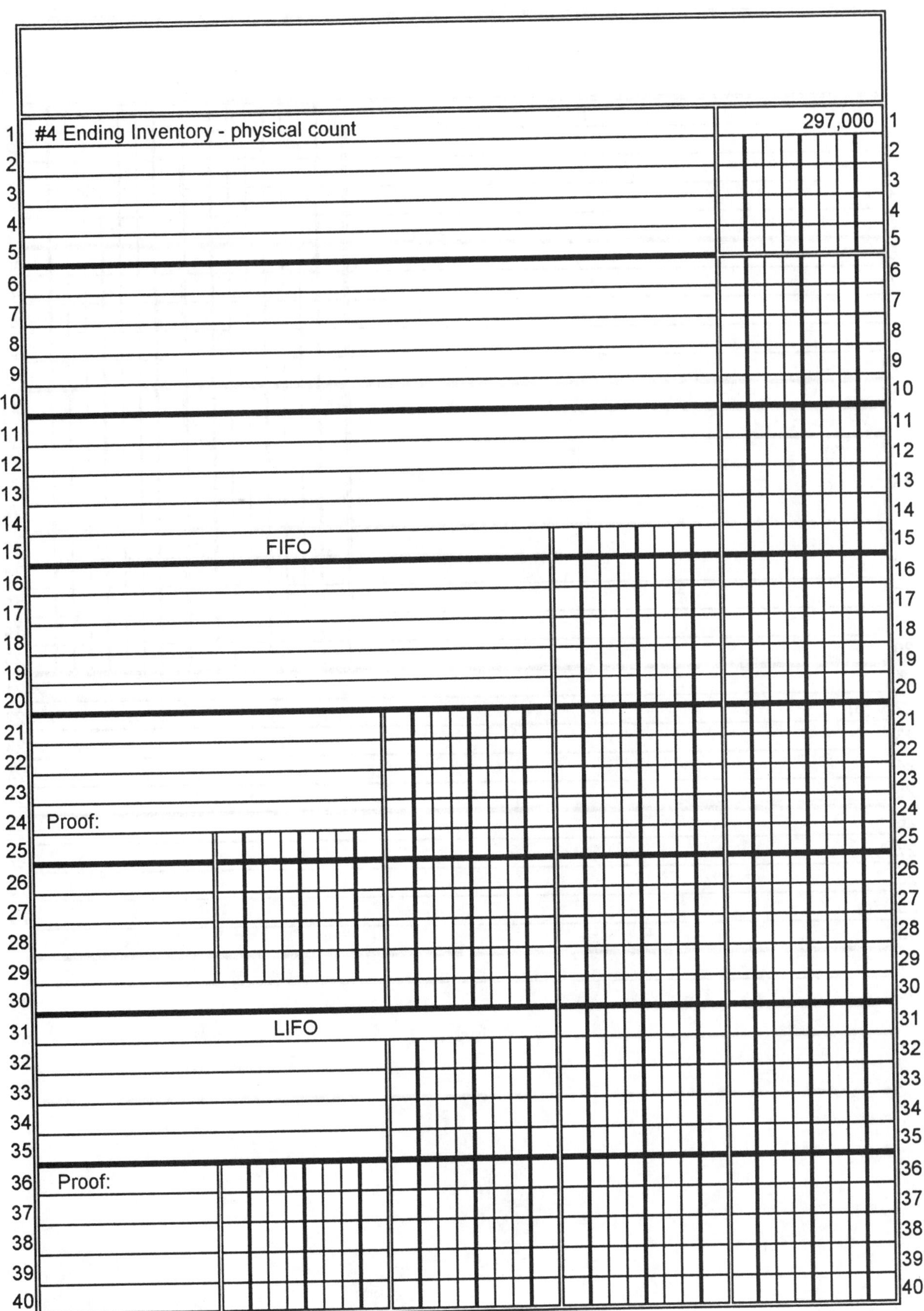

#4 Ending Inventory - physical count 297,000

FIFO

Proof:

LIFO

Proof:

Name

Section

Date

Exercise 6-6

Naperville Company

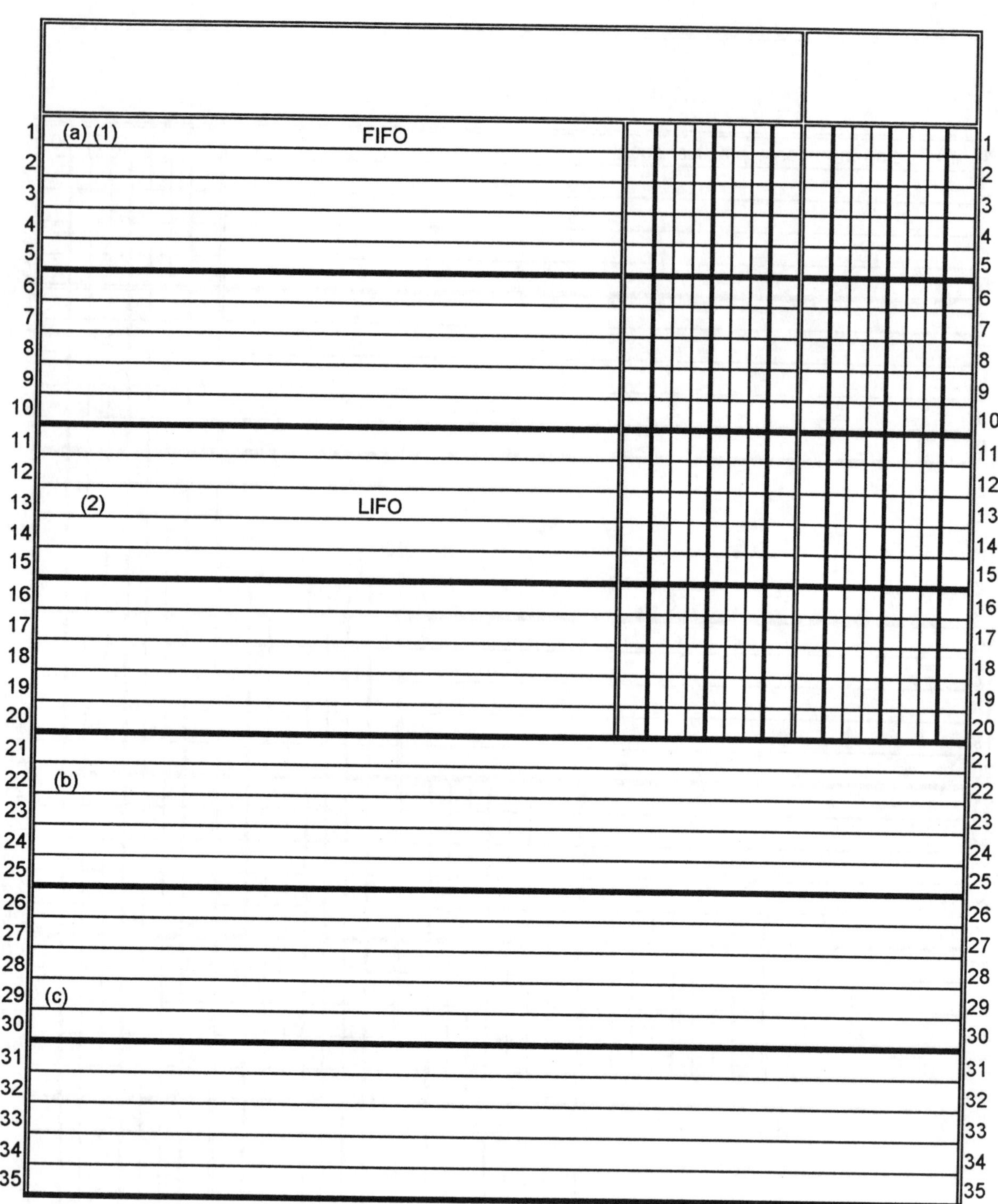

(a) (1) FIFO

(2) LIFO

(b)

(c)

Name

Section

Date

#7 (a)

(b)

(c)

#9	2002	2003

Name
Section
Date

Exercise 6-8

Oriental Camera Shop

Inventory Items	Total Cost	Market	Lower of Cost or Market by (a) Individual Items	Lower of Cost or Market by (b) Major Categories	Total Inventory
Cameras					
Minolta					
Canon					
Total					
Light Meters					
Vivitar					
Kodak					
Total					
Total Inventory					

Name

Section

Date

Exercise 6-10

Finlandia Watch Company

(a)	2002	2003

(b)

(c)

Name

Section

Date

Exercise 6-11

Wideangle Lens Corporation

	2000	2001	2002
Inventory turnover ratio			
Days in inventory			
Gross profit rate			

Name

Section

Date

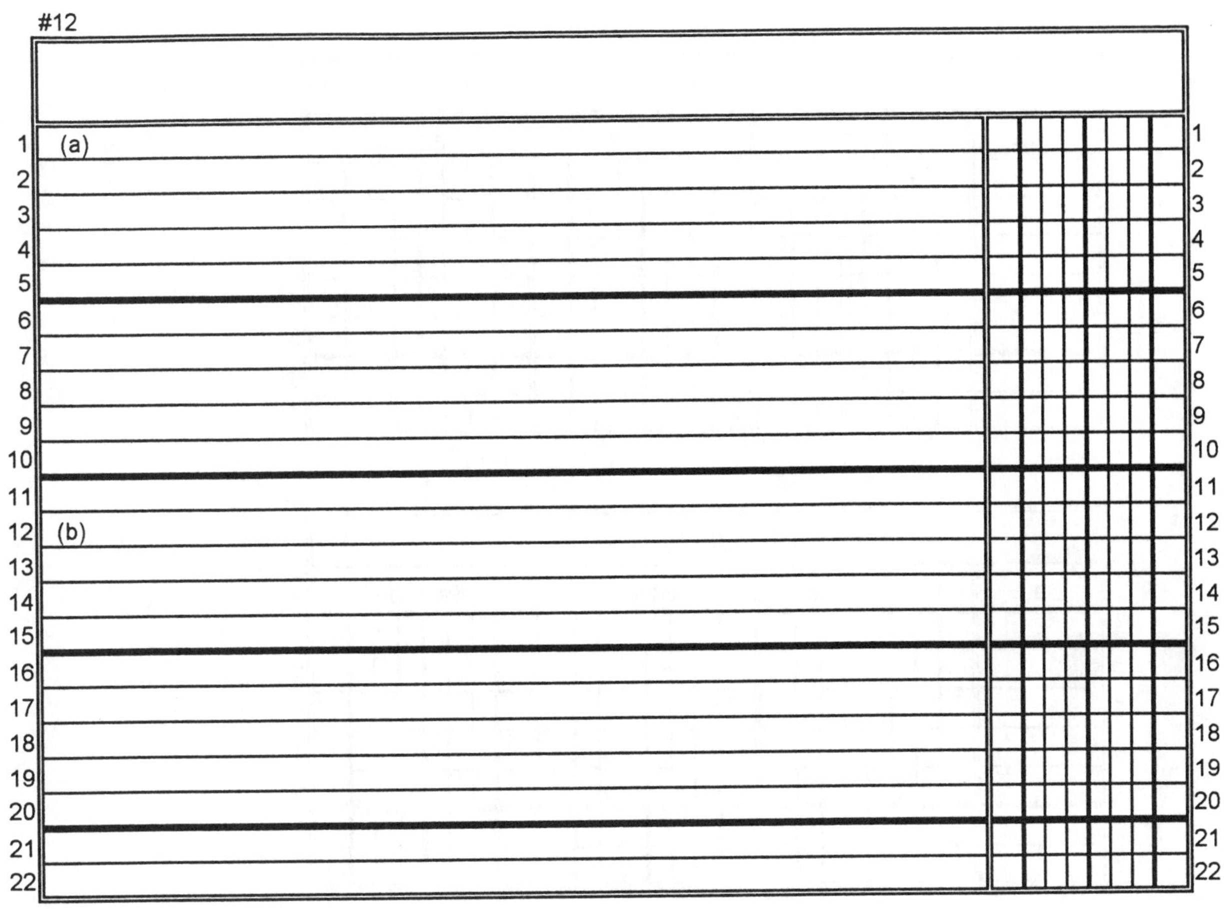

#12

(a)

(b)

#13

	Women's Department		Men's Department	
	Cost	Retail	Cost	Retail
Cost-to-retail ratio				
Estimated cost of ending inventory				

Name

Section

Date

Exercise 6-14

Alpine Appliance Company

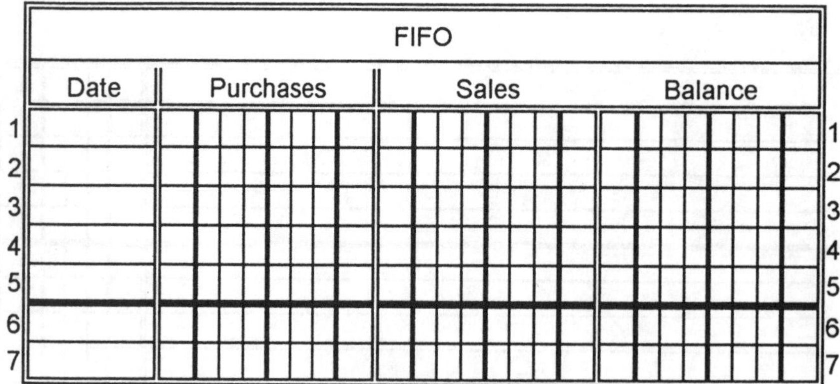

FIFO

Date	Purchases	Sales	Balance

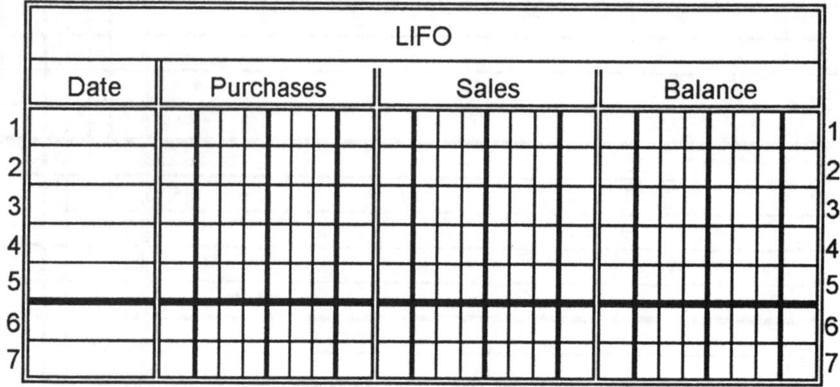

LIFO

Date	Purchases	Sales	Balance

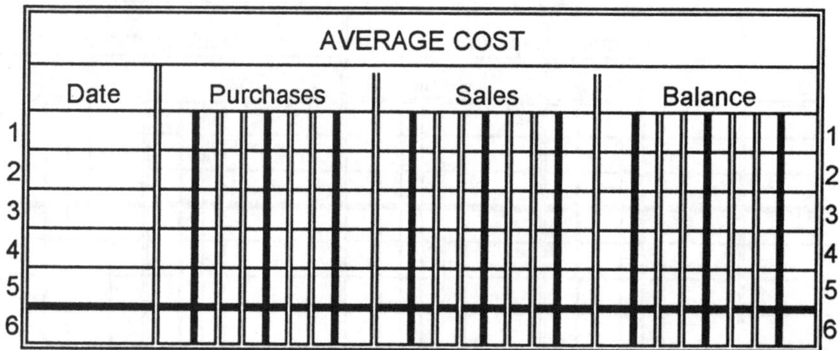

AVERAGE COST

Date	Purchases	Sales	Balance

Name Problem 6-1A

Section

Date VW's Tennis Shop

(a) General Journal

Date	Account Titles and Explanation	Ref.	Debit	Credit

Name

Problem 6-1A Continued

Section

Date

VW's Tennis Shop

(a) (Continued)

General Journal

	Date	Account Titles and Explanation	Ref.	Debit	Credit	
1						1
2						2
3						3
4						4
5						5
6						6
7						7
8						8

(b)

Cash

No. 101

Date	Explanation	Ref.	Debit	Credit	Balance

Accounts Receivable

No. 112

Date	Explanation	Ref.	Debit	Credit	Balance

Merchandise Inventory

No. 120

Date	Explanation	Ref.	Debit	Credit	Balance

(b)

Accounts Payable No. 201

Date	Explanation	Ref.	Debit	Credit	Balance

V. Williams, Capital No. 301

Date	Explanation	Ref.	Debit	Credit	Balance

Sales No. 401

Date	Explanation	Ref.	Debit	Credit	Balance

Sales Returns and Allowances No. 412

Date	Explanation	Ref.	Debit	Credit	Balance

Purchases No. 510

Date	Explanation	Ref.	Debit	Credit	Balance

(b)

Purchase Returns and Allowances No. 512

Date	Explanation	Ref.	Debit	Credit	Balance

Purchase Discounts No. 514

Date	Explanation	Ref.	Debit	Credit	Balance

Freight-in No. 516

Date	Explanation	Ref.	Debit	Credit	Balance

(c)

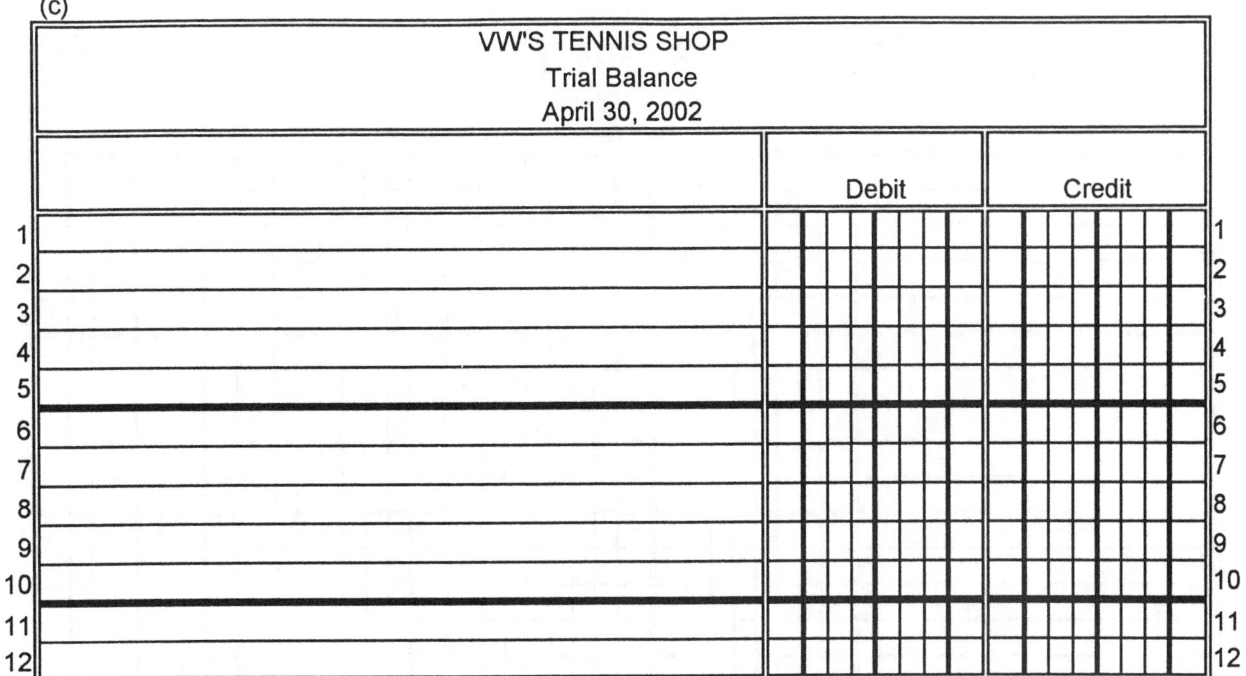

VW'S TENNIS SHOP
Trial Balance
April 30, 2002

	Debit	Credit
1		
2		
3		
4		
5		
6		
7		
8		
9		
10		
11		
12		

(d)

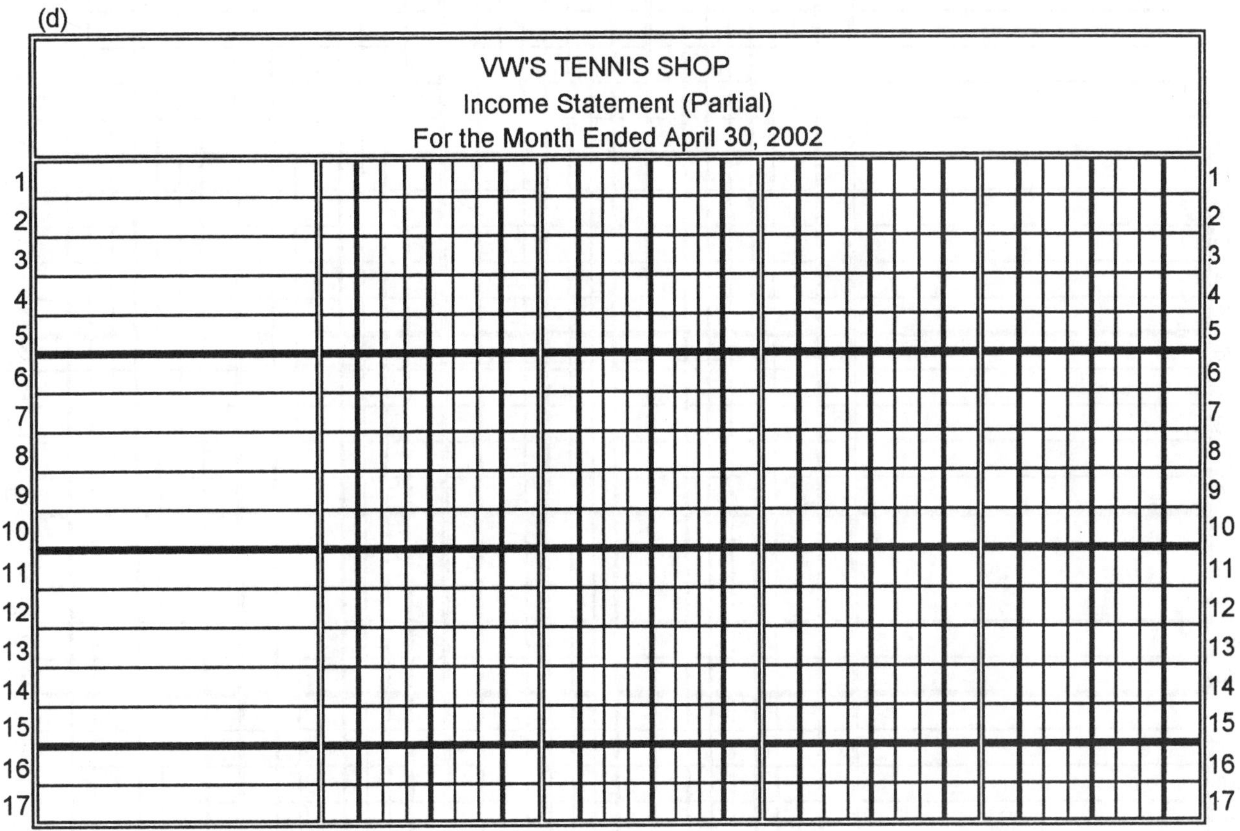

VW'S TENNIS SHOP
Income Statement (Partial)
For the Month Ended April 30, 2002

Name Problem 6-2A

Section

Date Anna Mossity Department Store

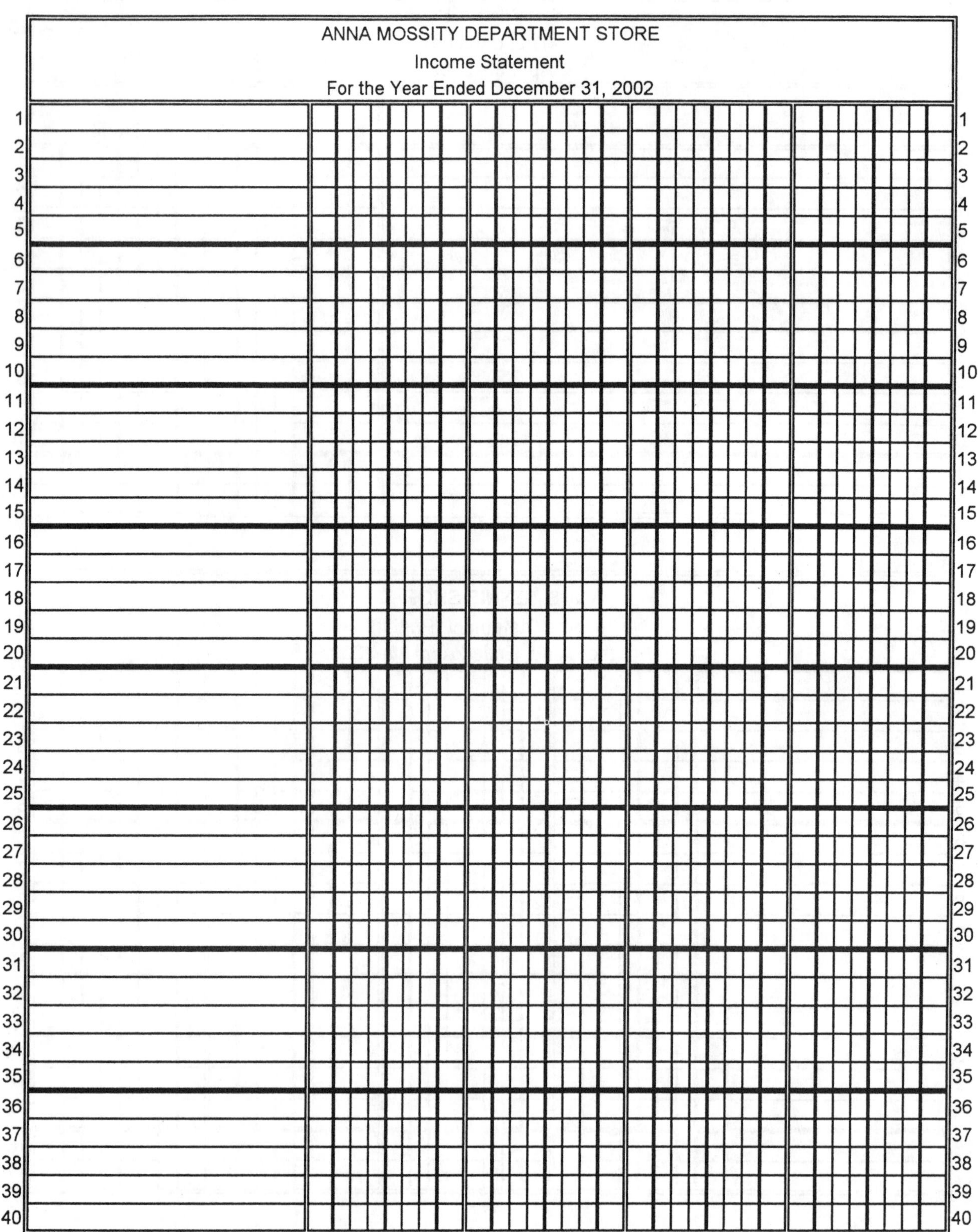

ANNA MOSSITY DEPARTMENT STORE

Income Statement

For the Year Ended December 31, 2002

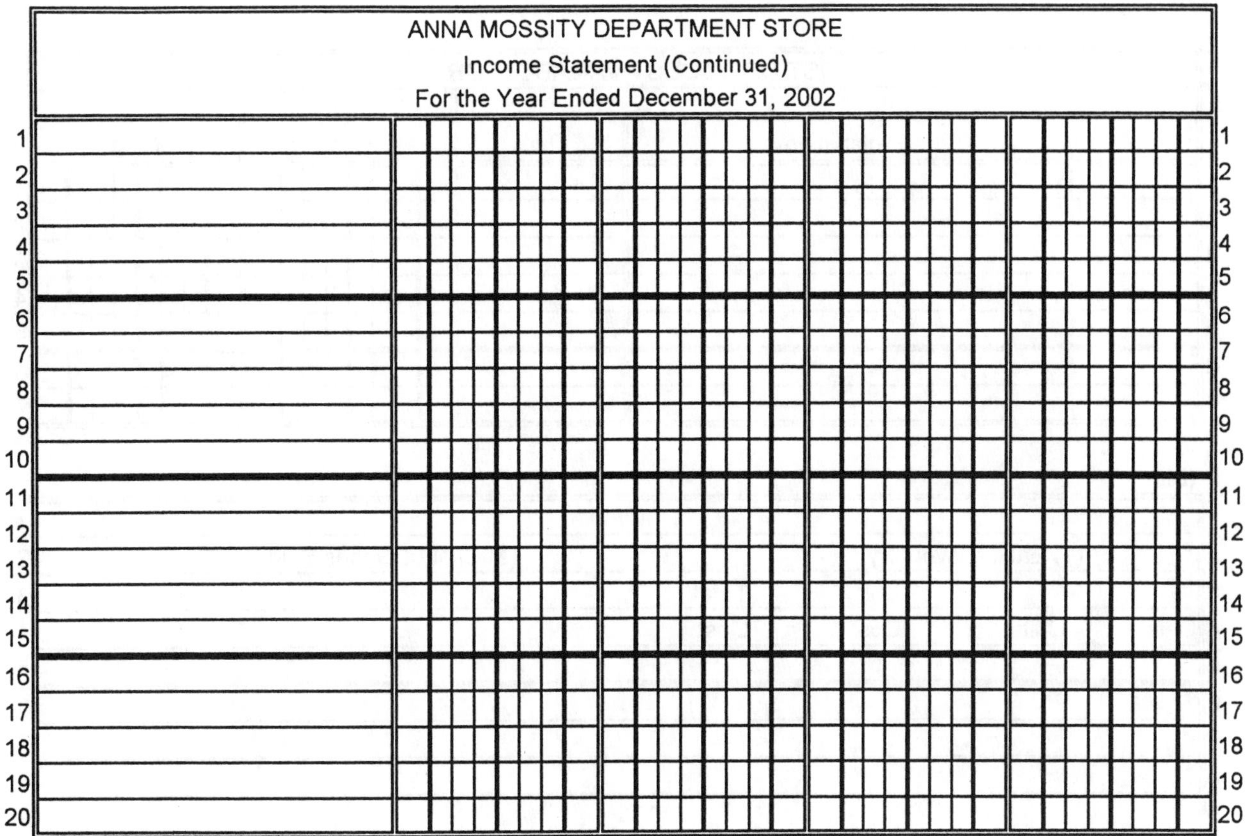
ANNA MOSSITY DEPARTMENT STORE
Income Statement (Continued)
For the Year Ended December 31, 2002

Name Problem 6-3A

Section

Date Scott Company

(a)

COST OF GOODS AVAILABLE FOR SALE				
Date	Explanation	Units	Unit Cost	Total Cost

(b)

FIFO

(1) Ending Inventory (2) Cost of Goods Sold

Date	Units	x	Unit Cost	=	Total Cost

Proof of Cost of Goods Sold

Date	Units	x	Unit Cost	=	Total Cost

LIFO

(1) Ending Inventory (2) Cost of Goods Sold

Date	Units	x	Unit Cost	=	Total Cost

Name — Problem 6-3A Concluded

Section

Date — Scott Company

(b) (Continued) and (c)

(b) Proof of Cost of Goods Sold

Date	Units	x	Unit Cost	=	Total Cost

AVERAGE COST

(1) Ending Inventory

(2) Cost of Goods Sold

Units	x	Unit Cost	=	Total Cost

Proof of Cost of Goods Sold

(c)

Name — Problem 6-4A

Section

Date — Aurora Co.

(a)

AURORA CO.
Condensed Income Statements
For the Year Ended December 31, 2002

	FIFO	LIFO

(b) (1)

(2)

(3)

(4)

(5)

Name | Problem 6-5A

Section

Date | Wayne E. Weather Company

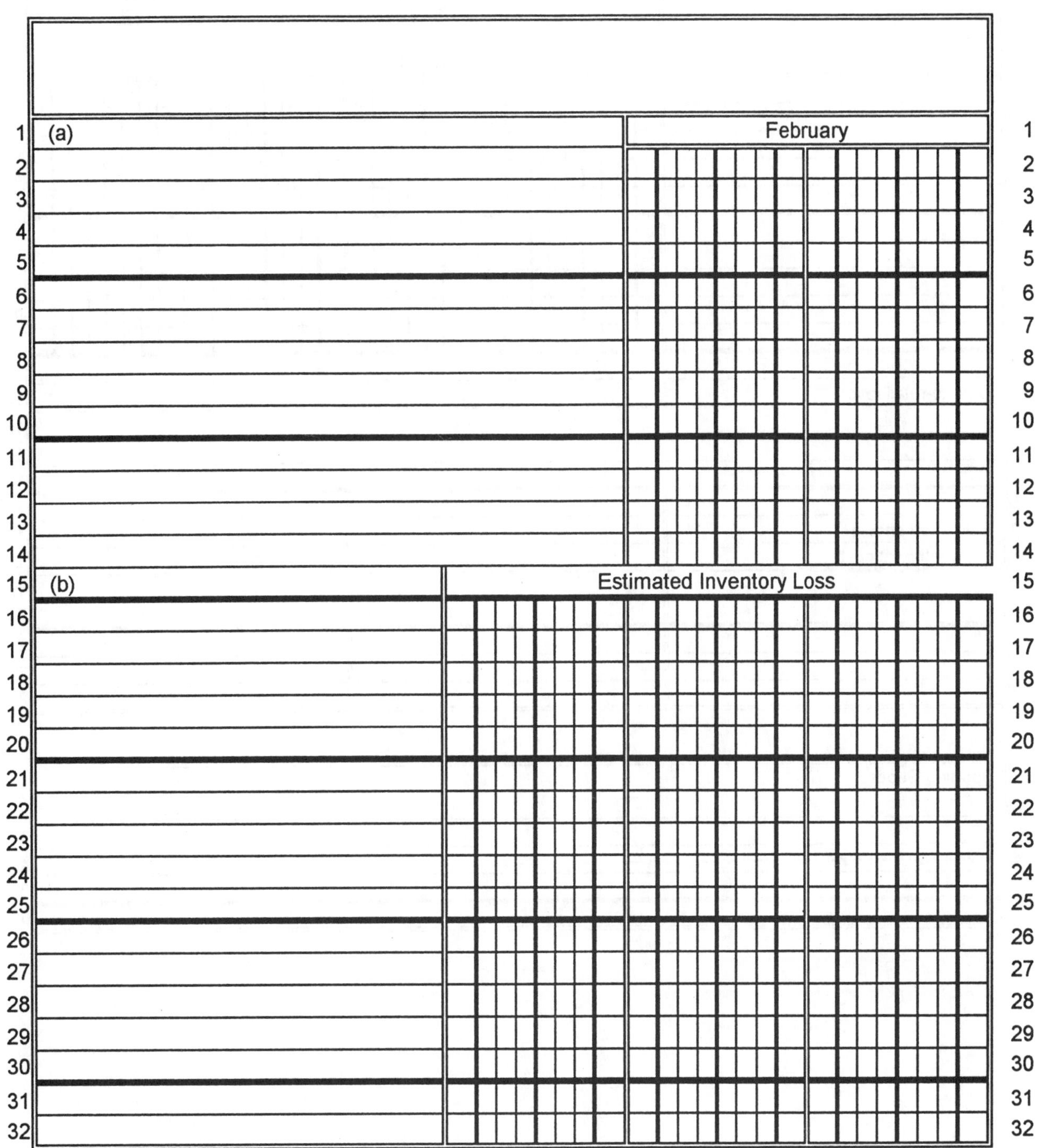

Name Problem 6-6A

Section

Date Korean Department Store

(a)

	Sporting Goods		Jewelry & Cosmetics	
	Cost	Retail	Cost	Retail

Cost-to-retail ratio:

Estimated ending inventory at cost:		

(b)

Sporting Goods:

Jewelry & Cosmetics:

Name Problem 6-7A

Section

Date Reliable Appliance Mart

(a) (1)

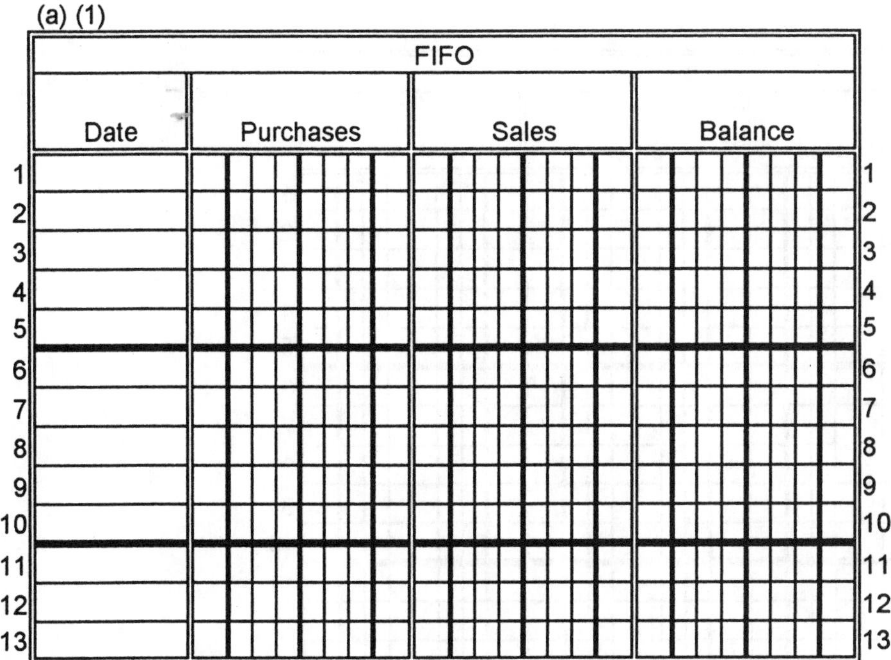

	FIFO				
	Date	Purchases	Sales	Balance	
1					1
2					2
3					3
4					4
5					5
6					6
7					7
8					8
9					9
10					10
11					11
12					12
13					13

(2)

	AVERAGE COST				
	Date	Purchases	Sales	Balance	
1					1
2					2
3					3
4					4
5					5
6					6
7					7
8					8
9					9
10					10

Name

Section

Date

Problem 6-7A Concluded

Reliable Appliance Mart

(a) (Continued)

(3)

LIFO			
Date	Purchases	Sales	Balance

(b)

Name Problem 6-1B

Section

Date Nick's Pro Shop

(a)

General Journal

Date	Account Titles and Explanation	Ref.	Debit	Credit

(a) (Continued) General Journal

	Date	Account Titles and Explanation	Ref.	Debit	Credit	
1						1
2						2
3						3
4						4
5						5
6						6
7						7
8						8
9						9

(b) Cash No. 101

Date	Explanation	Ref.	Debit	Credit	Balance

Accounts Receivable No. 112

Date	Explanation	Ref.	Debit	Credit	Balance

Merchandise Inventory No. 120

Date	Explanation	Ref.	Debit	Credit	Balance

(b)

Accounts Payable No. 201

Date	Explanation	Ref.	Debit	Credit	Balance

N. Bear, Capital No. 301

Date	Explanation	Ref.	Debit	Credit	Balance

Sales No. 401

Date	Explanation	Ref.	Debit	Credit	Balance

Sales Returns and Allowances No. 412

Date	Explanation	Ref.	Debit	Credit	Balance

Purchases No. 501

Date	Explanation	Ref.	Debit	Credit	Balance

(b) (Continued)

Purchase Returns and Allowances — No. 512

Date	Explanation	Ref.	Debit	Credit	Balance

Purchase Discounts — No. 514

Date	Explanation	Ref.	Debit	Credit	Balance

Freight-In — No. 516

Date	Explanation	Ref.	Debit	Credit	Balance

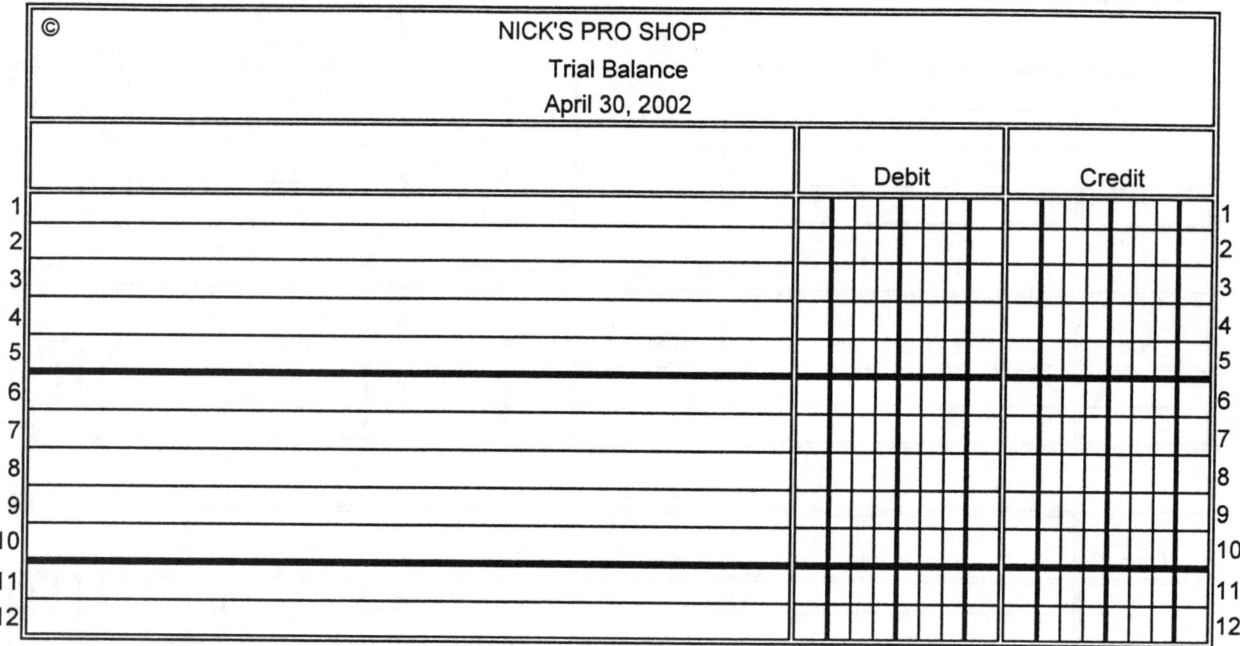

NICK'S PRO SHOP
Trial Balance
April 30, 2002

		Debit	Credit	
1				1
2				2
3				3
4				4
5				5
6				6
7				7
8				8
9				9
10				10
11				11
12				12

Name
Section
Date

Problem 6-1B Concluded

Nick's Pro Shop

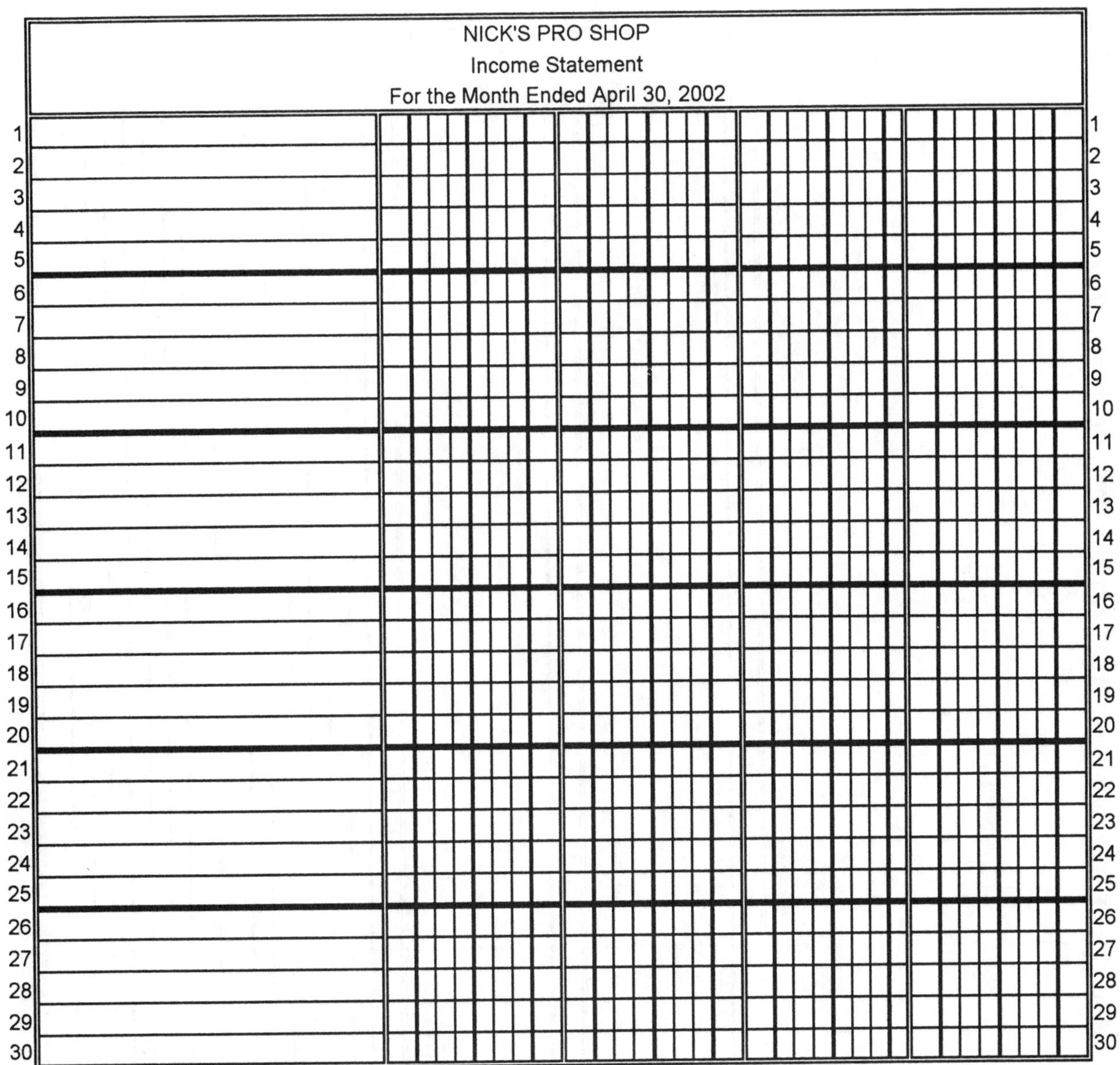

NICK'S PRO SHOP
Income Statement
For the Month Ended April 30, 2002

Name

Section

Date

Problem 6-2B

Bedazzle Department Store

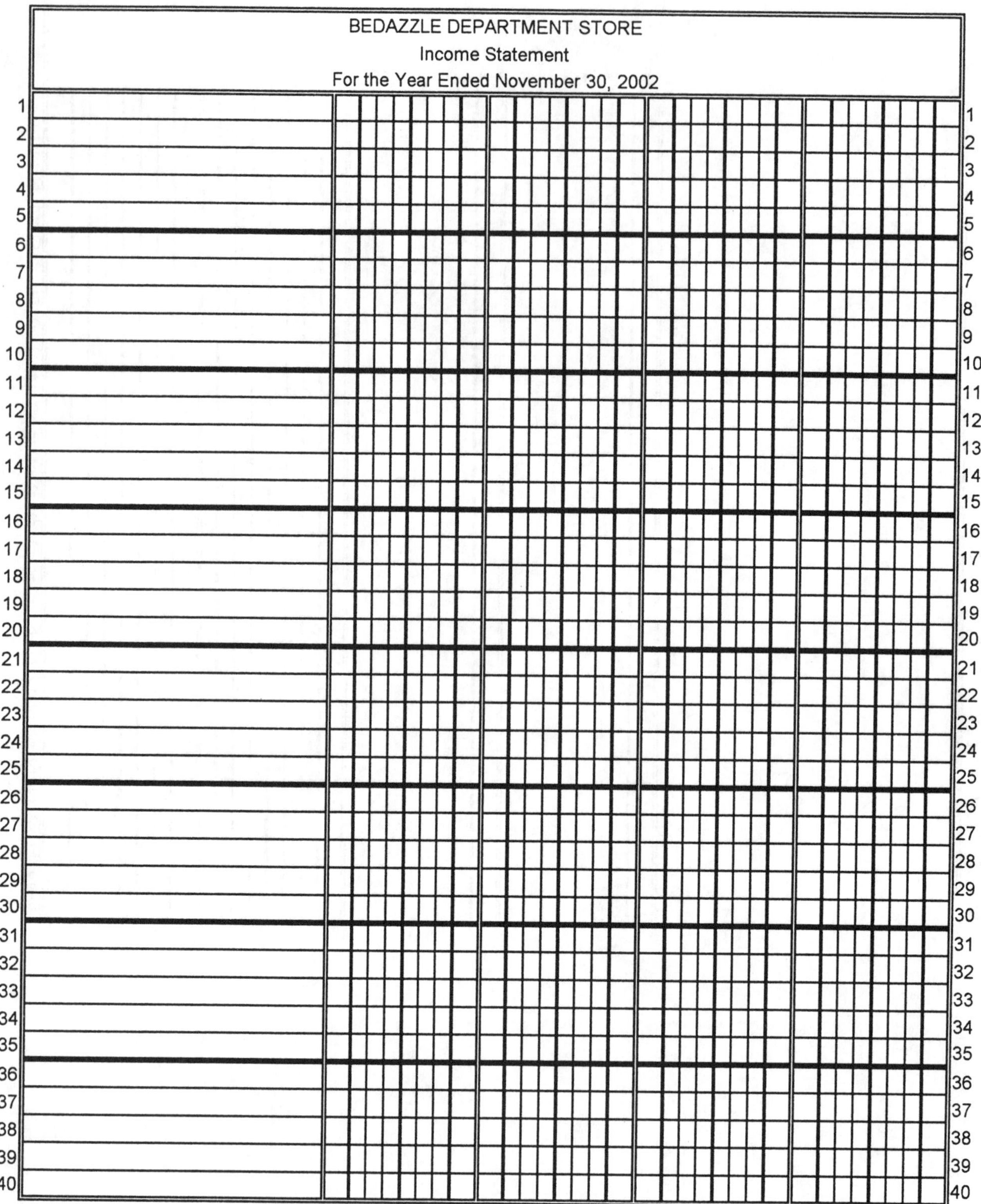

Name

Section

Date

Problem 6-2B Concluded

Bedazzle Department Store

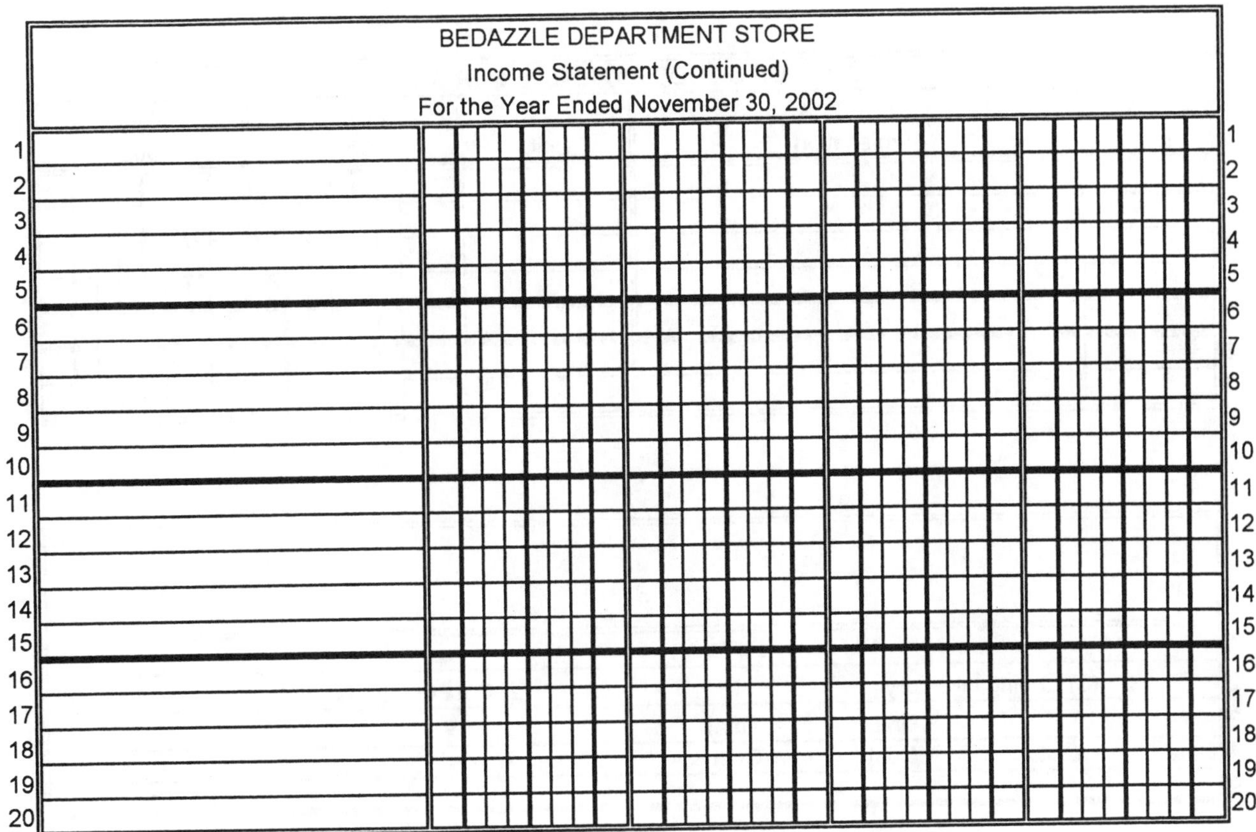

BEDAZZLE DEPARTMENT STORE

Income Statement (Continued)

For the Year Ended November 30, 2002

Name

Section

Date

Problem 6-3B

John Lewis Company

(a)

COST OF GOODS AVAILABLE FOR SALE				
Date	Explanation	Units	Unit Cost	Total Cost

FIFO

(1) Ending Inventory

Date	Units	x	Unit Cost	=	Total Cost

(2) Cost of Goods Sold

Proof of Cost of Goods Sold

Date	Units	x	Unit Cost	=	Total Cost

LIFO

(1) Ending Inventory

Date	Units	x	Unit Cost	=	Total Cost

(2) Cost of Goods Sold

Name

Section

Date

Problem 6-3B Concluded

John Lewis Company

(b) (Continued) and (c)

Proof of Cost of Goods Sold

Date	Units	x	Unit Cost	=	Total Cost

AVERAGE COST

(1) Ending Inventory

(2) Cost of Goods Sold

Units	x	Unit Cost	=	Total Cost

Proof of Cost of Goods Sold

(c)

Name

Section

Date

Problem 6-4B

Congo Co.

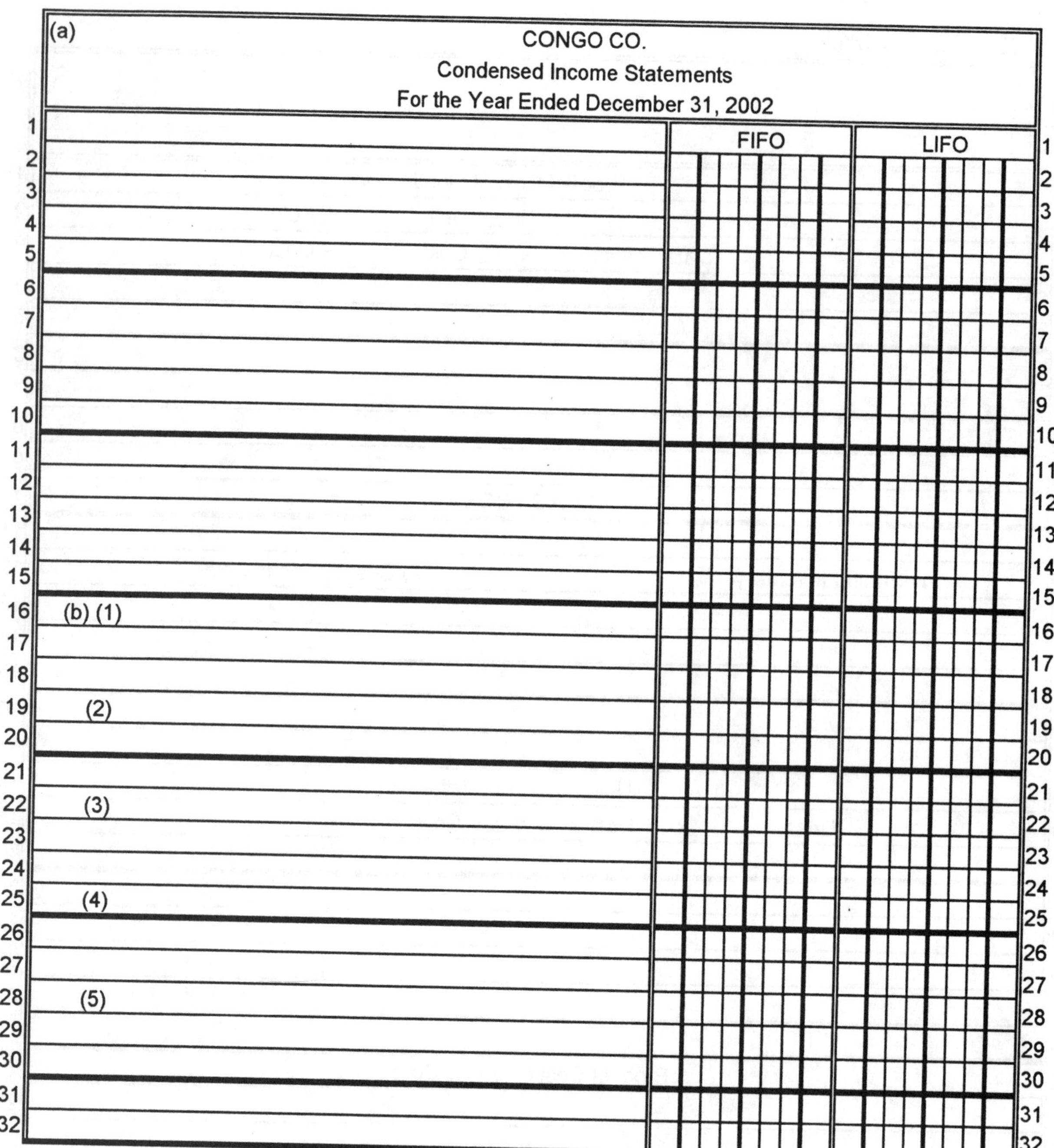

(a)

CONGO CO.
Condensed Income Statements
For the Year Ended December 31, 2002

	FIFO	LIFO
1		
2		
3		
4		
5		
6		
7		
8		
9		
10		
11		
12		
13		
14		
15		
16 (b) (1)		
17		
18		
19 (2)		
20		
21		
22 (3)		
23		
24		
25 (4)		
26		
27		
28 (5)		
29		
30		
31		
32		

Problem 6-5B

Name

Section

Date

Dutch Company

(a)

November

(b)

Estimated Inventory Loss

Name

Section

Date

Problem 6-6B

Enlighten Bookstore

(a)

	Hardcovers		Paperbacks	
	Cost	Retail	Cost	Retail

Cost-to-retail ratio:

Estimated ending inventory at cost:			

(b)

Hardcovers:

Paperbacks:

Name

Section

Date

Problem 6-7B

Angelina Jolie Co.

(a) (1)

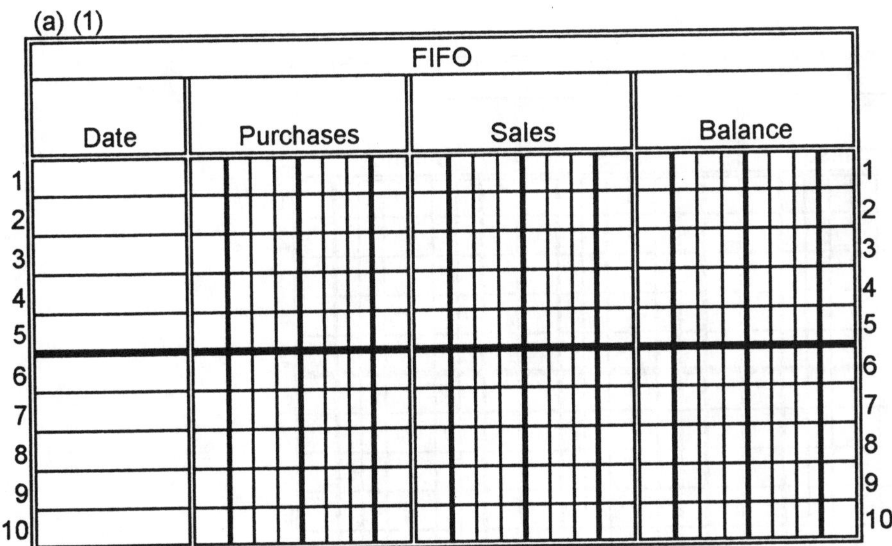

(2)

AVERAGE COST			
Date	Purchases	Sales	Balance

Name

Section

Date

Problem 6-7B Concluded

Angelina Jolie Co.

(a) (Continued) (3)

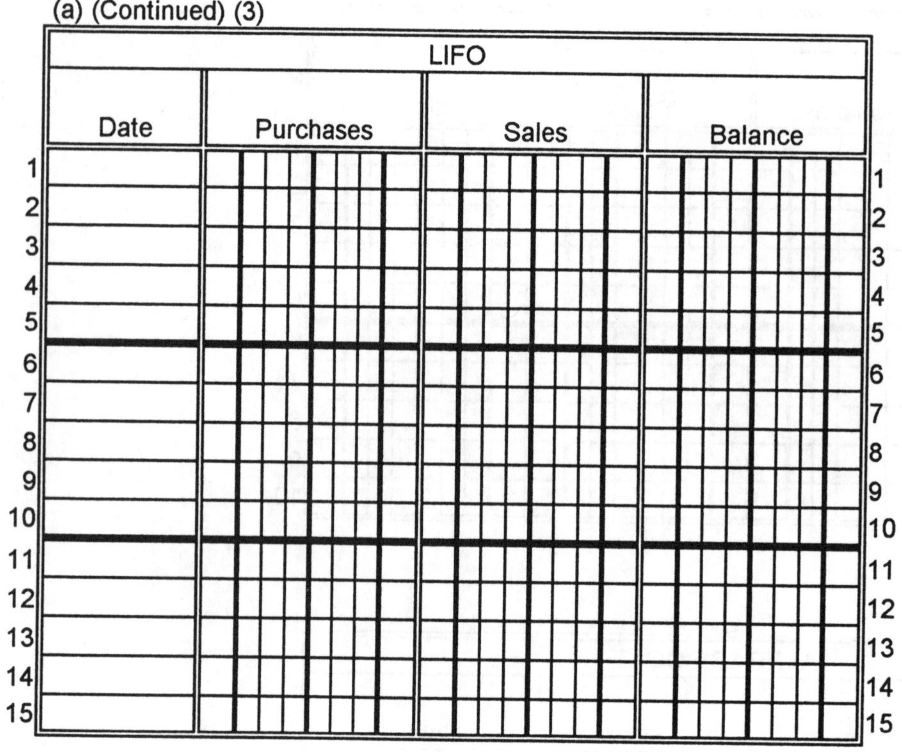

(b)

Name

Section

Date

(a)

(b)

(c)

(d)

Name

Section

Date

(a)	Lands' End	Abercrombie & Fitch
Inventory turnover ratio:		
Average days to sell inventory:		

(b)

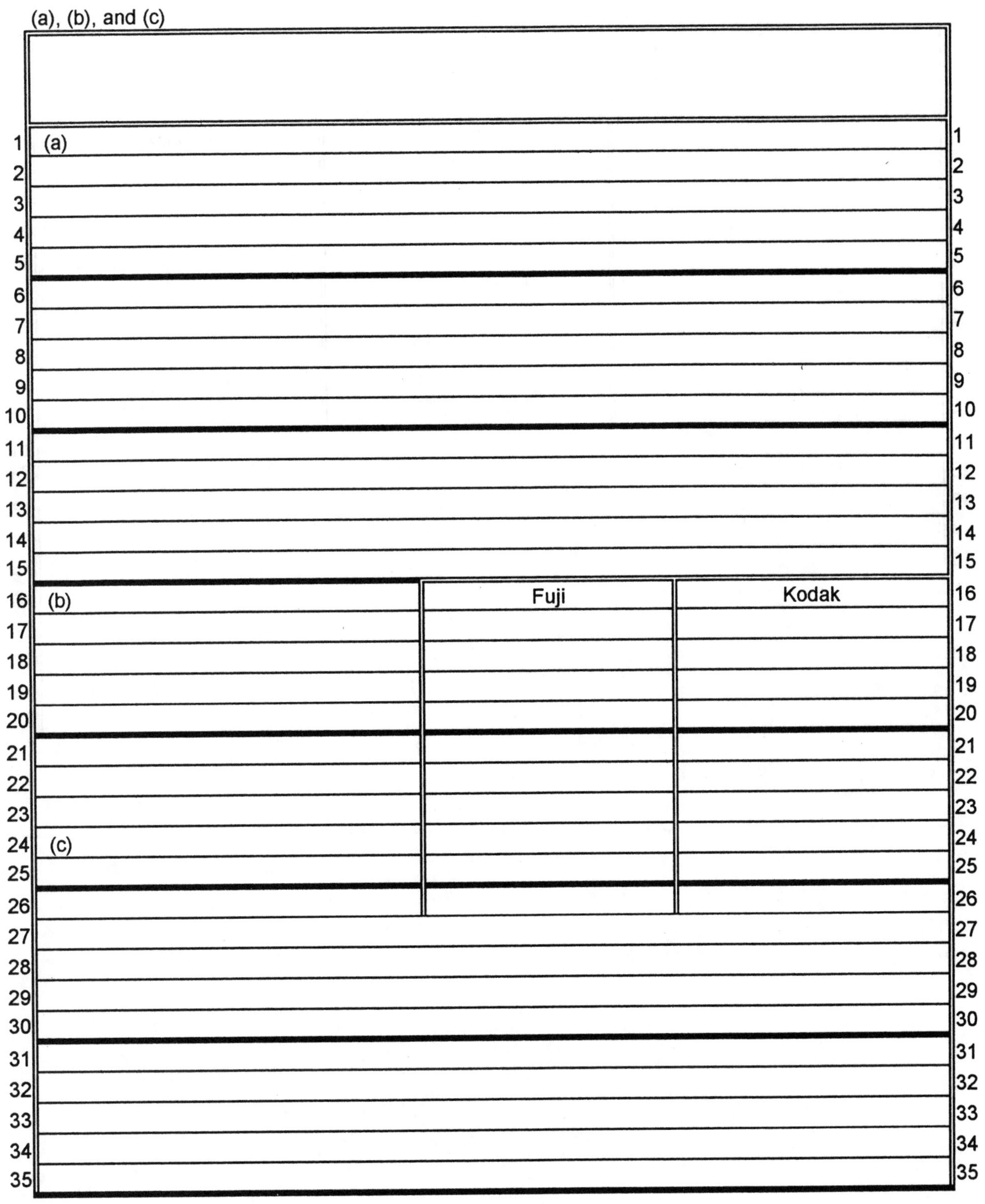

(a), (b), and (c)

(a)

(b)

	Fuji	Kodak

(c)

		Fuji	Kodak	
1		Fuji	Kodak	1
2				2
3				3
4				4
5				5
6				6
7				7
8				8
9				9
10				10
11				11
12				12
13				13
14				14
15				15
16				16
17				17
18				18
19				19
20				20

Name

Chapter 6 Exploring The Web

Section

Date

Cisco System

(a)

(b)

(c)

(d)

Name

Section

Date

Gibson Company

(a) (1) Sales

(2) Purchases

(b)

	2000	1999

(c)

Name

Section

Date

Small Toys Inc.

Name

Section

Date

Chapter 6 Ethics Case

J.K. Leask Wholesale Corp.

NOTES

NOTES

NOTES

NOTES

NOTES

APPENDIX